ISLAMOPHOBIC HATE CRIME

In recent years, there has been a sharp increase in anti-Muslim attacks. What is driving the proliferation of these hate crimes? Why are Muslims being demonised? Building on current research and drawing upon real-life examples and case studies, this book provides an accessible introduction to Islamophobia and Islamophobic hate crimes along with the various responses to this form of victimisation. Chapters cover a range of topics including:

- Definitions of hate crime and Islamophobia
- Islamophobic hate crime online
- Gender and Islamophobia
- Media representations of Islamophobia
- Institutional Islamophobia

As one of the first student resources dedicated to the subject of Islamophobia, this book will be instructive and important reading for those engaged in a range of topics in criminology, including hate crime, victimology and victimisation, crime and media, and gender and crime.

Imran Awan is a Professor in Criminology and Deputy Director of the Centre for Applied Criminology at Birmingham City University, UK.

Irene Zempi is a Senior Lecturer in Criminology at Nottingham Trent University, UK.

ISLAMOPHOBIC HATE CRIME

A Student Textbook

Imran Awan and Irene Zempi

LONDON AND NEW YORK

First published 2020
by Routledge
2 Park Square, Milton Park, Abingdon, Oxon OX14 4RN

and by Routledge
52 Vanderbilt Avenue, New York, NY 10017

Routledge is an imprint of the Taylor & Francis Group, an informa business

© 2020 Imran Awan and Irene Zempi

The right of Imran Awan and Irene Zempi to be identified as authors of this
work has been asserted by them in accordance with sections 77 and 78 of the
Copyright, Designs and Patents Act 1988.

All rights reserved. No part of this book may be reprinted or reproduced or
utilised in any form or by any electronic, mechanical, or other means, now
known or hereafter invented, including photocopying and recording, or in any
information storage or retrieval system, without permission in writing from the
publishers.

Trademark notice: Product or corporate names may be trademarks or registered
trademarks, and are used only for identification and explanation without intent to
infringe.

British Library Cataloguing in Publication Data
A catalogue record for this book is available from the British Library

Library of Congress Cataloging-in-Publication Data
A catalog record has been requested for this book

ISBN: 978-1-138-55268-5 (hbk)
ISBN: 978-1-138-55270-8 (pbk)
ISBN: 978-1-315-14827-4 (ebk)

Typeset in Bembo
by Taylor & Francis Books
Printed by CPI Group (UK) Ltd, Croydon CR0 4YY

CONTENTS

List of tables   *vi*

1	Introduction	1
2	Understanding Islamophobic hate crime	10
3	Islamophobia online and in the digital world	29
4	Gendered Islamophobia	42
5	Islamophobia and perceived Muslim identity	59
6	Using autoethnography for Islamophobic hate crimes	75
7	Institutional Islamophobia: policing, profiling, and hate	85
8	Islamophobia, terrorism, and the media	99
9	Impacts of Islamophobic hate crime	114
10	Islamophobic hate crime in Europe	126
11	Conclusion	134

Index   *147*

TABLES

8.1 Reference made to Woolwich in broadsheet newspapers   104
8.2 Reference made to Woolwich in regional newspapers   104

1

INTRODUCTION

Background and context

As authors of this book, we have spent our academic careers researching and investigating Islamophobic hate crimes. In our capacity as researchers and experts in this area, we have provided several impactful reports before high-profile parliamentary committees, published academic articles/books, and are passionate about the study of Islamophobic hate crimes. This has also led to independent advisory work with the British Government and working closely with politicians and Ministers on developing our understanding of Islamophobia in Britain and beyond. Following the 9/11 and 7/7 terrorist attacks, and more recently the terrorist attacks in Paris and Tunisia in 2015, and in Woolwich, south-east London, where British Army soldier Drummer Lee Rigby was murdered in 2013, there has been a significant increase in anti-Muslim hate attacks and hostility (Zempi and Awan 2016). Indeed, during Hate Crime Awareness Week in October 2018 (a campaign to help better understand hate crimes in Britain) the UK police force recorded a surge in hate crimes against people because of their religious beliefs. According to the Home Office official data, out of all the offences recorded, 52 per cent of offences were targeting Muslims (Home Office 2017 to 2018). Furthermore, following the appointment of the US President Donald Trump (at the time of writing) and the Brexit vote in Britain, these incidents have led to a sharp increase in Islamophobic hate crimes. There have been reports of mosques being vandalised, Muslim women having their hijab (headscarf) or niqab (face veil) pulled off, Muslim men being attacked, and racist graffiti has been scrawled against Muslim properties.

This book fills a gap in the current research literature on Islamophobia by bringing together a wide range of principles around Islamophobia and hate crimes. The aim of this book is to provide an original textbook on Islamophobic hate crime for students, practitioners, and policy-makers. In doing so, we challenge

2 Introduction

current thinking around Islamophobia and provide an in-depth academic textbook addressing a topic that, following recent events (discussed earlier) across the world, has become of critical importance. Our starting point for this book is based on our experiences with our students. As academics teaching hate crime and Islamophobia within Higher Education, our students have often expressed difficulties in the lack of choices regarding student academic textbooks on Islamophobia. With this in mind, we have embarked upon our vision to create the first ever student textbook on Islamophobia that helps students and also wider stakeholders, such as community groups, politicians, and the media, to better understand Islamophobia.

This book allows students the opportunity to examine the different processes of victimisation, whether by or of individuals, groups, families, communities, institutions, or the state, and gives them the opportunity to be able to evaluate the impacts of Islamophobia upon individuals and society. Students will also be able to examine the development, role, organisation, and governance of efforts to reduce and prevent Islamophobic crime and harm, and discuss how victims are able to ensure personal and public safety and security in different locations. Students will also be able to analyse and evaluate the effectiveness of such measures and human rights issues in relation to preventive measures in combating Islamophobic hate crimes. It will give readers the opportunity to formulate questions and investigate key areas of Islamophobia. The book will also help students to take account of the complexity and diversity of the ways in which Islamophobic hate crime is constituted, represented, and dealt with by different agencies and be able to make reasoned arguments. Students will also be able to use empirical evidence about Islamophobic hate crime, victimisation surveys, and wider responses towards Islamophobia. Some of the more technical skills students will acquire will include written and oral communication skills, including the clear presentation of research, participating in academic debates and interrogating the evidence. The book will work alongside the other criminology, policing, law, history, religious studies, education, and security studies modules where issues of victimisation within the criminal justice system are examined. This book builds on current research and disseminates new messages arising from Islamophobia, thus contributing towards our understanding of Islamophobia and responding to this form of hate crime. A book of this nature is long overdue and we hope students will be able to benefit from this textbook which they can use when studying about hate crimes.

Key themes and concepts

This book allows students the opportunity to develop a key understanding of criminological and sociological concepts and theoretical approaches, which have been developed in relation to Islamophobic hate crime. It gives students and others an opportunity to examine and conceptualise some of the key debates around Islamophobic hate crime, policy, human rights, and victimisation. The book identifies problems around the processes of Islamophobia and victimisation, the causes and organisation of Islamophobic hate crime, and the processes of preventing and managing crime and victimisation in relation to Islamophobia. The main themes and objectives of this book are focusing on Islamophobic hate crime. Empirical evidence shows that Muslims, particularly those with a 'visible' Muslim identity – including wearing a veil for women and a beard for men – are more vulnerable to verbal and physical attacks in public (see, for example, Craig 2002; Githens-Mazer and Lambert 2010; Poynting and Mason 2007; Zempi and Chakraborti 2014). This book examines a wide range of core principles around Islamophobic hate crime and discusses – through a student-led approach – the impact of this victimisation upon victims, their families, and wider communities. It provides empirical research, which examines the nature, scope, and impact of Islamophobia upon Muslims and the wider society. The book also highlights the multidimensional nature of Islamophobic hate crime, and recognises the fact that there is a relationship between anti-Muslim attacks, especially in the globalised world. As such, this book seeks to shed new light on a hitherto under-researched topic and to develop a more nuanced understanding of Islamophobic hate crime. The central themes of the book include a focus on our understanding of hate crime, globalised Islamophobic hate incidents, and also the impact on victims and wider society:

- Conceptualising the nature of Islamophobia
- Autoethnography research methods
- Barriers and victimisation
- Gendered forms of Islamophobia
- Online Islamophobic hate speech
- Marginalised communities
- Contemporary responses to Islamophobic crime
- Institutional forms of Islamophobia
- Islamophobic hate crimes and the media
- Policing and Islamophobia
- Islamophobia in the climate of Brexit and Donald Trump

How to use this textbook?

This textbook is an introduction to some of the key themes and debates surrounding Islamophobia today. It should be used alongside other key texts and should be more than a companion guide. It is not an exhaustive list of all issues to do with Islamophobia but picks out some of the core contemporary debates and uses an academic and student positioning to debate and get students to think more critically about these issues. The book will present students with insights towards a better understanding of criminology, sociology, and hate crime studies. It has also been designed to act as the main reference point for students undertaking summative and formative assessments. The book is split into 11 chapters.

Chapter 1 provides an introduction and discussion about how students should use this textbook. It examines some of the critical debates within Islamophobia and uses contemporary examples, from cases such as the Punish a Muslim Day letter

4 Introduction

sent to British Muslims. The chapter also provides students with some theoretical examples in relation to the roots of Islamophobia and how perpetrators use societal justifications to target those they perceive as being different. Chapter 2 examines the nature, scope, and impact of hate crime. It argues that hate crimes have a disproportionate impact on the victim on the basis that individuals are being targeted because of their identity. However, hate crimes not only impact the individual victim but also the wider community to which the victim belongs. In this regard, hate crimes send a 'message' to the victim and the victim's group members that they are neither safe nor welcome in the community. The chapter also discusses manifestations of Islamophobic hate crime. Furthermore, it examines the role of 'trigger' events with regards to the prevalence and severity of Islamophobic hate crimes. Finally, it outlines the impact of Islamophobia, racism, and discrimination in the workplace on young Muslims' career development and progression.

Chapter 3 examines the role of the digital space in relation to Islamophobia online. Using empirical research data, the chapter draws upon how certain 'trigger' events can lead to an escalation of online hostility. We specifically cite the example of the Woolwich terrorist attack and the social media reaction towards Muslims. This chapter also argues that online incidents cannot be isolated from offline attacks. Both online and offline incidents are a continuity of anti-Muslim hate and thus should not be examined in isolation. Drawing on evidence, the chapter demonstrates that the prevalence and severity of online Islamophobic hate crimes are influenced by 'trigger' events of local, national, and international significance. The visibility of people's Muslim identity is also key to triggering online Islamophobic hate crime.

Furthermore, Chapter 4 examines historical and contemporary discourses of the Muslim veil, and outlines the implications of this rhetoric for veiled Muslim women in the West. The chapter argues that through the colonial lens, the Muslim veil was seen as a symbol of gender oppression. From this perspective, the 'liberation' of veiled Muslim women became fused with the motivations of imperial expansion. In a post-9/11 climate, the wearing of the veil is routinely seen as a symbol of Islamist extremism and segregation as well as a sign of gender oppression. The chapter also examines contemporary legal restrictions upon the wearing of the niqab (face veil) in public places in the West, and suggests that banning the niqab potentially legitimises public acts of violence towards veiled Muslim women. The chapter concludes with a discussion of the gendered dimensions of Islamophobia.

Drawing on empirical research, Chapter 5 examines the experiences of non-Muslim men who suffer Islamophobic hate crime because they look Muslim. As will be discussed in detail, participants described being verbally and physically attacked, threatened, and harassed as well as their property being damaged. 'Trigger' events included the Brexit vote, Donald Trump's presidency, as well as ISIS-inspired terrorist attacks in European countries such as France, Germany, Sweden, and the UK. The impacts upon victims included physical, emotional, psychological, and economic damage. These experiences were also damaging to community cohesion and led to polarisation between different communities in the UK. Chapter 6 uses two real-life case studies in order to examine the advantages and limitations of using autoethnography when investigating Islamophobic hate crime. The chapter discusses our personal journey into becoming 'visibly' identifiable as Muslims and documents our experiences in relation to this autoethnography study. Autoethnography is a research method used by social scientists when immersing themselves in the footsteps of those they research about. We employ our diary extracts to describe in detail the impact of Islamophobic victimisation upon us and the coping strategies we used.

Chapter 7 explores an emerging theme in relation to policing, profiling, and institutional forms of Islamophobia. Unarguably, Islamophobia entails more than physical violence and verbal abuse. Rather, it has become part of a discussion in relation to racial inequality and structural abuse. Using contemporary examples of policing by force and discriminatory practices at airports, this chapter makes the case that Islamophobia has moved into institutional places. From a policing perspective, we argue that Muslims are under official suspicion and therefore treated as a 'suspect' community. Using the earlier examples, the chapter draws upon how these themes impact communities and are part of the new Islamophobia narrative.

Chapter 8 discusses Islamophobia in the media. It provides students with example scenarios, and uses an interactive discussion in relation to media stories about Muslims. The chapter also draws upon empirical research in relation to the media depiction of the murder of Mohammed Saleem and the Woolwich attacks. A further analysis of newspaper coverage is produced which reveals themes of how the media depict Muslims in a negative manner. Similar to other forms of hate crime, the impact of Islamophobia is felt at a variety of levels: by the direct victim, the wider community to which the victim belongs, and society as a whole. As such, Chapter 9 discusses the implications of Islamophobic hate crime on three broad levels: individual, community, and societal impacts.

Chapter 10 examines the nature and extent of Islamophobia in Europe. It argues that Muslims living in Europe face victimisation and discrimination in a broad range of settings and particularly when looking for work, at work, and when trying to access public or private services (FRA 2017). However, all the available data and statistics about Islamophobic hate crime in Europe show only the tip of the iceberg. The vast majority of European states do not record hate crime or anti-Muslim/Islamophobic incidents as a separate category of hate crime. Chapter 11 concludes by raising awareness and issues of Islamophobia from a global context and in particular discusses the role of Donald Trump and the rise of the right. This chapter also provides some key learning points for students and ends with key tips for essay writing and exam writing, by giving students advice in relation to essays. It concludes with discussion about the hate crime action plan and how the UK Government intends to tackle Islamophobic hate crimes.

Why study Islamophobia?

Current events both in Britain and internationally have raised the issue of Islamophobia more prominently in the public eye. When Boris Johnson, the former Foreign

6 Introduction

Secretary, described Muslim women wearing the burqa as being 'bank robbers' and 'letterboxes' it caused a huge public outrage. This was not an isolated incident because in early 2018, a letter also emerged titled 'Punish a Muslim' Day. The letter set out different points to score regarding verbally and physically attacking Muslims.

The significance of the letter is important as it led to a wide police and criminal investigation into both the nature and contents of the letter. The letter called for a national day of action against Muslim communities, which aimed to instil both fear and anxiety. In June 2018, David Parnham was eventually charged with 14 offences, including five counts of packages containing substances that were noxious (BBC News 2018). As the growth of hatred against Muslims continues, the need to tackle the root causes of Islamophobia has become critical. This student textbook acts as a student reading text, which is part of every student's essential reading list within the field of hate crime studies and beyond. The text also provides a list of further reading, key questions, and case studies. Islamophobia, as noted earlier, in recent years has become more prominent following the rise of groups such as Britain First and Donald Trump who proposed a Muslim travel ban. Islamophobia has therefore become normalised or in the words of the former Minister for Faith and Communities, Baroness Sayeeda Warsi, "it has passed the dinner table test". With the current development of modules, courses, undergraduate and postgraduate programmes, Islamophobia has become a 'hot' topic and one that requires further reading and investigation. If anyone is a victim of Islamophobic hate crimes, they can report incidents to the police and other third-party reporting agencies such as Tell MAMA (Measuring Anti-Muslim Attacks) who measure the volume and reported incidents of Islamophobia. With the rapid rise in Islamophobic incidents, this textbook provides the reader with a better understanding of how the criminal justice system should deal with victims and offenders. We also hope that beyond being a student textbook that prepares students wanting to study Islamophobia, they can use what they learn in their daily lives in helping improve society with the knowledge they have gained.

What is Islamophobia? Checklist

✓ Islamophobia is the fear, prejudice, and hatred of Muslims or non-Muslim individuals.
✓ Islamophobia leads to provocation, hostility, and intolerance.
✓ Islamophobia is based upon threatening, harassment, abuse, incitement, and intimidation of Muslims and non-Muslims.
✓ Islamophobia can happen both in the online and offline world.
✓ Islamophobia is motivated by institutional, ideological, political, and religious hostility.
✓ Islamophobia transcends into structural and cultural racism.
✓ Islamophobia targets the symbols and markers of being a Muslim.

Key theories in relation to Islamophobia

Islamophobia is linked to perceptions of fear and threat. Evidence shows that such threats can often be linked back to how society perceives the 'other'. Often this is used by perpetrators to argue issues such as economic stability and values/belonging. Fear is much more part of the view that Islamophobia is a social construct and therefore a distinct form of aggression and hate. Islamophobic hate crime victimisation serves as a visible indicator of the motives of the perpetrators and it indicates the perpetrator's bias and prejudice towards a specific group. Islamophobia therefore becomes a symbolic way in which groups are despised and victimized because of who they are perceived to be. As with hate crimes in general, Islamophobic hate crimes serve to send a message, which is instrumental in targeting victims. Some of the key theories in relation to Islamophobia and hate crimes in general are based on sociological, criminological, economic, and psychological explanations. Some of these theories include:

- Allport's Scale of Prejudice
- Strain theory
- Social Identity Theory
- Scapegoat theory

Allport (1958)

One of the most important theories in relation to hate crime and prejudice is Allport's (1958) scale of prejudice. Allport's scale of prejudice includes different stages of bias and prejudice. They are: Antilocution; Avoidance; Discrimination; Physical attack and Extermination. In this context, Islamophobia is seen as normal and can lead to issues of 'in-groups' and 'out-groups'. In our view, Islamophobia like hate crime in general will start with low-level abuse that can escalate and lead to physical manifestations of discrimination and prejudice. In some cases, it can also lead to ethnic cleansing of a particular group as was the case with the Srebrenica massacre where in July 1995 Bosnian Serb forces killed more than 8,000 Bosnian Muslims who were meant to be under UN protection. At the time of writing this book, a similar crisis is emerging in Myanmar where Rohingya Muslims have been killed for practicing their faith and in China where Muslims have been forced to leave their faith.

Merton (1957)

Another theory used in relation to hate crimes is strain theory. Strain theory occurs when individuals feel they have no choice but to react and act in a violent manner (Merton 1957). With respect to Islamophobia, perpetrators use the power imbalance to target minorities who they perceive as being given preferential treatment. This is important because in a climate of Islamophobia, far-right groups will often use effects of 'strain' to target minorities because of social and economic issues (Hall 2013). Strain theory can thus lead to issues around identity, belonging, fear, and anger. For example, Ezekiel (1995)

8 Introduction

found a strong link between neo-Nazis, poverty, and hate crimes. In Britain, the strain theory has led to political rhetoric that has impacted upon society. For example, this was demonstrated with the Brexit campaign and the posters used by the UKIP and Nigel Farage, which suggested that immigrants were coming to the UK to 'steal our jobs'.

Tajfel and Turner (1986)

Prejudice and hate crimes can also be learnt through access/contact with peers and those closest to perpetrators such as family members whose biased views can be adopted by children (social learning theory). Just as the strain theory identified issues of power and inequality, perceptions of behaviour and how they can be learnt are important when grounding where Islamophobia and hate crimes emerge from (Sharma 2012). For example, after the Paris terrorist attacks, there was a spike in Islamophobic hate crimes reported in schools in the UK (Tajfel and Turner 1986). These images are intertwined with perceptions of self-esteem and the issue to gain control and a sense of identity. This can also help to formulate ideas around 'in-groups' and 'out-groups' (Gerstenfeld 2013).

A scapegoat

The scapegoat theory is well-documented in the literature around hate crime and was used initially to discuss how certain groups are targeted because they are perceived as a 'problem-group'. Within the scapegoat theory, we see how offenders target victims because of economic difficulties (Gerstenfeld 2013). Gerstenfeld (2013) and Walters (2011) argue that this happens because of perceived competition over jobs, housing, and other resources between different groups. The scapegoat theory is intertwined with issues around the welfare state. It also extends to the debate and conflict concerning finding in the traditional sense a scapegoat because of perceived issues around economics, social cohesion, and social mobility (see Chapter 2 for further details).

Key questions

- How can theories help us better understand Islamophobia today?
- How would you define Islamophobia?
- What are the implications of the Punish a Muslim Day letter?
- Do you think Islamophobia is going to get worse?
- What is your checklist of key issues in relation to Islamophobia?

Further reading

- Law, I. 2010. *Racism and Ethnicity: Global Debates, Dilemmas, Directions.* London: Pearson Education.
- Lambert, B. and Githens-Mazer, J. 2011. *Islamophobia and Anti-Muslim Hate Crime: UK Case Studies 2010 – An Introduction to a Ten Year Europe-Wide Research Project.* London: European Muslim Research Centre.

- Meer, N., Dwyer, C., and Modood, T. 2010. Embodying nationhood? Conceptions of British national identity, citizenship and gender in the 'veil affair'. *The Sociological Review*, 58(1): 84–111.
- Modood, T. 1997. 'Difference', cultural racism and anti-racism. In: T. Modood and P. Werbner (eds) *Debating Cultural Hybridity*. London: Zed Books.
- Parekh, B. 2000. *The Future of Multi-Ethnic Britain*. London: Profile Books.
- Zebiri, K. 2008. The redeployment of orientalist themes in contemporary Islamophobia. *Studies in Contemporary Islam*, 10: 4–44.

References

Allport, G. W. 1958. *The Nature of Prejudice*. Garden City, NY, USA: Doubleday Anchor Books.

BBC News. 2018. Lincoln man admits sending 'Punish a Muslim Day' letters. Available at: www.bbc.co.uk/news/uk-england-45838506

Craig, K. M. 2002. Examining hate-motivated aggression. *Aggression and Violent Behaviour*, 7, 85–101.

Ezekiel, R. S. 1995. *The Racist Mind*. New York: Viking.

FRA (European Union Agency for Fundamental Rights). 2017.

Gerstenfeld, P. B. 2013. *Hate Crimes: Causes, Controls and Controversies*, 3rd ed. London: Sage.

Githens-Mazer, J. and Lambert, R. 2010. *Islamophobia and Anti-Muslim Hate Crime: A London Case Study*. London: European Muslim Research Centre.

Hall, N. 2013. *Hate Crime*, 2nd ed. London: Routledge.

Home Office. 2017 to 2018. Statistics recorded by the police. Available at: www.gov.uk/government/statistics/hate-crime-england-and-wales-2017-to-2018

Merton, R. K. 1957. *Social Theory and Social Structure*. Glencoe, IL: Free Press.

Poynting, S. and Mason, V. 2007. The resistible rise of Islamophobia: Anti-Muslim racism in the UK and Australia before 11 September 2001. *Journal of Sociology*, 43(1): 61–86.

Sharma, S. 2012. Hate crimes in India: An economic analysis of violence and atrocities against scheduled castes and scheduled tribes. Available at: http://dx.doi. org/10.2139/ssrn.2055549

Tajfel, H. and Turner, J. C. 1986. The social identity theory of inter-group behaviour. In: S. Worchel and L. W. Austin (eds) *Psychology of Intergroup Relations*. Nelson-Hall.

Walters, M. A. 2011. A general theories of hate crime? *Critical Criminology*, 19, 313–330.

Zempi, I. and Chakraborti, N. 2014. *Islamophobia, Victimisation and the Veil*. Basingstoke: Palgrave Macmillan.

Zempi, I. and Awan, I. 2016. *Islamophobia: Lived Experiences of Online and Offline Victimisation*. Bristol University Press.

2

UNDERSTANDING ISLAMOPHOBIC HATE CRIME

Introduction

This chapter examines the nature and impact of hate crime. It argues that hate crimes have a disproportionate impact on the victim on the basis that individuals are being targeted because of their identity. However, hate crimes not only impact the individual victim but also the wider community to which the victim belongs. In this regard, hate crimes send a message to the victim and the victim's group members that they are neither safe nor welcome in the community. The chapter also discusses the nature and scope of Islamophobic hate crime. It examines the role of 'trigger' events with regards to the prevalence and severity of Islamophobic hate crimes. Finally, it outlines the impact of Islamophobia, racism, and discrimination in the workplace on young Muslims' career development and progression.

Defining hate crime

Hate crime is the umbrella concept used in its broadest sense to describe incidents motivated by hate, hostility, or prejudice towards an individual's identity (Chakraborti and Garland 2015). As Copsey et al. (2013) point out, definitions of hate crime vary from one country to the next, and even within countries (the US, for example). In England and Wales, the central point of reference is the operational definition offered by the College of Policing (2014, p. 4), which defines hate crime as:

> Any criminal offence which is perceived by the victim or any other person, to be motivated by a hostility or prejudice based on a person's race or perceived race; religion or perceived religion; sexual orientation or perceived sexual orientation; disability or perceived disability and any non-crime incident motivated by a hostility or prejudice against a person who is transgender or perceived to be transgender.

The College of Policing (2014) states that the alleged actions of the perpetrator must amount to a criminal offence (under normal crime recording rules) in order to be recorded as a hate crime. If the facts do not identify any recordable crime but the victim perceives it to be a hate crime, the police should record it as a non-crime hate incident and not a hate crime. Relatedly, hate incidents are defined as:

> Any non-crime incident which is perceived by the victim or any other person, to be motivated by a hostility or prejudice based on a person's race or perceived race; religion or perceived religion; sexual orientation or perceived sexual orientation; disability or perceived disability and any non-crime incident motivated by a hostility or prejudice against a person who is transgender or perceived to be transgender.
>
> *(College of Policing 2014, p. 4)*

In addition to the five officially protected characteristics (namely race, religion, disability, sexual orientation, and transgender identity), police forces locally can record other aspects of identity that they think are at risk. For example, in 2013 Greater Manchester police was the first force in the UK to monitor hate crimes directed towards members of alternative subcultures such as goths and punks, whilst in 2016 Nottinghamshire police was the first force in the UK to record misogyny as a hate crime.

Hate crimes can be one-off events or form part of a series of repeated and targeted offending. Evidence shows that many hate crime incidents form part of an ongoing process of victimisation (Bowling 1998; Chakraborti, Garland, and Hardy 2014; Williams and Tregidga 2013). Individuals can be targeted for a combination of reasons, including disability, sexual orientation, or transgender identity, in addition to their race or religion. Hate crime can be perpetrated online or offline, or there can be a pattern of behaviour that includes both. The Internet, and social media in particular, have provided new platforms for offending behaviour. Crown Prosecution Service (CPS) is committed to prosecuting complaints of hate crime online with the same robust and proactive approach used with offline offending. The new CPS (2018) revised guidance on the prosecution of social media cases provides more detail.

Hate crimes often have a disproportionate impact on the victim on the basis that they are being targeted because of their identity. Hate crimes not only impact the individual victim but also the wider community to which the victim belongs. Whether one-off events or a series of repeated and targeted offending, hate crimes can send reverberations through communities as they reinforce established patterns of bias, prejudice, and discrimination. Referring to the powerful symbolic nature of hate crimes, Chakraborti and Garland (2015) state that hate crimes transmit a 'message' not just to the immediate victim but to fellow members of their minority community that reminds them of their 'othered' status: that 'their kind' are not welcome.

McDevitt et al. (2001) observe that 'hate' is absent from the vast majority of hate crimes. Rather, hate crimes may be driven by bias, prejudice, or "negative feelings held by the offender towards a social group that, in their eyes, have an 'outsider status'" (Garland and Chakraborti 2012, p. 40). It is useful to note that an 'in-group' is any group to which a person belongs and with which they identify; in contrast, an 'out-group' is one which people do not belong to or identify with. A key element of hate crime is that offenders target potential victims because of their membership of despised 'out-groups'. According to Gerstenfeld (2013), it is the fact that the victim is targeted because of their actual or perceived membership of a social grouping – rather than the presence of any bias or hatred – that is the most significant factor when defining hate crime: it is the attack on their identity that sets these acts apart. Implicit in this argument is that these are 'stranger danger' offences (namely, random acts carried out by strangers unknown to the victim) in which the perpetrator selects the victim not because of who they are as an individual but because they are part of a despised 'out-group' in the eyes of the aggressor (Perry 2001). Indeed, the Leicester Hate Crime Project found that 49 per cent of hate crimes are committed by perpetrators who are unknown to their victim (Chakraborti, Garland, and Hardy 2014). These incidents usually occurred in public spaces including streets, parks, and city centres, as well as in and around public transport infrastructures (Chakraborti, Garland, and Hardy 2014).

According to the typology of hate crime perpetrators, first developed by Levin and McDevitt in 1993 and updated in 2002, there are four 'types' of perpetrators including: thrill seekers (those motivated by the thrill and excitement of offending); defensive (those motivated by a perceived threat to their 'territory' or 'turf' that must be defended); retaliators (those who act in retaliation for a perceived attack against their in-group); and mission (perpetrators who make it their mission in life to eradicate 'difference'). However, it could be argued that there is no single 'type' of person who commits hate crime. As Walters and Brown (2016) point out, compartmentalising perpetrators into single 'types' may be overly simplistic, with many perpetrators having multiple motivations for offending. Moreover, the various 'types' of perpetrators may influence each other. 'Mission' perpetrators may, alongside other factors, help to fuel wider climates of hate, fostering an environment within which 'thrill seekers' and 'defensive' perpetrators feel justified in committing offences (Walters and Brown 2016). Along similar lines, 'defensive' offences may give rise to 'retaliatory' ones, and so a vicious circle between (perceived) victimisation and perpetration is perpetuated (Walters and Brown 2016).

Walters and Brown (2016) suggest that despite dissimilarities between types of hate crime, most, if not all, hate crimes are linked by perceptions of 'threat'. In other words, perpetrators are likely to be influenced by their perception that certain groups pose a 'threat' to them. According to Walters and Brown (2016), these threats can be divided into 'realistic' threats and 'symbolic' threats. Realistic threats include tangible conflicts of interest such as perceived competition over jobs, housing and other social/state resources, and physical harm to themselves or others; for example, a perpetrator of racist or anti-immigrant abuse fears that minority ethnic groups are encroaching upon his/her dominant group identity as well as 'unfairly' taking, jobs, housing, and social welfare (Walters and Brown 2016). Symbolic threats relate to people's social identities, such as the in-group's 'way of life', including values and social norms. Walters and Brown (2016) argue that both survey and experimental evidence support the link between perceived threats (both realistic and symbolic) and out-group prejudice. Using FBI statistics, Kaplan (2006) showed how there was a sharp spike in Islamophobic hate crime in the US immediately following the terrorist attacks in September 2001.

Conceptualising Islamophobia

Drawing on the operational definition offered by the College of Policing (2014), Islamophobic hate crime is defined as any criminal offence which is perceived, by the victim or any other person, to be motivated wholly or partly by hostility or prejudice based upon a person's religion or perceived religion, that is, their Muslim religion. In 1996 the Runnymede Trust, an independent research and social policy agency, established the Commission on British Muslims and Islamophobia. In November 1997, the Commission produced a report entitled 'Islamophobia: A Challenge for Us All' (Runnymede Trust 1997). The aim of the Commission was twofold: (a) to counter Islamophobic assumptions that Islam is a single monolithic system, without internal development, diversity, and dialogue, and (b) to draw attention to the principal dangers which Islamophobia creates or exacerbates for Muslim communities, and therefore for the well-being of society as a whole. The report described the nature of Islamophobic prejudice and drew a key distinction between closed views of Islam on the one hand and open views on the other. Islamophobia is equated with closed views and eight main features are itemised (Runnymede Trust 1997).

Importantly, this report raised awareness about the problem of Islamophobia in the UK and elsewhere. It brought the term to public and policy prominence, in Britain and indeed beyond. It defined Islamophobia as "the shorthand way of referring to dread or hatred of Islam – and, therefore, to fear or dislike all or most Muslims" (Runnymede Trust 1997, p. 2). It also defined Islamophobia as "unfounded hostility towards Islam" and noted that "It also refers to the practical consequences of such hostility in unfair discrimination against Muslim individuals and communities, and to the exclusion of Muslims from mainstream political and social affairs" (Runnymede Trust 1997, p. 4). In essence, the report stated that the term Islamophobia refers to three phenomena:

- Unfounded hostility towards Islam;
- Practical consequences of such hostility in unfair discrimination against Muslim individuals and communities;
- Exclusion of Muslims from mainstream political and social affairs.

Since the publication of the report 'Islamophobia: A Challenge for Us All' in 1997, Islamophobia has grown considerably. On the 20th anniversary of the initial

14 Understanding Islamophobic hate crime

report, Runnymede Trust has published a new report, which offered the following definition of Islamophobia:

> Islamophobia is any distinction, exclusion, or restriction towards, or preference against, Muslims (or those perceived to be Muslims) that has the purpose or effect of nullifying or impairing the recognition, enjoyment or exercise, on an equal footing, of human rights and fundamental freedoms in the political, economic, social, cultural or any other field of public life.
>
> *(Runnymede Trust 2017, p. 1)*

This definition, which derives from the United Nations definition of racism, highlights the ways in which racism operates: not simply as a prejudicial attitude but by denying people dignity, rights, and liberties across a range of political, economic, social, and cultural institutions (Elahi and Khan 2017). Referring only to 'anti-Muslim hate' does not fully capture the widespread (or structural) ways in which racial inequalities persist, whereby Muslims face particular economic or political disadvantages both historically and in a contemporary context; thus Elahi and Khan (2017) argue that a definition of Islamophobia as 'anti-Muslim racism' fits with historical and academic accounts of racism. Indeed, in a landmark report, the All Party Parliamentary Group on British Muslims (2018, p. 11) proposed the following definition of Islamophobia: "Islamophobia is rooted in racism, and is a type of racism that targets expressions of Muslimness or perceived Muslimness." In light of this, the following paragraphs consider the relationship between Islamophobia and racism.

Islamophobia and racism

Racism can occur in situations where neither the reality nor concept of race actually exists (Allen 2010a). As Meer, Dwyer, and Modood (2010) point out, understandings of racism should not focus exclusively on race thereby overlooking religion and culture. Conceptualising racism exclusively as a form of 'biological determinism' ignores the ways in which cultural racism draws upon other markers of 'difference' to identify minority groups and individuals that do not conform with 'mainstream' society. Modood (1997, p. 165) states that:

> Cultural racism is likely to be particularly aggressive against those minority communities that want to maintain – and not just defensively – some of the basic elements of their culture or religion; if, far from denying their difference (beyond the colour of their skin), they want to assert this difference in public, and demand that they be respected just as they are.

Taking a similar position, Law (2010) highlights the complex chameleon like character of racism, which changes in terms of form and content across different times and contexts. Law (2010) observes that racism takes many forms and links this reality to contemporary perceptions of Western superiority and to this end, legitimised violence towards Muslims. This new form of racism can be interpreted as racism of 'reaction', based on the perceived 'threat' to traditional social and cultural identities. It can also be understood as racism of 'surveillance' premised on the notion that cultural difference slides into the demonisation and stigmatisation of 'Other' cultures in the interests of 'protecting' the European people, which is a different entity to the European population as a whole (Law 2010). This line of argument suggests that the key element of contemporary racism is the attribution of negative cultural characteristics to 'Other' minority groups.

In light of popular debates about national identity, immigration, and community cohesion, colour racism has ceased to be acceptable; nevertheless, a cultural racism which emphasises the 'Other', 'alien' values of Muslims has increased (Zebiri 2008). In this context, cultural difference is understood as 'cultural deviance' and equated with the notion of cultural threat. Parekh (2000, p. 60) observes that contemporary anti-Muslim racism is "one of the most serious forms of cultural hostility in modern Europe". Similarly, Modood (1997) identifies that Islamophobia is at the heart of contemporary British and European cultural racism. In this context, Islam is routinely portrayed as an external 'threat' to distinctly European norms and values. For advocates of the 'clash of civilisations' thesis, there is a cultural war between Islam and the West. In the British context, Islam and Muslims have increasingly been seen to be 'culturally dangerous' and threatening the 'British way of life'. Whilst recognising that Muslim minorities differ in the context of European countries – predominantly Algerian in France, Turkish in Germany and Austria, Pakistani in the UK – it is increasingly Islamic religion, tradition, and culture that have been seen as a 'threat' to the Western ideals of democracy, freedom of speech, and gender equality.

Nevertheless, it is often argued that Islamophobia 'does not exist' as a form of racism. Alexander (2017) suggests that the de-raceing of Islamophobia can be traced to four interlinked arguments:

- First, the reduction of our understanding of racism to narrow biological markers strips it to its social, structural, and historical context;
- Second, the denial of 'Muslim' as a racial or ethnic category (unlike, for example, Sikhs or Jews) and relatedly, the denial of Muslims being victims of racism as Muslims;
- Third, the placing of Islam as a category of choice rather than ascription, and thus as separate from the embodied being of its adherents ('culture' rather than 'race');
- Fourth, the over-emphasis on Muslim/Islamic culture as a foundational explanation for the 'demonisation' of Muslims.

The racialisation of Muslim identity

In the present context, Muslims have been labelled as being both deviant and evil. As Islamophobia becomes more rampant, the conflation between race, ethnicity,

16 Understanding Islamophobic hate crime

and appearance with the Islamic faith has constructed non-Muslim men as dangerous too. As a result, non-Muslim men have experienced racism and similar treatment through institutional forms of Islamophobia. Part of this polarisation and moral panic is the conflation of Islam and terrorism, which has led to questions around non-Muslim men and their loyalty, citizenship, and identity.

The racialisation of crime has led to a drastic upsurge, following terrorist attacks. Islamophobia has now evolved into attacks against Muslim-looking people because of factors such as their skin colour, facial hair, and clothing. Ahmad (2002, p. 101) argues: "Among the enormous violence done by the United States since the tragedies suffered on September 11 has been an unrelenting, multivalent assault on the bodies, psyches, and rights of Arabs, Muslim, and South Asian immigrants." The increased attention around people's perceived 'Muslimness' has led to the intersection between race, ethnicity, and faith. Research has shown that this intersection can lead to experiences of discrimination and minority communities suffering victimisation. Understanding that Islamophobia can also mean racism is critical if we are to get an understanding of how racial stereotypes and attitudes target communities because of their perceived identities.

In America, an Indian man wearing a turban was mistaken as a Muslim and shot dead while working at the gas station he owned (Basu 2016). Victims of these anti-Muslim incidents include not only Muslims but also anyone who looks like a Muslim or an Arab. Many non-Muslims such as Sikh men (with readily identifiable turbans and long beards) and Hindus, and many non-Arabs such as Indians, Pakistanis, and other South Asians are affected. Racism and Islamophobia are inextricably linked. Participants in Awan and Zempi's (2019) study noted how their appearances acted as a 'trigger' for the types of hate and abuse they suffered. For example, if they had a beard or were perceived to be from a Muslim background because of their skin colour then they were more likely to be targeted for racial abuse.

Using a race-based traumatic stress injury model, Abu-Ras and Suarez (2009) argue that perceived or actual forms of racism will lead to different forms of discrimination, i.e. racial prejudice, profiling, verbal assaults, and hate crimes. The trauma experienced by participants in this case would mean uncontrollable anger but also impacting an individual's quality of life. Ahmad (2002) states that these forms of hatred perpetuated against people who look like Muslims manifests itself in the form of racial discrimination and harassment. For example, according to a YouGov poll about the "UK attitudes toward the Arab world" it showed that when respondents were asked if they would support racial profiling against Arabs or Muslims for security reasons, 55 per cent agreed (Dearden 2017). The types of hate incidents reported can be used to discuss structural racism inflicted within different segments of society. This hate violence can be thus understood, as Ahmad (2002, p. 104) argues, as the result of "racial profiling's flawed logic (people who 'look Muslim' are more likely to be terrorists, therefore if we are attacking terrorism we should attack people who 'look Muslim')".

Legislation for racially and religiously motivated hate crime

There is no single piece of legislation for hate crime in the UK. The five monitored strands of hate crime are covered by legislation (sections 28–32 of the Crime and Disorder Act 1998 and sections 145 and 146 of the Criminal Justice Act 2003), which allows prosecutors to apply for a 'sentence uplift' (increased punishment for the crime) for those convicted of a hate crime. The legal framework for racially and religiously aggravated crime includes (a) specific aggravated offences and sentence uplift under section 145 and (b) stirring up hatred on the grounds of race and religion.

Specific aggravated offences and sentence uplift under s.145 of the Criminal Justice Act 2003

Racially and religiously aggravated offences were introduced by the Crime and Disorder Act 1998 (CDA 1998). These specific offences cover wounding, assault, criminal damage, harassment, stalking, and threatening/abusive behaviour. To prove that an offence is racially or religiously aggravated, the prosecution has to prove the 'basic' offence and racial or religious aggravation, as defined in section 28 CDA 1998. Section 145 Criminal Justice Act 2003 (CJA 2003) gives the court power to increase the sentence of any other offence that is racially or religiously aggravated. An offence is racially or religiously aggravated if:

- At the time of committing the offence, or immediately before or after doing so, the offender demonstrated towards the victim of the offence hostility based on the victim's membership (or presumed membership) of a racial or religious group, or
- The offence was motivated (wholly or partly) by hostility towards members of a racial or religious group based on their membership of that group.

It is important to note that the legal framework and the police/CPS definition refer to hostility, not hatred. There is no statutory definition of hostility and the everyday or dictionary definition is applied, encompassing a broad spectrum of behaviour including ill-will, ill-feeling, spite, prejudice, unfriendliness, antagonism, resentment, and dislike.

Stirring up hatred on the grounds of race and religion

Parts 3 and 3A Public Order Act 1986 cover stirring up hatred on the grounds of race and religion. Stirring up racial hatred, defined by reference to colour, race, nationality (including citizenship), ethnic, or national origin is committed when someone says or does something which is threatening, abusive, or insulting, and the person either intends to stir up racial hatred, or make it likely that racial hatred will be stirred up. It covers behaviour such as making a speech, posting material online, displaying a poster, performing a play, or broadcasting on the media. Stirring up religious hatred is committed if a person uses threatening words or behaviour, or displays any threatening written material, and intends to stir up religious hatred against a group of persons defined by reference to religious belief or lack of religious belief. It covers the same behaviour applicable to stirring up racial hatred. Stirring up religious hatred is limited to threatening words or behaviour and the CPS have to prove intent. Additionally, there is a freedom of expression defence contained in section 29J, but no corresponding statutory defence for the racial offence. Any prosecution for the offence of stirring up hatred on the grounds of race or religion requires the consent of the Attorney General.

Contemporary Islamophobia

Contemporary Islamophobia is a reflection of a historical anti-Muslim, anti-Islamic phenomenon, which was constructed in colonial times but has increased significantly after the 9/11 and 7/7 terrorist attacks. Indeed, Islamophobia is not a new phenomenon. Rather, contemporary Islamophobic discourses draw on Orientalist discourses emerging from colonialism (Said 1978). In this respect, Islamophobic sentiments reflect notions of medieval cultures, barbarism, and timeless antagonism to the West (Alexander 2017). Contemporary Islamophobic discourses also draw on decolonisation and mass post-war migration. Alexander (1998; 2002) notes that 'Muslims' in post-war Britain were configured as 'coloured', then 'Black', then 'Asian', then 'Pakistani' and 'Bangladeshi' before they appeared as 'Muslims' – although the labels may have changed, the racist sentiments remain. These older racial and ethnic stereotypes feed into contemporary Islamophobic discourse.

In the aftermath of the attacks on the World Trade Center in 2001, the launch of the 'war on terror' and the 'home-grown' terror attacks in London in 2005, Islamophobic hate crime has increased dramatically. In other words, the 9/11 and 7/7 terrorist attacks played a major role in heightening Islamophobic perceptions of Muslims in the West. These attacks and subsequent media portrayals of the events facilitated a deeper resentment and fear of Islam and Muslims than existed before. The Council of Europe's Commission on Racism and Intolerance 2010 UK country report (ECRI 2016) noted that "Muslims, migrants and asylum seekers [and] Gypsies/Travelers are regularly presented in a negative light in the mainstream media". These concerns were picked up by the Leveson inquiry and subsequent report into UK press standards (House of Commons 2012), which also stated that "discriminatory, sensational or unbalanced reporting in relation to ethnic minorities, immigrants and/or asylum seekers is a feature of journalistic practice in parts of the press, rather than an aberration".

The popular press has had a massive impact in terms of determining notions of the 'threat' of Islam. The political rhetoric and sensational media reporting in the aftermath of Islamist terrorist attacks illustrates the ways in which Muslim identities can be transformed across time and space. The effect of these transformations has been the construction of hate and fear, resulting in the rise in the level of Islamophobia through the construction of Muslims as synonymous with 'deviance', 'un-

Britishness', and terrorism (Poole 2006; Saeed 2007). This discourse has positioned 'the Muslim community' as homogeneous, outside of, and opposed to Britishness, and understood through stereotypes of 'us versus them' (Alexander 2017).

Concurrently, counter-terrorism measures have contributed to the 'demonisation' of Muslims in political, media, and public discourses, portraying Islam and Muslims as a security 'threat'. A series of policies around securitisation and 'tackling extremism' have positioned all Muslims as a 'suspect community'. There has been an institution(alisation) of surveillance of Muslim groups on the streets (as in the Birmingham 'spycam' affair; Awan 2014; Hussain 2014), by police, in prisons, in the immigration system, in their own homes, and on the Internet and, particularly worryingly, across the education system from primary schools to universities (Alexander 2017). This has particularly affected young people, who bear the brunt of this hostility, creating a climate of fear and suspicion (Alexander 2017).

Relatedly, Spalek and Lambert (2008) point out that since 9/11 and 7/7, terrorism has been the subject of intense media interest, political discourse, and public scrutiny in the British context, whilst a major concern has been that the 7/7 terrorists were British-born. The terminology of the 'new terrorism' has helped to justify a re-configuration of security systems, legislation, and police powers. Post the 9/11 attacks, the number of Asian people stopped and searched under anti-terrorism laws in the UK quadrupled in a single year, from 744 in 2001–2002 to 2,989 in 2002–2003 (Morris 2004). Following the 2005 bombing of London's transport infrastructure, there was a seven-fold increase in the number of people of Asian appearance stopped and searched by British Transport Police under the use of counter-terrorism police powers (Dodd 2005).

The notion of 'new terrorism' is based on the construction of Muslim minorities as 'suspect communities' who should be monitored by state agencies, casting new questions about national identity, security, and loyalty (Spalek and Lambert 2008). Clearly, this approach has created a climate of fear and suspicion towards Muslims. Following the 7/7 bombings, the then Prime Minister Tony Blair stated: "Let no one be in doubt. The rules of the game have changed" (quoted in Wintour 2005) echoing Bush's false dilemma in 2001 "You're either with us, or against us" (quoted in CNN 2001). Afshar (2008) states that immediately after 7/7 there was a 'shoot to kill' policy that could threaten anyone assumed to have been 'a Muslim terrorist'. Jean Charles de Menezes was mistakenly shot dead by the Metropolitan Police who followed him on to a tube train at Stockwell station in London the day after the failed attacks of 21 July 2005 as he was misidentified as one of the suspects (Siddique 2010).

The UK Government's anti-terrorism strategy has caused further feelings of stigmatisation and alienation amongst Muslims. Awan (2012, p. 1168) states that:

> while counterterrorism policies such as Prevent have an overall goal of community engagement to combat extremism, it may alienate sections of the Muslim community through counterterrorism policing tactics. Such policies have, in effect, constructed a 'suspect' community within the dictum of community engagement for counterterrorism purposes.

20 Understanding Islamophobic hate crime

British Muslims have reported feeling increasingly alienated and isolated (Choudhury and Fenwick 2011). Seen through the prism of security risk, incompatible 'difference' and self-segregation, Muslims in the West have emerged as the new "folk devils" (Cohen 1972) of popular and media imagination. This is particularly apparent in the gendering of Muslim identities. Islam is understood as a violent political ideology, religion, and culture; Muslim men are perceived as the embodiment of terrorism, fundamentalism, and extremism; and Muslim women are viewed as the personification of gender oppression in Islam, especially if they are veiled. Such stereotypes provide fertile ground for public expressions of Islamophobia including verbal abuse, threats and intimidation, harassment, physical assault and violence, property damage, hate mail and literature, as well as online abuse.

Manifestations of Islamophobia

Islamophobic hate crimes and incidents often occur in public spaces such as streets, city centres, and public transport networks. Common locations for these incidents also include shops, restaurants, gyms, and other business environments accessed by members of the public, as well as surrounding public areas (Tell MAMA 2017). Rather than being single, one-off incidents, Islamophobic hate crimes can sometimes form part of an ongoing process of victimisation that often makes up part of a victim's everyday experiences of hostility. Individuals can also be targeted in schools or Higher Education, the workplace, household, or private property. Indeed, a significant proportion of hate crimes are committed by perpetrators who are known to the victim such as neighbours, local community members, and even friends, carers, family members, and work colleagues (Chakraborti, Garland, and Hardy 2014; Mason 2005; Quarmby 2008; Roxwell 2011; Sibbitt 1997). The All Wales Hate Crime Project found that 43 per cent of victims reported that they knew their perpetrator (Williams and Tregidga 2013).

Tell MAMA supports victims of anti-Muslim hate and is a public service which also measures and monitors anti-Muslim incidents. In the report entitled 'The Geography of Anti-Muslim Hatred', Tell MAMA (2016) found that a high proportion of Islamophobic incidents occurred near public transport hubs. Islamophobic hate crime on public transport networks is a particularly stressful social situation in which passengers may feel trapped in enclosed and overcrowded spaces where people of 'difference' come into close contact with one another, and where micro aggressions can quickly escalate into violent altercations (Walters and Brown 2016). Yeung and Duncan (2016) note that there has been a 37 per cent increase in the number of race hate crimes reported to British Transport Police over the past five years. Finally, Muslims who work in the night-time economy such as security guards, late night takeaway, restaurant staff, and taxi drivers appear to be particularly vulnerable to Islamophobic attacks. In this case, incidents appear to be fuelled by alcohol, which lowers perpetrators' inhibitions (Tell MAMA 2017).

The visibility of Muslim identity

Evidence shows that Islamophobia is highly gendered. Muslim women are more likely to be attacked or abused than men in public settings, particularly if they are visibly Muslim (for example, wearing Islamic clothing such as a headscarf, face veil, abaya), and the largest proportion of perpetrators remain white males (Tell MAMA 2017). In a report published by the European Monitoring Centre for Racism and Xenophobia (EUMC), Allen and Nielsen (2002, p. 35) found that the stimulant behind the vast majority of Islamophobic incidents was the fact that victims were identified as Muslims by 'visual identifiers', namely something that could be recognisably associated with Islam:

> It seems that behind the vast majority of attacks and infringements upon specific communities and individuals was the fact that they were identified as Muslims, whether they in fact were or not, by something that could be recognisably associated with Islam; this we call visual identifiers. Whilst these were not necessarily in themselves the reason for any attacks, it would seem that they were the single most predominant factor in determining who or what became the victim of retaliation.

Within this paradigm, the visual identifiers of Islam are the tools for identification upon which Islamophobia can be expressed. This approach demonstrates why certain individuals and groups are more likely to become targets for hostility than others. As Allen (2010b) points out, when the visual identifiers of Islam hold such primacy in determining who or what become the targets for violence, it is veiled Muslim women in particular – possibly the most visually identifiable religious adherents in the West – who become the primary foci for retaliation. This ties in with the suggestions of Githens-Mazer and Lambert (2010; also see Lambert and Githens-Mazer 2011) who documented the heightened sense of vulnerability of Muslim women who wore hijab or niqab in public places in London.

Certainly, another focus for manifestations of Islamophobia has been mosques. As Allen and Nielsen (2002, p. 37) point out, mosques have become a 'very easy and readily identifiable target' due to their visible nature. Between May 2013 and June 2017, 167 mosques in the UK were targeted in Islamophobic incidents and attacks (Tell MAMA 2017). Taken together, these equate to an average of one incident against a mosque every week. In the deadliest mass shooting attack New Zealand has ever seen, Brenton Tarrant is believed to be responsible for the shootings at the Al Noor mosque and the Linwood Islamic centre both located in Christchurch, New Zealand on 15 March 2019. The attacks killed 51 people and injured 49 others (Hollingsworth 2019).

'Trigger' events

The prevalence and severity of Islamophobic hate crimes are influenced by 'trigger' events of local, national, and international significance. Williams and Burnap (2015) argue that hate crimes are communicative acts, which are often provoked by antecedent events that incite a desire for retribution in the targeted group, towards the group that share similar characteristics to the perpetrators. Hate crimes increase following 'trigger' events as they operate to galvanise tensions and sentiments against the suspected perpetrators and groups associated with them. Indeed, evidence shows that Islamophobic hate crimes have increased significantly following 'trigger' attacks including terrorist attacks carried out by individuals who choose to identify themselves as being Muslim or acting in the name of Islam (Hanes and Machin 2014). Spikes in Islamophobic hate crimes and incidents following 'trigger' events are not confided to offline settings; rather, the offline pattern is replicated online (Awan 2014).

Following the murder of British army soldier drummer Lee Rigby in Woolwich, London by two Islamist extremists in May 2013, there was a clear spike in attacks on Muslims. For example, more than 140 Islamophobic incidents were reported to Tell MAMA in the 48 hours following the Woolwich murder (Jivanda 2013). Attacks in 2017 alone included those at Westminster Bridge, Manchester Arena, London Bridge, Finsbury Park, and Parsons Green tube station. Police in Manchester and London registered surges in Islamophobic hate crime in the immediate aftermaths of the Manchester Arena bombing and the London Bridge attack. The number of Islamophobic attacks in Manchester went up five-fold in the week after the concert bombing, with 139 incidents reported to Tell MAMA, compared to 25 incidents the previous week. The Finsbury Park terrorist attack was in fact an Islamophobic attack deliberately targeting British Muslims. That said, the Finsbury Park attack was not the first act of terrorism against Muslim communities. In 2013, a Ukrainian neo-Nazi, Pavlo Lapshyn, murdered 82-year-old Mohammed Saleem and tried to bomb several West Midlands mosques in the hope of instigating a 'race war'. A year later, a neo-Nazi named Ian Forman was jailed for ten years after plotting to bomb mosques in Merseyside (Travis 2017).

On 13 November 2016, Paris and Saint-Denis in France were targeted in a coordinated attack by ISIS. The attacks by gunmen and suicide bombers hit Bataclan music hall, the national stadium, and restaurants and bars, almost simultaneously; the attacks left 130 people dead and hundreds wounded, with more than 100 in a critical condition. Cuerden and Rogers (2017) found an increase in the number of referrals for race hate crime at the time of the Paris attacks, before returning to more stabilised numbers in the following week. On 22 March 2016, ISIS claimed responsibility for the coordinated attacks at Brussels Airport Zaventem and Maalbeek Metro Station, which killed 32 people and injured over 300 people. Cuerden and Rogers (2017) found that the number of referrals of race hate crime increased during the time period when the attacks took place.

According to BBC (2019), Islamophobic hate crimes in London have increased significantly since the Christchurch mosque shootings in New Zealand. There were 1,630 hate offences recorded by the Metropolitan Police in March 2019. Of these, 156 were Islamophobic – almost double the number recorded the previous month.

Furthermore, in the wake of high-profile events such as the EU referendum and the Syrian refugee crisis in 2016, debates around immigration have promoted Islamophobic sentiments. According to the National Police Chiefs Council (NPCC), racist or religious offences recorded by police forces in England and Wales increased by 41 per cent in the month after the referendum vote with 5,468 hate crimes recorded in July 2016, up from 3,886 such crimes in the same period a year earlier (Home Office 2016). Tell MAMA (2017) recorded a 475 per cent increase in the number of Islamophobic incidents in the week following the EU referendum vote (from 12 incidents in the week beginning 17 June to 69 incidents in the week beginning 24 June 2016). Cuerden and Rogers (2017) argue that the toxic rhetoric around Brexit encouraged some individuals to engage in open hostility towards immigrants across the country. For example, incidents have been reported in the media of racial abuse being hurled at minority ethnic individuals in places such as Manchester, Basingstoke, and Cardiff amongst many other places, as well as online race hate abuse towards individuals (Cuerden and Rogers 2017). Islamophobic narratives are reproduced and shared globally, and the reach of social media has amplified those voices (Elahi and Khan 2017).

Moreover, there is a media influence upon reporting whereby Muslim men have been constructed as "The New Folk Devils" (Shain 2011; Cohen 1972). National scandals such as the grooming of young girls across the UK by groups of organised criminal 'grooming gangs', twisted by the far-right into a 'Muslim' issue has also been identified as a 'trigger' event. Awan and Zempi (2015) found that in the wake of the Rotherham scandal, 'Muslim' is deployed in order to cast *all* Muslims as synonymous with child abusers. Indeed, evidence shows that widespread child sexual exploitation by 'Asian/Muslim gangs' in Rotherham led to a rise in Islamophobia towards Muslims in Rotherham and elsewhere in the UK (Tufail 2015). Finally, the next section outlines the impact of Islamophobia, racism, and discrimination in the workplace on young Muslims' career development and progression.

Social mobility

Muslims are the most disadvantaged faith group in the labour market in the UK. According to Social Mobility Commission (2017), Muslims experience the greatest economic disadvantages than any other faith group in the UK. For example, they are more likely than non-Muslims to experience neighbourhood deprivation, housing, educational and health disadvantage, and unemployment.

According to the 2011 Census (Nomis/Office for National Statistics 2013), 19.8 per cent of the Muslim population is in full-time employment, compared to 34.9 per cent in the overall population whilst 7.2 per cent of Muslims are unemployed compared to 4 per cent in the overall population. Only 6 per cent of Muslims are in "higher managerial, administrative and professional occupations" compared to 10 per cent of the overall population. In contrast, 24 per cent of Muslims are classified as having "Never worked/long-term unemployed" compared to just 6

24 Understanding Islamophobic hate crime

per cent for the overall population (Nomis/Office for National Statistics 2013). Muslim women seeking employment are not finding commensurate support and equal opportunities: 71.2 per cent of Muslim women aged 16–24 are not in employment (Muslim Council of Britain 2015). Furthermore, 46 per cent of the Muslim population live in the 10 per cent of the most deprived local authority districts. Social Mobility Commission (2017) argues that this has implications for access to resources, school attainment, progression to Higher Education, and the availability of jobs, including those at postgraduate or managerial levels. According to the Muslim Council of Britain (2015), Muslims face a 'double penalty' in entering the labour market, that is, Islamophobia and racial discrimination, and this is one of the key reasons for this data.

Social Mobility Commission (2017) examined the causes of low social mobility for young Muslims. It found that Muslims experience Islamophobia, discrimination, and/or racism at all stages of their careers – including transitioning from education to employment at every stage (see also McGregor-Smith 2017). Young Muslims were excluded, discriminated against, or failed, at all stages of their transition from education to employment. As might be expected, this has profound implications for social mobility amongst Muslims. Specifically, the Social Mobility Commission (2017) found that with respect to school and Higher Education:

- Incidences of Islamophobia or racism affect young Muslims' self-esteem and self-confidence, which in turn impacts on their aspiration and ultimately their attainment.
- The failure to accommodate religious norms and/or develop understanding of Muslims' needs directly impacts on young Muslims' sense of belonging, which compounds feelings of isolation and can limit their aspirations.
- Perceptions that they will be targets for overt bullying/harassment based on their appearance, beliefs, and their overall 'difference' means that young Muslims may avoid asking for help in classes at school, which affects their academic attainment.

The Social Mobility Commission (2017) found that with respect to young Muslims' transition to the labour market and career progression:

- They face repeated rejection at application and interview stages, perceiving this to be the result of both direct and indirect discrimination. Participants also felt that employers are reluctant to recruit them because they are prejudiced or hold stereotypical views.
- Discrimination and Islamophobia in the recruitment process were perceived to be more of a threat further from home, thus restricting their opportunities and job searches to their local area. Respondents argued that they felt safer, better integrated, or less visibly 'different' in areas with high number of Muslims. However, they were concerned that remaining within Muslim communities would limit aspirations and that navigating wider non-Muslim society was

imperative for succeeding in relation to education or employment. As a consequence, young Muslims are more likely to be unemployed, underemployed, in insecure employment, and/or in receipt of low pay.

- With respect to their career progression, Islamophobia, racism, discrimination, harassment, and lack of cultural awareness in the workplace impacted on young Muslims' career development and progression.

Key questions

- What is the difference between hate crime and hate incident?
- What is the relationship between Islamophobia and racism?
- What is the role of 'trigger' events in recorded levels of Islamophobic hate crime attacks?
- What are the key findings from Social Mobility Commission (2017)?

Further reading

- All Party Parliamentary Group on British Muslims. 2018. *Islamophobia Defined: Report on the Inquiry into a Working Definition of Islamophobia/Anti-Muslim Hatred*. London: All Party Parliamentary Group on British Muslims.
- Allen, C. 2010. *Islamophobia*, Surrey: Ashgate.
- Chakraborti, N. and Garland, J. 2015. *Hate Crime*. London: Sage.
- CPS. 2018. Social Media – Guidelines on prosecuting cases involving communications sent via social media. Available at: www.cps.gov.uk/legal-guidance/social-media-guidelines-prosecuting-cases-involving-communications-sent-social-media

References

Abu-Ras, W. M. and Suarez, Z. E. 2009. Muslim men and women's perception of discrimination, hate crimes, and PTSD symptoms post 9/11. *Traumatology*, 15: 48–63.

Afshar, H. 2008. Can I see your hair? Choice, agency and attitudes: The dilemma of faith and feminism for Muslim women who cover. *Ethnic and Racial Studies*, 31(2): 411–427.

Ahmad, M. 2002. Homeland insecurities: Racial violence the day after September 11. *Race / Ethnicity Multidisciplinary Global Contexts*, 4. doi:10.1215/01642472-20-3_72-101.

Alexander, C. 1998. Re-imagining the Muslim community. *Innovation*, 11(4): 439–450.

Alexander, C. 2000. *The Asian Gang*. Oxford: Berg.

Alexander, C. 2017. Raceing Islamophobia. In: Runnymede Trust (ed.) *Islamophobia: Still a Challenge for us All*. London: Runnymede Trust, pp. 13–16.

Alexander, C. 2002. Beyond black: Rethinking the colour/culture divide. *Ethnic and Racial Studies*, 25(4): 552–571.

All Party Parliamentary Group on British Muslims. 2018. *Islamophobia Defined: Report on the Inquiry into a Working Definition of Islamophobia/Anti-Muslim Hatred*. London: All Party Parliamentary Group on British Muslims.

Allen, C. 2010a. *Islamophobia*. Surrey: Ashgate.

Allen, C. 2010b. *An Overview of Key Islamophobia Research*. Birmingham: The National Association of Muslim Police.

26 Understanding Islamophobic hate crime

Allen, C. and Nielsen, J. 2002. *Summary Report on Islamophobia in the EU after 11 September 2001*. Vienna: European Monitoring Centre on Racism and Xenophobia.

Awan, I. 2012. "I am a Muslim not an extremist": How the Prevent Strategy has constructed a "suspect" community. *Politics & Policy*, 40(6): 1158–1185.

Awan, I. 2014. Islamophobia on Twitter: A typology of online hate against Muslims on social media. *Policy & Internet*, 6(2): 133–150.

Awan, I. and Zempi, I. 2015. 'I will blow your face off'—Virtual and physical world anti-Muslim hate crime. *British Journal of Criminology*, doi:10.1093/bjc/azv122

Awan, I. and Zempi, I. 2019. 'You all look the same': Non-Muslim men who suffer Islamophobic hate crime in the post-Brexit era. *European Journal of Criminology*, doi:10.1177/1477370818812735

Basu, M. 2016. 15 years after 9/11, Sikhs still victims of anti-Muslim hate crimes. Available at: https://edition.cnn.com/2016/09/15/us/sikh-hate-crime-victims/index.html

BBC. 2019. Hate crime in London soars since Christchurch attacks. *BBC*. 1 May. Available at: www.bbc.co.uk/news/uk-england-london-48120278

Bowling, B. 1998. *Violent Racism: Victimization, Policing, and Social Context*. Oxford: Oxford University Press.

Chakraborti, N. and Garland, J. 2015. *Hate Crime*. London: Sage.

Chakraborti, N., Garland, J., and Hardy, S. J. 2014. *The Leicester Hate Crime Project: Findings and Conclusions*. Leicester: University of Leicester.

Choudhury, T. and Fenwick, H. 2011. *The Impact of Counter – Terrorism Measures on Muslim Communities*. Manchester: Equality and Human Rights Commission.

CNN. 2001. 'You are either with us or against us'. *CNN*. 6 November. Available at: http://edition.cnn.com/2001/US/11/06/gen.attack.on.terror/

Cohen, S. 1972. *Folk Devils and Moral Panics: The Creation of the Mods and Rockers*. London: Routledge.

College of Policing. 2014. *Hate Crime Operational Guidance*. London: College of Policing.

Copsey, N., Dack, J., Littler, M., and Feldman, M. 2013. *Anti-Muslim Hate Crime and the Far Right*. Teeside: Teeside University.

CPS. 2018. *Social Media – Guidelines on Prosecuting Cases Involving Communications Sent Via Social Media*. Available at: www.cps.gov.uk/legal-guidance/social-media-guidelines-prosecuting-cases-involving-communications-sent-social-media

Cuerden, G. and Rogers, C. 2017. Exploring race hate crime reporting in Wales following Brexit. *Review of European Studies*, 9(1): 158–164.

Dearden, L. 2017. More than half British people support racial profiling of Muslims and Arabs for security reasons, survey reveals. *The Independent*. 25 September. Available at: www.independent.co.uk/news/uk/home-news/racial-profiling-british-people-muslims-arabs-support-security-anti-terrorism-attacks-survey-caabu-a7966666.html

Dodd, V. 2005. Asian men targeted in stop and search. *The Guardian*. 17 August: 6.

ECRI (European Commission against Racism and Intolerance). 2016. *ECRI Report on the United Kingdom*. Available at: https://www.coe.int/t/dghl/monitoring/ecri/Country-by-country/United_Kingdom/GBR- CbC-V-2016-038-ENG.pdf

Elahi, F. and Khan, O. 2017. Introduction: What is Islamophobia? In: Runnymede Trust (ed.) *Islamophobia: Still a Challenge for us All*. London: Runnymede Trust, pp. 5–12.

Garland, J. and Chakraborti, N. 2012. Divided by a common concept? Assessing the implications of different conceptualizations of hate crime in the European Union. *European Journal of Criminology*, 9(1): 38–51.

Gerstenfeld, P. 2013. *Hate Crimes: Causes, Controls, and Controversies*. London: Sage.

Githens-Mazer, J. and Lambert, R. 2010. *Islamophobia and Anti-Muslim Hate Crime: A London Case Study*. Exeter: European Muslim Research Centre.

Hanes, E. and Machin, S. 2014. Hate crime in the wake of terror attacks: Evidence from 7/7 and 9/11. *Journal of Contemporary Criminal Justice*, 30: 247–267.

Hollingsworth, J. 2019. Christchurch terror attack death toll increases to 51. *CNN*. 2 May (updated). Available at: https://edition.cnn.com/2019/05/02/asia/nz-christchurch-atta ck-death-toll-intl/index.html

Home Office. 2016. Hate Crime, England and Wales, 2015/16. Available at: https://assets. publishing.service.gov.uk/government/uploads/system/uploads/attachment_data/file/ 559319/hate-crime-1516-hosb1116.pdf

House of Commons. 2012. *The Leveson Inquiry: An Inquiry Into the Culture, Practices and Ethics of the Press*. Available at: www.gov.uk/government/uploads/system/uploads/atta chment_data/file/27094 1/0780_ii.pdf

Hussain, A. 2014. Transgressing community: The case of Muslims in a twenty-first-century British city. *Ethnic and Racial Studies*, 37(4): 621–635.

Jivanda, T. 2013. Islamophobia: Surge revealed in anti-Muslin hate crimes. *The Independent*. 27 December. Available at: www.independent.co.uk/news/uk/crime/islamophobia-sur ge-revealed-in-anti-muslim-hate-crimes-9026873.html

Kaplan, J. 2006. Islamophobia in America? September 11 and Islamophobic hate crime. *Terrorism and Political Violence*, 18(1): 1–33.

Law, I. 2010. *Racism and Ethnicity: Global Debates, Dilemmas, Directions*. London: Pearson Education.

Lambert, B. and Githens-Mazer, J. 2011. *Islamophobia and Anti-Muslim Hate Crime: UK Case Studies 2010 – An Introduction to a Ten Year Europe-Wide Research Project*. London: European Muslim Research Centre.

Levin, J. and McDevitt, J. 1993. *Hate Crimes: The Rising Tide of Bigotry and Bloodshed*. New York: Plenum.

Mason, G. 2005. Hate crime and the image of the stranger. *The British Journal of Criminology*, 45(6): 837–859.

McGregor-Smith. 2017. Race in the workplace. The McGregor-Smith Review. Available at: https://assets.publishing.service.gov.uk/government/uploads/system/uploads/attachm ent_data/file/594336/race-in-workplace-mcgregor-smith-review.pdf

Meer, N., Dwyer, C., and Modood, T. 2010. Embodying nationhood? Conceptions of British national identity, citizenship and gender in the 'veil affair'. *The Sociological Review*, 58(1): 84–111.

Meer, N. and Modood, T. 2009. The multicultural state we're in: Muslims, 'multiculture' and the 'civic re-balancing' of British multiculturalism. *Political Studies*, 57(3): 473–497.

McDevitt, J., Balboni, J., Garcia, L., and Gu, J. 2001. Consequences for victims: A comparison of bias and non-bias motivated assaults. *American Behavioral Scientist*, 45(4): 697–713.

Modood, T. 1997. 'Difference', cultural racism and anti-racism. In: T. Modood and P. Werbner (eds) *Debating Cultural Hybridity*. London: Zed Books, pp. 13–16.

Morris, N. 2004. The politics of fear. *The Independent*. 23 November.

Muslim Council of Britain. 2015. British Muslims in numbers. Available at: www.mcb.org. uk/wp-content/uploads/2015/02/MCBCensusReport_2015.pdf

Nomis/Office for National Statistics. 2013. 2011 Census Data on Nomis. Available at: www.nomisweb.co.uk/census/2011

Parekh, B. 2000. *The Future of Multi-Ethnic Britain*. London: Profile Books.

Perry, B. 2001. *In the Name of Hate: Understanding Hate Crimes*. London: Routledge.

Poole, E., 2006. Reporting Islam: Media representations of British Muslims. In: E. Poole and J. Richardson (eds) *Muslims and the News Media*. London: I.B. Tauris.

Quarmby, K. 2008. *Getting Away with Murder: Disabled People's Experiences of Hate Crime in the UK*. London: SCOPE.

Roxwell, L. 2011. Hate, threats, and violence. A register study of persons suspected of hate crime. *Journal of Scandinavian Studies in Criminology and Crime Prevention*, 12(12), 198–215.

Runnymede Trust. 1997. *Islamophobia: A Challenge for us All*. London: Runnymede Trust.

Runnymede Trust. 2017. *Islamophobia: Still a challenge for us all*. London: Runnymede Trust.

Saeed, A. 2007. Media, racism and Islamophobia: The representation of Islam and Muslims in the media. *Sociology Compass*, 1(2), 443–462.

Said, E. W. 1978. *Orientalism*. New York: Pantheon Books.

Shain, F. 2011. *The New Folk Devils: Muslim Boys and Education in England*. Stoke-on-Trent: Trentham Books Ltd.

Sibbitt, R. 1997. *The Perpetrators of Racial Harassment and Racial Violence, Home Office Research Study 176*. London: Home Office.

Siddique, H. 2010. Jean Charles de Menezes memorial unveiled at Stockwell station. *The Guardian*. Available at: www.theguardian.com/uk/2010/jan/07/jean-charles-de-mene zes-memorial

Social Mobility Commission. 2017. *The Social Mobility Challenges Faced by Young Muslims*, London: Social Mobility Commission.

Spalek, B. and Lambert, R. 2008. Muslim communities, counter-terrorism and counter-radicalisation. *International Journal of Law, Crime and Justice*, 36(4): 257–270.

Tell MAMA. 2016. *The Geography of Anti-Muslim Hatred*. Available at: www.tellmamauk. org/wp-content/uploads/pdf/tell_mama_2015_annual_report.pdf

Tell MAMA. 2017. *A Constructed Threat: Identity, Intolerance and the Impact of Anti-Muslim Hatred. Tell MAMA Annual Report 2016*. London: Tell MAMA.

Travis, A. 2017. Anti-Muslim hate crime surges after Manchester and London Bridge attacks. *The Guardian*. Available at: www.theguardian.com/society/2017/jun/20/anti-m uslim-hate-surges-after-manchester-and-london-bridge-attacks

Tufail, W. 2015. Rotherham, Rochdale, and the racialised threat of the 'Muslim Grooming Gang'. *Crime Justice Journal*, 4(3): 30–34.

Walters, M. and Brown, R. 2016. *Causes and Motivations of Hate crime. Project Report*. London: Equality and Human Rights Commission.

Williams, M. L. and Burnap, P. 2015. Cyberhate on social media in the aftermath of Woolwich: A case study in computational criminology and big data. *British Journal of Criminology*, 54(4): 946–967.

Williams, M. and Tregidga, J. 2013. *All Wales Hate Crime Project*. Cardiff: Race Equality First and Cardiff University.

Wintour, P. 2005. Blair vows to root out extremism. *The Guardian*. 6 August. Available at: www.theguardian.com/politics/2005/aug/06/terrorism.july7

Yeung, P. and Duncan, P. 2016. Race hate crimes reported on UK railways rise 37% in five years. *The Guardian*. Available at: www.theguardian.com/uk-news/2016/jan/27/race-ha te-crimes-uk-railways-rise-37-per-cent-five-years

Zebiri, K. 2008. The redeployment of Orientalist themes in contemporary Islamophobia. *Studies in Contemporary Islam*, 10: 4–44.

3

ISLAMOPHOBIA ONLINE AND IN THE DIGITAL WORLD

Introduction

Islamophobia has often been viewed in the lens of offline hate crimes and prejudice. Yet, a new emerging threat in the realm of the online world has meant Islamophobia has now become a digital phenomenon too. This chapter examines this emerging threat and whilst major terrorist incidents, such as Woolwich, can provoke public outrage and anger, they also can lead to communities and people being victimised online. The power of social media, with anonymity and accessibility issues, has meant it has become a popular arena for offenders who can use it in order to intimidate, harass, and threaten people. Just as the dark net remains an unregulated platform, Islamophobia online has been overlooked by policy-makers, academics, and wider stakeholders. This chapter also explores the role of cyberspace when it comes to key debates and issues around tackling online hate speech.

As outlined earlier in this book, Islamophobic hate crimes fall under the category of religious hate crime which is where it is perceived, by the victim or any other person, to be motivated by hostility or prejudice based upon a person's religion or perceived religion. Online Islamophobia remains under-researched. Indeed, a report conducted by Feldman et al. (2013, p. 10) regarding online anti-Muslim prejudice highlighted how: "The online domain remains under-researched" and "much less attention has been paid to online hate crime, which can be the precursor to more physically threatening offline incidents." As noted earlier, the debate about Islamophobia is often centred on street-level incidents, including pulling of headscarves and attacks against mosques (Allen 2010). However, increasingly a number of cases reported to organisations such as Tell MAMA include online anti-Muslim abuse which is directed against Muslim communities, including high-profile Muslim figures such as Baroness Sayeeda Warsi (the former Minister of Faith and Communities) and Jemima Khan (ex-wife of the Pakistani

30 Islamophobia online

cricketer turned politician, Imran Khan) both of whom were subjected to online threats which were reported to the police by Tell MAMA (Keats 2014).

Cyberspace is a virtual minefield where offenders or 'trolls or trolling' specifically target people through online pre-meditated abuse and specific targeting of a victim, which a perpetrator has identified (Perry and Olsson 2009). Online hate speech can come in many different forms including racial harassment, religiously motivated abuse such as anti-Semitic abuse, and directed abuse more generally which targets someone because of their disability, gender, culture, race, and beliefs (Gerstenfeld 2013). Key trigger events, such as Woolwich and the death of drummer Lee Rigby in the UK, showed an increase in online Islamophobic hate crimes. Indeed, this chapter sheds light on this 'new' digital form of anti-Muslim racism, which following the Woolwich, Tunisia, and Paris attacks has become the prime focus for the police and other agencies who have to investigate online hate crime. Moreover, this is reinforced by statistics from the police and organisations such as Tell MAMA (Measuring Anti-Muslim Attacks) who are based in the UK and who have reported a significant increase in the amount of people reporting online anti-Muslim abuse to them. Feldman et al. (2013, p. 21) found that: "The majority of the incidents of Muslim hate crime reported to Tell MAMA are online incidents and 300 – 69 per cent – of these online cases reported a link to the far right."

Cyberspace can become a safe environment for some offenders but equally internal and external mechanisms are required to support victims of online hate (Douglas et al. 2005). Online Islamophobia can be categorised as being forms of 'cyber harassment', 'cyber bullying', 'cyber abuse', 'cyber incitement/threats', and 'cyber hate'. This chapter argues that online Islamophobic hate therefore requires a multi-faceted and international approach from different agencies, including the police, social networking sites, and a government-led approach that tackles online Islamophobia as a separate phenomenon.

Islamophobia online – *a definition*

Cyber hate has become a nexus of online communications and concepts where a perpetrator utilises electronic technology and the convergence of space, movement, and behaviour in a 'safe' virtual environment to 'control' and target 'opponents' considered to be a threat (Awan and Blakemore 2012). This type of control allows the perpetrator to act in a dominant way against groups they deem to be subordinate often in the case of Muslims being attacked for their faith and ethnicity (Perry 2001). It also allows offenders to use the online world and other social networking platforms to target individuals they deem to be 'different' from them both in an ideological, political, and religious sense. Academics such as Taras (2012) make the point that Islamophobia has become a term that is misunderstood and indeed lacking in clarity. Taras (2012, p. 4) states that Islamophobia entails: "...the spread of hostile public attitudes towards Muslims, in this case across Europe. The spread of Islamophobia is based on a conviction that Europe is in peril because of Islamisation..." This sense of securitisation and fear is based upon the visual representations of Islam which have become synonymous with people who fear the pervading sense of Islamic history and Muslims more generally. For example, the depiction of mosques, headscarves, and minarets helps contribute towards the 'othering' of Muslim communities. Taras (2012, p. 4) notes that: "Islamophobia thus entails a cultural racism that sets Muslims apart. As a result, the Islamic migrant is constructed as someone burdened by alien attributes and as a carrier of antagonistic, threatening values." In the online space, the depiction of Muslims, through visual cartoons and language, as being dangerous, extremists, and fundamentalists has become critical.

The Forum Against Islamophobia and Racism (2013) argues that Islamophobia constitutes fear and hostility against Muslim communities. However, the earlier interpretation confines Islamophobia to physical abuse and targeted violence against Muslim women, men, mosques, cemeteries, and discrimination in places of education (Allen 2001). Islamophobia, therefore, is seen as 'dangerous' because of the 'expansion' of Muslim communities. Whilst this definition remains limited in scope with regards the online dimension of Islamophobia, it does, however, give us a starting point for further discussion and discourse in this area. We argue that we need a separate definition of online Islamophobia, which is recognisable both at a policy level and an academic level.

The definition for online Islamophobia could include: Islamophobic hate crimes that target a victim in order to provoke, cause hostility and promote intolerance by means of harassment, stalking, abuse, incitement, threatening behaviour, bullying and intimidation of the person or persons, via all platforms of social media, chatrooms, blogs and forums.

This definition could be used as a means to help assist the police and social media companies when confronting Islamophobia online. Cyber Islamophobic hate groups and individuals are promoting a particular ideology that incites racial hatred, religious intolerance, and also allows 'lone actors' and 'hate groups' to exert cyber power and social control in a systematic and targeted manner that has no respect for Muslims (Perry 2001). This, therefore, can result in them trying to use online methods as a means of self-protectionism and false patriotism for groups like the far-right which fuel Islamophobic hate and abuse (Cole and Cole 2009). In the online world, this can often be played out by abusive, threatening, and coordinated tweets or through the use of sites like Twitter or Facebook to send messages of hate crime, which include the use of visual images to target particular individuals (Whine 2003). Clearly, it should be noted that cyberspace can also be an extremely valuable tool in helping detect and tackle online cybercrime and increasingly is being used by the police to help engage with the communities. The use of social networking sites by the police can have an important impact on people's level of 'fear of cybercrime' and also can help assist them report such incidents to the police. The phenomenon of online Islamophobia, and trying to conceptualise it through a criminological lens, is required in order to better understand the causes and motivations behind online hate crimes.

Impacts of online Islamophobia

Social media companies such as Twitter and Facebook have been slow to react to the dangers posed by far-right groups and individuals who promote hate speech online. However, in a progressive move to tackle hate speech, Twitter and Facebook took the decision to remove the former leader of the English Defence League, Tommy Robinson, because his views breached their values and community guidelines. Similarly, Facebook took the decision to remove the far-right group Britain First from its platform. Social media sites have a global reach and audience; with this growth and expansion of the Internet it has created many positive opportunities for people to communicate and engage in a manner not seen previously. However, it has also acted as a 'double-edged' sword by creating an online vacuum and platform for people using an ideology of hate as a means to appeal to a wider audience, often under the cloak of anonymity that allows them to supersede and bypass editorial control or regulation. It should also be noted that whilst there is a dearth of online material that could cause offence, this does not equate to it necessarily being illegal in the UK. The notion of freedom of speech and freedom of expression are used by those who post such material with their constitutional right to do so but, at the same time, balancing freedom of speech.

The Internet, therefore, provides new opportunities for associated crimes to be committed. Messages can be spread online at great speed, people can remain anonymous, and the nature of cyberspace remains unregulated. For example, after the Paris terrorist attacks, it was reported that one the key hashtags that had been trending on Twitter was the hashtag #KillAllMuslims. In particular, for hate groups wanting to recruit people for their cause this can also give them a platform to spread unsolicited material, which can go unnoticed. This allows them to capture new audiences and use the Internet as a propaganda tool for those purposes. Indeed, these communicative messages can spread and cause a lot of discontent and these hate-based groups are quick to create websites that create more hate through blogs and forums of hate and Islamophobia. This is important because in the case of Tommy Robinson and Britain First, social media sites have taken the appropriate steps to tackle the hate online. Keats and Norton (2011), for example, found that social media sites were being used to facilitate this form of online hate. Hall (2013, p. 204) states that: "The increase in the use of the Internet as a vehicle for hate is therefore seemingly undeniable, be it organized hate groups or those expressing prejudice and hostility in a more casual manner."

Hate on the Internet can also have direct and indirect experiences for victims and communities being targeted. In one sense, it can be used to harass and intimidate victims and on the other hand it can also be used for opportunistic crimes. The Internet, therefore, is a powerful tool by which people can be influenced to act in a certain way and manner. Zempi and Awan (2016) found that these impacts are psychological, emotional, and anxiety related. What also is left in terms of direct impact is important because it impacts upon local communities and the understanding of how this could constitute acts of violence offline. This is particularly strong when considering hate speech online that aims to threaten and incite violence. Hate speech in this context is any form of language used to depict someone in a negative fashion in regards to their race, ethnicity, gender, religion, sexual orientation, or physical and mental disability which promotes hate and incites violence (Yar 2013). This also links into the convergence of emotional distress caused by hate online, the nature of intimidation and harassment online, and the prejudice that seeks to defame groups through speech intending to injure and intimidate.

Another problem with Internet hate crime is the issue of how to police it. This can be problematic when individuals are using hate material from outside the UK and as such it becomes very difficult to prosecute anyone, because they are outside the jurisdiction of UK courts. Indeed, a lot of the material online can also cause a lot of fear and it is imperative that the police and other agencies work together to tackle hate crime on the Internet. Hate crimes on the Internet have also been used as a means to create storage and communicative messages that go beyond the physical to the virtual dimension. For Perry (2003, p. 19) this means the spectrum of hate crime goes further and targets people because of who they are and as such Coliandris (2012, p. 82) argues hate crimes "are capable of 'sending a message' to particular communities".

The Internet, therefore, has become a safe haven for many of these groups and individuals who are using it effectively to target, marginalise, and demonise a group or community. A lot of this has been dedicated to far-right groups and lone actors who have engaged in what has been defined as cybersquatting and Google bombing. These are anti-hate webpages and online sources, which are used to create content that creates a measure of intolerance and targets specific individuals or groups. For example, this has been used by far-right groups and those such as Britain First, the Anti-Defamation League, and the English Defence League who have used the Internet to create a public presence and been successful in using the Internet as a platform to disseminate further hate and intolerance. Moreover, Feldman et al. (2013) found that from the 74 per cent of online hate incidents reported to Tell MAMA, the majority of online incidents did also include threats made about offline action. They also found that most of the online hate was committed by males and 70 per cent of online incidents had a link to the far-right, specifically to the English Defence League (EDL) and the British National Party (BNP). As noted earlier, in England and Wales it can be an offence to stir up and incite hatred through illegal hate content on the grounds of race, religion, and sexual orientation. Indeed, there are also other offences such as using the content of a website which can be illegal when it threatens or harasses a person or a group of people. Furthermore, if it can be proved that such material was posted because of hostility based on race, religion, sexual orientation, disability, or transgender then it is also a hate crime offence. In practice this is not confined to words or pictures but could include videos, chatrooms, and even music.

The Woolwich attacks, for example, triggered a backlash against Muslims across the world mainly because Islam was being used to justify the terror attacks. Whilst Islamophobia has been viewed as a new term it has long roots back from the time

34 Islamophobia online

of the Christian Crusades to the Prophet Muhammad (Allen 2010). Taras (2012, p. 119) notes how "Islamophobia is a backlash to the expanded presence of Muslim communities in Europe." Indeed, a BBC Radio 1 Newsbeat poll found that one in four young people in Britain distrust Muslims. Additionally, 16 per cent said they did not trust Hindus or Sikhs, 15 per cent said they did not trust Jewish people, 13 per cent for Buddhists, and 12 per cent said they did not trust Christians. Also, 44 per cent said they believe Muslims did not share the same values, whilst 28 per cent said the UK would be a better place with fewer Muslims there (Kotecha 2013).

Clearly, prejudice towards Muslim communities post events such as 9/11, 7/7, and more recently Woolwich are intensified. This marginalisation of Muslim communities appears to be rooted in the narrative that Islam is a barbaric faith and that Islam and the West are in actual fact in the realms of a clash of civilizations. This belief often creates the space whereby Muslims are targeted and also vilified for what they believe in, both offline and online. This demonisation is captured in studies with Muslim communities conducted by Awan and Blakemore (2012) that found that Muslims were being targeted both online and offline which had culminated in Muslims feeling isolated and alienated.

The Association of Chief Police Officers (ACPO) revealed a similar trend that had seen them receive over 136 complaints of online Islamophobic abuse reported through its 'True Vision website' which deals with hate crimes, since the death of Lee Rigby (Khaleeli 2013) . True Vision is the police's main cyber tool in tackling online hate and is used as a means of helping the police create a safer online environment. The website states that it will examine illegal content that threatens or harasses a person or group of persons because of hostility towards their race, religion, sexual orientation, disability, or transgender. It adds, however that: "Most hateful or violent website content is not illegal" and gives victims of online hate three options in dealing with the incident. These include reporting the material to the police, or reporting the material to a hosting company, or contacting the website administrator to remove the material (True Vision 2019).

Case study: Woolwich and online Islamophobia

The Woolwich attack in May 2013 in the UK has led to a spate of hate crimes committed against Muslim communities. These incidents included Muslim women being targeted for wearing the headscarf and mosques being vandalised. For example, the Al-Rahma community centre in Muswell Hill in North London was burnt down soon after the Woolwich incident (BBC News 2013). Other examples of hate incidents included graffiti being scrawled against mosque walls and petrol bombs being left outside mosques (Saul 2013). All these incidents have led to a heightened atmosphere for British Muslims, fearful of reprisal attacks against them because of the Woolwich incident. In May 2013, Michael Adebowale and Michael Adebolajo murdered British soldier Lee Rigby in Woolwich, south-east London. Adebowale and Adebolajo were both convicted of the murder of Lee Rigby in December 2013. At the time, the incident provoked strong public anger and outrage by politicians, policy-makers, and the media. The former British Prime Minister David Cameron argued that the Woolwich attack would not 'divide us' but instead make us 'stronger' in the fight against global and home-grown terrorism. However, the tragic events of that day also led to a series of attacks against Muslims, mosques, and Islamic institutions which amounted to a sharp increase in Islamophobic related incidents. Indeed, a number of police forces saw a dramatic surge in the number of reported hate crimes against Muslims, with the Metropolitan police recording 500 Islamophobic crimes since Woolwich (The Guardian 2013).

Whilst a number of these incidents took place offline there were also people who used social media sites to either vent their anger or to make actual death threats against Muslim communities (BBC News 2013). Clearly, major incidents such as the Woolwich attack can provoke public outrage, anger, and can lead to stereotyping of all Muslim communities as being violent extremists (Larsson 2007). Indeed, the Internet and social media sites, such as Twitter, have become a popular arena for online hate, partly due to their accessibility and the anonymity they offer for offenders who use it to intimidate, harass, and bully others (Christopherson 2007). Moreover, following the Woolwich attack, we also witnessed how Twitter was used by offenders who were promoting this type of online Islamophobic hate, which was loaded with tactics of harassment and threats of reprisal attacks.

On the face of it, a number of offenders who use Twitter to target Muslims after Woolwich share similar characteristics but were uniquely different in their approaches to targeting Muslim communities online. Using an online content behavioural offender typology, we can categorise the tweets together in different categories and create a typology based on the following. These are: **the trawler** (a person who has gone through other people's Twitter accounts to specifically target people with a Muslim connection); **the apprentice** (someone who is fairly new to Twitter but nonetheless has begun to target people with the help of more experienced online abusers); **the disseminator** (someone who has tweeted about and retweeted messages, pictures, and documents of online hate that are specifically targeting Muslims); **the impersonator** (a person who is using a fake profile, account, and images to target individuals); **the accessory** (a person who is joining in with other people's conversations via Twitter to target vulnerable people); **the reactive** (a person who, following a major incident such as Woolwich, or issues on immigration, will begin an online campaign targeting that specific group and individual); **the mover** (someone who regularly changes their Twitter account in order to continue targeting someone from a different profile); and finally, **the professional** (a person who has a huge following on Twitter and regardless of consequences has and will launch a major campaign of hate against an individual or group of people because they are Muslim. This person will also likely have multiple Twitter accounts all aimed at targeting Muslim communities) (Zempi and Awan 2016).

Many of these tweets are often used by perpetrators to target a particular group or person. This is often personified by racist jokes and stereotypical 'banter' (Weaver 2013). If these incidents go unchecked physical attacks can also take place and could culminate from extreme online prejudice and discrimination, which are

36 Islamophobia online

intertwined together. Indeed, this type of negativity can also lead to an escalation of online abuse and the normalisation of such behaviour. For example, a number of sites, such as the http://anti–islam.blogspot.co.uk/ and www.jihadwatch.org/, all aim to tackle what they call the 'anti-civilisation of Islam'. Whilst many of these blogs and websites use the cloak of freedom of expression to perpetuate an anti-Muslim rhetoric, it does inevitably attract users who are quick to post comments on pieces that have a deeply embedded anti-Muslim narrative (see www.jihadwa tch.org/ in 2018).

Challenging and reporting online Islamophobia

As noted previously, online Islamophobia is under-researched both at a policy level and an academic level, and this chapter argues that a new cyber hate policy is much needed both at government level and policing level which would be timely considering the recent spike of online Islamophobic abuse. Interestingly, cyber hate has been used by the far-right and white supremacists who have used it to inflame religious and racial tensions. For example, a study for the British-based think-tank group Demos (2011) found that far-right populist movements are gaining support across Europe and playing upon a small perception of public disenfranchisement within society to promote an agenda of protecting national identity as a method to whip up online anti-Muslim hate.

The Demos (2011) study is interesting because its findings would seem to suggest that the EDL have become a web-based far-right group that is using social networking sites such as Facebook and Twitter where it has gained a core group of online sympathisers to target Muslim communities (Awan and Blakemore 2012). The Demos study found that on a national scale 72 per cent of supporters for the EDL were under the age of 30 and 36 per cent of people were aged between 16 and 20; thus, reflecting the movement's desire to attract a 'younger' audience on social networking sites such as Facebook. The Online Hate Prevention Institute (2013) report into online Islamophobia searched over 50 different Facebook pages and showed how online hate speeches had targeted Muslims. Overall, they found 349 separate instances of online hate speeches directed against Muslims. Indeed, they also included a number of those Facebook pages that were created in order to specifically target Muslim communities. For example, they found a number of group pages that had a number of people who had visited and 'liked' certain posts and pages. For example, the 'Boycott all Halal products in Australia!' page had over 520 likes (see www.facebook.com/pages/boy cott-all-halal-products-in-australia/171203192936626). Furthermore, is the online Facebook page 'The truth about Islam' which has over 150,000 likes (see www.fa cebook.com/TheIslamicThreat); the 'Islam is Evil' page (418 likes) (see www.fa cebook.com/IslamIsEvil); and the 'Prophet Muhammad Still Burns in Hell' page (470 likes) (see www.facebook.com/pages/The-Prophet-Muhammad-STILL-Burns-In-Hell-Fire/281538198643648). This report is significant because it documents the rise of online Islamophobia post-Woolwich through Facebook.

Communications via social media sites, like Twitter, can also be a criminal offence. The CPS guidelines state that there must be either a credible threat of violence, communications which specifically target an individual or group of people, communications which amount to a breach of a court order, and communications which may be considered grossly offensive, indecent, obscene or false (Crown Prosecution Service 2014). In many of these cases people can be charged for comments made via social networking sites under 'racially motivated' or 'religiously motivated' crimes through the Crime and Disorder Act 1998, the Malicious Communications Act 1988, the Communications Act 2003, and the Public Order Act 1986 (Coliandris 2012). Overall, policing cyberspace and people's activity via social media sites remains difficult and the recent Leveson Inquiry (2012) in the UK, which was set up by the British Government to investigate the culture, practices, and ethics of the Press also acknowledges that it is problematic to regulate. Following the Woolwich attack, a number of arrests were made where people had posted comments on Twitter and Facebook, which were deemed to incite racial hatred or violence. In one case, a person was convicted under the Malicious Communications Act 1988 after an offensive message was posted on Facebook (Urquhart 2013). Cyber hate regulation therefore requires the police and other agencies to act quickly and more effectively in relation to online Islamophobic abuse. At the moment cyberspace does resemble a virtual minefield of hate and therefore policing it requires a shift in thinking from authorities which gets them thinking and acting not in an abstract black and white way, but in a more innovative and nuanced way that helps the police prosecute people for cyber hate issues and can educate people of the dangers of online abuse (Chan 2007).

In 2007, the Police Service, Crown Prosecution Service (CPS), Prison Service (which is now the National Offender Management Service), and other similar agencies that make up the criminal justice system agreed that hate crime should only consist of five separate strands and that this could be monitored centrally. Interestingly, UK policy also deems crimes committed against a person because of hostility towards someone's age, gender, and/or appearance could also constitute a hate crime, despite not being part of the five monitored strands. Hall (2013, p. 5) argues that: "These definitions are notable because they allow for anyone to be a victim of hate crime, and for any offence or incident to be recorded and investigated by the police as a hate crime." The UK policy and legal interpretation of hate crime has also divided the term into different areas from hate motivation, hate incidents, and hate crimes. The operational definition in England and Wales states that hate motivation is where: "Hate crimes and incidents are taken to mean any crime or incident where the perpetrator's hostility or prejudice against an identifiable group of people is a factor in determining who is victimized" (College of Policing 2014, p. 3). The definition included here is broader in the sense that the victim does not have to be a member of a group.

As noted earlier, policing cyberspace is difficult. Indeed, Feldman et al. (2013) found that 74 per cent of anti-Muslim prejudice occurred online, in comparison to 26 per cent of offline incidents. Worryingly, critics argue that the difficult nature of policing cyberspace has therefore led to Muslim communities being failed by their local police forces in the UK. Indeed, Tell MAMA, which records anti-Muslim attacks, argued that not enough was being done to investigate online anti-Muslim abuse. Another problem for the police appears to be the way in which data is recorded and collected by local police forces. The problem for the police, therefore, is helping root out far-right groups and lone actors and extremists who are using social networking sites like Twitter to post malicious statements (Esposito and Kalin 2011). This realm of cyber activism used by groups like the EDL and others who are promoting online hate means the police require more people to report what they see and what they read so that they can take the necessary actions required to either remove the online hate material or in some cases arrest and charge people. At the moment those who use online hate to disguise themselves in a cloak of anonymity remain at large because they understand that unless someone reports them they can remain anonymous. Feldman et al. (2013, p. 23) state that a number of online incidents reported included direct threats from burning down mosques to killing Muslim babies. They state that: "Racist remarks were, in turn, mainly anti-Pakistani comments and references to dirt and filth. More generally there were comments accusing Muslims of rape; paedophilia; incest; interbreeding; being terrorists; and killing Jews."

Conclusion

Clearly, threatening and abusive comments, whether it be by visual images, fake online profiles, Facebook messages, YouTube videos and tweets, such as the previous, can have a detrimental direct effect on the victims who are targeted and their families (Waddington 2010). What the previous cases demonstrate is that online behaviour can be normalised by offenders which allows a perpetrator to use, in many cases, anonymity, manipulation, and social control to target their victims (Douglas et al. 2005). However, whilst this form of cyber hate often remains invisible, sometimes due to offenders deleting tweets, comments, or posts and also because the perpetrator can hide their identity, the threat remains very real for the victims it targets (Hall 2013). Indeed, trying to ascertain all the potential threats and risks posed online does pose a major challenge for the security services, the police, and the Government. Cyber hate within the policing context, therefore, requires due diligence and an investigation that determines potential online offenders, offensive online messages, and those they believe can be prosecuted alongside the CPS rules. Furthermore, this involves dialogue and discussion about the issues around policing cyberspace since hate crime on the Internet has become a more widespread problem since the rapid growth of the Internet (Iganski 2008). Indeed, the convergence of hate crime and Islamophobia on the Internet has provided a new platform by which a number of anti-hate websites and groups have appeared online in order to perpetuate a level of cyber hate not seen previously. Sheffield (1995, p. 438) argues therefore that hate crime is: "violence motivated by social and political factors and is bolstered by belief systems which (attempt to) legitimize such violence..."

Since the emergence of key events such as 9/11, 7/7, Woolwich, Tunisia, and the Westminster attacks, there has been an increase in hate crimes committed against Muslim communities. Whilst many of these incidents have led to offline violence, there is also a sense that such incidents are now commonplace online. Such attacks online mean that the police, social media companies, and Government must do more to tackle online Islamophobic hate crime. One way is to help build trust and confidence, so that victims of online hate crime can come forward and report such incidents. This is important because victims of online hate crime can feel isolated and alienated. For example, the UK-based charity ChildLine recently found an increase in the number of children contacting them with concerns about online bullying. They saw 4,507 cases of cyber bullying in 2012–2013, which was up from 2,410 from the previous year in 2011–2012 (Sellgren 2014). The use of social media and the Internet provides safe online spaces which has allowed, in some cases, a vacuum for perpetrators to target vulnerable people by using anti-Semitic abuse, racist abuse, homophobic abuse, gender-based abuse, anti-disability abuse, and Islamophobic abuse. As a result, online Islamophobic hate crime has also been increasing and there is an urgent need to examine the implications this has for community cohesion and society as a whole.

Key questions

- What definition would you use for cyber Islamophobia?
- How do trigger events lead to an escalation of Islamophobic hate crime online?
- Why is social media used to perpetuate hate speech?
- Do you think the reporting mechanism via True Vision works?
- What ideas do you have to help victims of Islamophobic abuse online?

Further reading

- Grabosky, P., Wright, P., and Smith, R. 1998. *Crime in the Digital Age: Controlling Telecommunications and Cyberspace Illegalities*. New Brunswick, NJ: Transaction.
- Jewkes, Y. and Yar, M. 2010. *Handbook of Internet Crime*. Cullompton: Willan.
- Mansell, R. and Collins, B. 2005. *Trust and Crime in Information Societies*. Cheltenham: Edward Elgar.

References

Allen, C. 2010. *Islamophobia*. Farnham: Ashgate.

Allen, C. 2001. *Islamophobia in the Media Since September 11th, Forum against Islamophobia and Racism*. Available at: www.fairuk.org/docs/islamophobia-in-the-media-since-911-christop herallen.pdf

Awan, I. and Blakemore, B. 2012. *Policing Cyber Hate, Cyber Threats and Cyber Terrorism*. Farnham: Ashgate.

BBC News. 2013. Woolwich aftermath: Key facts. Available at: www.bbc.co.uk/news/ uk-22635318

40 Islamophobia online

Chan, J. B. L. 2007. Police and new technologies. In: T. Newburn (ed.) *Handbook of Policing*. Cullompton: Willan Publishing.

Christopherson, K. 2007. The positive and negative implications of anonymity in Internet, nobody knows you're a dog. *Computers in Human Behavior*, 23: 3038–3056.

Cole, J. and Cole, B. 2009. *Martyrdom: Radicalisation and Terrorist Violence Among British Muslims*. London: Pennant Books.

Coliandris, G. 2012. Hate in a cyber age. In: I. Awan and B. Blakemore (eds) *Policing Cyber Hate, Cyber Threats and Cyber Terrorism*. Farnham: Ashgate, pp. 75–95.

College of Policing. 2014. *Hate Crime Operational Guidance*. Available at: www.report-it.org. uk/files/hate_crime_operational_guidance.pdf

Crown Prosecution Service. 2014. Guidelines on Prosecuting Cases Involving Communications Sent via Social Media. Available at: www.cps.gov.uk/legal/a_to_c/communica tions_sent_via_social_media/

Demos. 2011. *The Rise of Populism in Europe can be Traced through Online Behaviour*. Available at: www.demos.co.uk/files/Demos_OSIPOP_Bookweb_03.pdf?1320601634

Douglas, K., McGarty, C., Bliuc, A., and Lala, G. 2005. Understanding cyberhate: Social competition and social creativity in online white supremacist groups. *Social Science Computer Review*, 23(1): 68–76.

Esposito, L. J. and Kalin, I. 2011. *Islamophobia: The Challenge of Pluralism in the 21st Century*. Oxford: Oxford University Press.

Feldman, M., Littler, M., Dack, J., and Copsey, N. 2013. *Anti-Muslim Hate Crime and the Far Right*, Teeside University. Available at: http://tellmamauk.org/wp-content/uploads/ 2013/07/antimuslim2.pdf

Forum Against Islamophobia and Racism. 2013 [Online]. Available at: www.fairuk.org/ introduction.htm [accessed: 10 July 2018].

Gerstenfeld, P. B. 2013. *Hate Crimes: Causes, Controls and Controversies*, 3rd ed. Thousand Oaks, CA: Sage.

Hall, N. 2013. *Hate Crime*, 2nd ed. London: Routledge.

Iganski, P. 2008. *'Hate Crime' and the City*. Bristol: The Policy Press.

Keats, C. and Norton, H. 2011. Intermediaries and hate speech: Fostering digital citizenship for our information age. *Boston University Law Review*, 91: 1435.

Keats, D. 2014. *Hate Crimes in Cyberspace*. Cambridge, MA: Harvard University Press.

Khaleeli, H. 2013. Islamophobic hate crime: Is it getting worse? *The Guardian*. Available at: www.theguardian.com/uk/2013/jun/05/islamophobic-hate-crime-getting-worse

Kotecha, S. 2013. Quarter of young British people 'do not trust Muslims', *BBC Newsbeat*. Available at: www.bbc.co.uk/newsbeat/24204742

Larsson, G. 2007. Cyber-Islamophobia? The case of WikiIslam. *Contemporary Islam*, 1(1): 53–67.

Leveson Inquiry. 2012. *Culture, Practice and Ethics of the Press*. Available at: www.leveso ninquiry.org.uk/about/the-report/

Online Hate Prevention Institute. 2013. *Islamophobia on the Internet: The Growth of Online Hate Targeting Muslims*. Available at: http://ohpi.org.au/islamophobia-on-the-internet- the-growth-of-online-hate-targeting-muslims/

Perry, B. 2001. *In the Name of Hate: Understanding Hate Crimes*. London: Routledge.

Perry, B. 2003. Where do we go from here? Researching hate crime. *Internet Journal of Criminology*. Available at: www.internetjournalofcriminology.com/where%20do%20we% 20go%20from%20here.%20researching%20hate%20crime.pdf

Perry, B. and Olsson, P. 2009. Cyber hate: The globalisation of hate. *Information & Communications Technology Law*, 18(2): 185–199. Available at: www.informaworld.com/smpp/ content-content=a912569634db=all~jumptype=rss

Saul, H. 2013. Police call home-made bomb outside Walsall's Ashia Mosque a 'hate crime' and draft in counter-terror police. *The Independent*. Available at: www.independent.co.uk/news/uk/crime/police-call-homemade-bomb-outside-walsalls-ashia-mosque-a-hate-crime-and-draft-in-counterterror-police-8670548.html

Sellgren, K. 2014. Cyberbullying 'on rise' – ChildLine. *BBC News*. Available at: www.bbc.co.uk/news/education-25639839

Sheffield, C. 1995. Hate violence. In: R. Rothenberg (ed.) *Race, Class and Gender in the United States*. New York: St Martin's Press, pp. 431–441.

Taras, R. 2012. *Xenophobia and Islamophobia in Europe*. Edinburgh University Press.

The Guardian. 2013. UK anti-Muslim hate crime soars, police figures show. Available at: www.theguardian.com/society/2013/dec/27/uk-anti-muslim-hate-crime-soars

True Vision. 2019. Internet hate crime. Available at: www.report-it.org.uk/reporting_internet_hate_crime

Urquhart, C. 2013. Attacks on Muslims soar in wake of Woolwich murder. *The Guardian*. Available at: www.theguardian.com/uk/2013/may/25/woolwich-murder-attacks-on-muslims

Waddington, P. A. J. 2010. An examination of hate crime. *Police Review*, 23 April, 118 (6077): 14–15.

Weaver, S. 2013. A rhetorical discourse analysis of online anti-Muslim and anti-Semitic jokes. *Ethnic and Racial Studies*, 36(3): 483–499.

Whine, M. 2003. Far right extremists on the Internet. In: D. Thomas and B. Loader (eds) *Cyber Crime: Law Enforcement, Security and Surveillance in the Information Age*. London: Routledge, pp. 234–250.

Yar, M. 2013. *Cybercrime and Society*. London: Sage.

Zempi, I. and Awan, I. 2016. *Islamophobia: Lived Experiences of Online and Offline Victimisation*. Bristol University Press.

4

GENDERED ISLAMOPHOBIA

Introduction

This chapter examines historical and contemporary discourses of the Muslim veil, and outlines the implications of this rhetoric for veiled Muslim women in the West. The chapter argues that through the colonial lens, the Muslim veil was seen as a symbol of gender oppression. From this perspective, the 'liberation' of veiled Muslim women became fused with the motivations of imperial expansion. In a post-9/11 climate, the wearing of the veil is routinely seen as a symbol of Islamist extremism and segregation as well as a sign of gender oppression. The chapter also examines contemporary legal restrictions upon the wearing of the niqab (face veil) in public places in the West, and suggests that banning the niqab potentially legitimises public acts of violence towards veiled Muslim women. The chapter concludes with a discussion of the gendered dimensions of Islamophobia.

Colonial understandings of the veil

Historically, Western contact with veiled Muslim women was rare before colonial exploration. Prior to the 17th century, colonial perceptions of veiled Muslim women were the product of male travellers' tales and poor translations of Arabic texts (Ahmed 1992). From the late 17th century, colonial interaction with veiled Muslim women remained limited until the next century when colonial expansion began to produce a "Western narrative of women in Islam" (Ahmed 1992, p. 149). In 1978, Said coined the term 'Orientalism' to portray the way that Western scholarship reflected a distorted image of the East. In particular, the 'Orientalist framework' stemmed from "an imaginative and yet drastically polarized geography dividing the world into two unequal parts, the larger, 'different' one called the Orient, the other, also known as 'our' world, called the Occident or the West"

(Said 1981, p. 4). This imaginative geography was characterised by the rigid dichotomy of 'us' and 'them' whereby the West was privileged over the Orient.

The ideology associated with Orientalism served to construct a Western identity based on opposition to the Orient. In this respect, the production of knowledge about the colonial 'Other' was a simultaneous constitution of the 'Self' (Bradford 1999). The Orient was seen as inferior and uncivilised whilst the Oriental woman was perceived to be alluring, bewitching, and extremely dangerous (Stott 1992). Based on the binary of 'us' and 'them', the act of veiling is constructed as evidence of the misogyny and violence associated with Islam whilst the act of unveiling is identified as an example of the equation of the West with gender equality and freedom (Klaus and Kassel 2005). As such, the veil is understood as a symbol for the oppression of Muslim women against which the West prides itself as being emancipator (Klaus and Kassel 2005). In striking contrast to the image of the oppressed veiled Muslim woman stands the image of the emancipated Western (and non-Muslim) woman who has "control over her income, her body and her sexuality" (Kapur 2002, p. 16).

Within the Orientalist framework, the veiled female Muslim body became the symbol for Islam. The wearing of the veil was seen as a symbol of the gender oppression in Islam on the basis that women were forced to wear the veil by Muslim men. In other words, the veil became the symbol of the 'backwardness' of Islam itself. From this perspective, the 'liberation' of veiled Muslim women became the justification for colonialism. During the late 19th and early 20th century, colonial officials adopted a 'civilising mission' in relation to colonised countries (Bradford 1999). To this end, the image of the oppressed Muslim woman in need of 'rescue' by Western men was employed to legitimise the build-up of French and British colonial empires. In other words, the 'liberation' of veiled Muslim women became fused with the motivations of imperial expansion, at least from the gaze of the coloniser. Colonial ways of seeing the veil as a symbol of gender oppression still function today as a lens through which to view veiled Muslim women, thereby promoting the 'Othering' of Islam and Muslims.

Contemporary perceptions of the veil

The Orientalist roots of the process of 'Othering' of Islam and Muslims paved the way for the current climate of Islamophobia. In a post-9/11 climate, veiled Muslim women are typically seen as oppressed, failing to integrate into society, and as potential extremists or terrorist sympathisers. The following paragraphs outline these stereotypes in more detail, and demonstrate how they promote Islamophobia towards veiled Muslim women.

Gender oppression

The wearing of the veil in public places in the West is routinely perceived as oppressive and representative of the presumed inferior position of women in

Islam (Rashid 2017). According to Runnymede Trust (1997, p. 28), "the claim that Islam oppresses women, in ways significantly different from and worse than the ways in which women are treated in other religions and cultures, is a recurring theme of much press coverage and comment". As a marker of patriarchy, the veil represents the subjugation of women in Islam on the basis that they are coerced into wearing it by Muslim men (Mancini 2013). The assumption of patriarchal domination and matriarchal submissiveness in Islam consolidates and re-produces Oriental views of Islam as culturally inferior to the West. This representation of Muslim women can be seen in David Cameron's controversial comments in 2016 about Muslim women being "traditionally submissive" (Hughes 2016).

Common perceptions about veiled Muslim women's lack of agency further entrench dangerous notions of a 'Muslim problem' whereby Muslim men deny Muslim women the freedom to exercise their autonomy. Indeed, as Rashid (2017, p. 61) points out, the stereotypes of Muslim women and Muslim men are formed in relation to each other whereby "Muslim women are seen as 'oppressed', passive victims and Muslim men are seen as exceptionally misogynistic". Both perceptions stem from stereotypes of Islam as a patriarchal religion (Kumar 2012). This widely held stereotype denies Muslim women the possibility of agency (Rashid 2017). Ahmad (2010) notes that this discourse silences and obscures alternative forms of agency, repeats simplistic 'Western' versus 'Muslim' dichotomous frameworks, and contributes to the separation between 'us' and 'them'. Ultimately, this narrative relies upon denying veiled Muslim women any agency, the presumption being that all Muslim women are being forced to wear the veil by male family members (Rashid 2017). While acknowledging that the social status and life conditions of many Muslim women need to be improved to achieve gender equality, it should also be recognised that to consider all Muslim women as passive victims is not an accurate reflection of how many Muslim women perceive their lives. Rather, the articulation of the female Muslim body as the 'victim subject' fails to accommodate a multi-layered experience and therefore denies the possibility of genuine choice. Rather, Muslim women are being pressured to remove their veils out of fear of Islamophobic discrimination or violence (Rashid 2017).

Islamist terrorism

The wearing of the veil in public places in the West is stereotypically seen as a symbol of Islamist fundamentalism. In a post-9/11 climate, the West is allegedly facing a global 'threat' by Islamist extremism and the veil is a visual representation of that 'threat'. Ghumman and Ryan (2013) argue that although Muslim women are perceived as oppressed and Muslim men are seen as dangerous, Muslim women are not free from popular stereotypes whereby Muslims *per se* are seen as potential terrorists or terrorist sympathisers. In particular, the niqab (face veil) is perceived as a danger to public safety on the basis that the covering of the face hinders identification and as such it could be used as camouflage for a terrorist.

Rashid (2017) notes that while there may be valid practical questions about whether the niqab should be worn in particular professions (e.g. by nursery nurses) or contexts (e.g. in court or during security checks at airports), these can be largely accommodated; more problematic is that it continues to be associated with Islamist extremism. Banning the niqab is often seen as the only way to ensure public safety. As it stands, there is no veil ban in the UK but schools and educational institutions are allowed to set their own uniform guidelines. In 2005, Imperial College in London banned its students from wearing the niqab on campus over security concerns raised by the terrorist attacks of 7/7 (Garner 2005). In 2006, Birmingham Medical School banned its medical students from wearing the niqab when talking to patients in hospitals and surgeries, and when they were in meetings with other medical staff (Leggatt, Dixon, and Milland 2006). In September 2013, Birmingham Metropolitan College banned its students from wearing the niqab on campus so that they were easily identifiable. Birmingham Metropolitan College has now reversed its decision after more than 9,000 people signed an online petition set up by the NUS Black Students' Campaign calling on the College to remove the ban (The Guardian 2013).

As a sign of Islamist terrorism and extremism, the niqab is also understood as a tool of religious fundamentalism whereby it serves to proselytise non-Muslims to Islam. In this regard, it is seen as an act of religious propaganda with the aim to infiltrate into Western society. In the words of Tissot (2011, p. 43), "Women in niqab are the Trojan horse of extremist Islamism". Seen in this light, the niqab hides not only the face but 'secret intentions' as well, namely, to impose Sharia law in the West. As such, the niqab represents the type of political Islamism that is also found in Iraq and Afghanistan, characterising the implementation of Sharia law as interpreted by the Taliban.

National cohesion

The wearing of the veil in public in the West is routinely understood as a sign of a lack of integration and a failure to conform to British/Western values. Seen in this light, the wearing of the veil mirrors the notion of 'parallel lives' (Cantle 2001) and self-enclosed communities. Also, it allegedly hinders integration and fosters the social isolation of Muslim women. Within this paradigm, multiculturalism is seen as a 'threat' to the existence of Western values and the veil – by virtue of its public visibility as the sign of Islam in the West – is a visual symbol of that 'threat' (Meer, Dwyer, and Modood 2010). In the British context, national identity and examples of Muslim 'difference' are cast as mutually exclusive. As such, the veil is rejected on the grounds that it is non-British in inception and adoption, thereby erasing the principle of integration as a two-way process of mutual accommodation by all; rather, it is integration at the price of becoming less 'Muslim' (Meer, Dwyer, and Modood 2010). Thus, the argument goes, veiled Muslim women must remove their veils in order to integrate into Western society.

In 2006, Jack Straw, then Labour home secretary, infamously asked a niqab-wearing constituent to remove her niqab. He described niqabs as "a visible statement of separation and difference" that made "better, positive relations between the two communities more difficult" (Meer, Dwyer, and Modood 2010). Media coverage of integration invariably includes stock photos of women wearing niqabs, thus making the association very explicit (Rashid 2017). Unsurprisingly, the veil has been incorporated into discussions about inclusivity and Britishness. Specifically, the niqab is 'unique' on the basis that it prevents a basic form of human contact in a way that the Muslim headscarf, the Sikh turban, the Buddhist robe, and the Christian Cross do not. Unlike other examples of religious attire that allow for the face to be visible, the niqab allegedly cancels the wearer's identity. According to this line of argument, the niqab relegates the wearer to a condition of isolation and segregation due to the perceived difficulty in communicating with a person whose face is covered. From this perspective, it is seen as a hindrance to direct communication because it makes inter-personal communication less open and transparent. Robert (2005, p. 28) states:

> It is as if, once you put on the niqab you cease to have a human identity. I know that the niqab is a shock to the system for most people in non-Muslim societies – we are used to seeing so much personal information about people around us, being able to tell their race, their age, their physique and their attractiveness. The niqab gives none of this information.

Mancini (2013, p. 27) argues that a covered face cancels transparency and reciprocity in communication, highlighting "the objective and undeniable difficulty of communication that derives from the almost total covering of a woman's face". Seen in this light, transparency and reciprocity is impeded by the covering of the face with the niqab. Along similar lines, Tourkochoriti (2012) observes that in Christianity the face has become the 'quintessence of the person', the 'noble part of the body', whilst the covering of the face marks an 'undignified' existence. Thus, it could be argued that the niqab is contrary to contemporary Christian/Western societies, which value the face and in which interactions amongst citizens are necessarily unveiled. Clearly, the fact that veiling has historically formed part of Christian traditions is ignored.

This discussion shows that the wearing of the niqab is routinely seen as an obstacle to face-to-face interaction and thus as a sign of social isolation and self-segregation. It would appear then that the community cohesion agenda is based exclusively upon the obligation of Muslim minorities for integration, and as a result the problem of non-integration rests with Muslims themselves (Meer, Dwyer, and Modood 2010). The concept of integration does not allow for 'difference' in general and 'Muslim distinctiveness' in particular; rather, 'real' integration can only be achieved through greater public conformity in sharp contrast to a multicultural integration that sustains 'difference'. From this perspective, the removal of the niqab is an essential step to community cohesion on the basis that the covering of the face is a visible barrier to community relations.

Indeed, the practice of veiling has acquired huge significance in the discourse on Muslim integration. Muslim women are viewed as the main vehicles of integration but simultaneously they are the first victims of the failure of integration. Ironically, choosing to veil is a greater offence than being forced to veil, or as Khiabany and Williamson (2008, p. 69) put it: "Veiled women are considered to be ungrateful subjects who have failed to assimilate and are deemed to threaten the British way of life". Even in cases where women choose to wear the veil, they are seen as deliberately isolating themselves and rejecting Western values. Ultimately, the parameters of the veil debate demonstrate that multiculturalism is an implicit expression of the degree of tolerance of the 'host' state that demands the integration of the Muslim 'Other' on its own terms. Such stereotypes are key to the criminalisation of the veil in public places in the West.

Case study: the lived experiences of Muslim women in niqab

Zempi (2014) examined the experiences of Islamophobic victimisation of Muslim women who wear the niqab. Throughout interviews and focus group discussions, participants made explicit reference to the type of language used by the perpetrators, which signified their motivations for the attack. For example, most participants had been called names such as 'Terrorists', 'Muslim bombers', and 'Suicide bombers', which indicate the perpetrators' perceptions of veiled Muslim women as a security or terrorist 'threat'. Along similar lines, the following comments demonstrate that the wearing of the niqab was perceived as a camouflage for a terrorist.

Have you got a bomb under there?

(Nisha, 28 years old)

Are you carrying belts full of explosives?

(Jahidah, 22 years old)

When are you going to blow us up?

(Shelina, 36 years old)

Why are you dressed like that? Are you a suicide bomber?

(Amtullah, 24 years old)

Importantly, participants argued that even if they were not seen to be involved in a terrorist plot – because veiled Muslim women are supposedly too oppressed, uneducated, and incapable of autonomy – they were nevertheless perceived as the mothers of home-grown terrorists; hence perpetrators often called them names such as "Bin Laden's wife". Research highlights that 'visible' Muslims and veiled Muslim women in particular are often targeted because their abusers hold the view that all Muslims are terrorists or terrorist sympathisers (Ameli, Elahi, and Merali 2004; Sheridan and Gillett 2005; Khan 2007; Choudhury 2010; Githens-Mazer

48 Gendered Islamophobia

and Lambert 2010). Additionally, participants described examples of verbal abuse, which illustrated the racist and xenophobic sentiments of the perpetrators such as:

> Go back to your country, you don't belong here!
>
> *(Nadia, 29 years old)*

> Go back to where from you came from! Go back to Afghanistan!
>
> *(Focus group participant)*

> If you want Sharia go back to Iraq!
>
> *(Nabeeha, 22 years old)*

> Take it off! You are in my country now!
>
> *(Layla, 38 years old)*

In the eyes of their abusers, veiled Muslim women are seen as immigrants who "don't belong" despite the fact that they have been born or largely raised in the UK. Within this paradigm, the wearing of the veil marks an unwelcome religious, cultural, and racial presence (Grillo and Shah 2012). Crucially, this type of language can be linked to the alleged 'Islamification' of the UK. In the current climate of economic instability, Muslims are supposedly 'taking over' Britain and as a result the visibility of the veil poses a 'threat' to national identity.

Moreover, there were incidents where the nature of the verbal abuse suggested both racist and Islamophobic hatred. For example, some Black Muslim women who took part in this study revealed that they had bananas thrown at them whilst others heard monkey noises or comments such as 'Go home Muslim monkey' or 'Black terrorist' being made when they were walking on the street. As Sallah (2010) points out, bananas and monkey noises are known symbols of racism. At one level, this indicates that the targeted victimisation of veiled Muslim women can be attributed to Islamophobic attitudes as well as to racist and xenophobic sentiments by virtue of the fact that these elements are often inextricably inter-twined. In this regard, Islamophobia, racism, and xenophobia become mutually reinforcing phenomena, and hostility against veiled Muslim women should also be considered in the context of a more general climate of hostility towards 'Otherness'. However, this is not to overlook the fact that veiled Muslim women have been victims of targeted violence because their abusers have been motivated either solely or partially by other factors. For example, the sight of the veiled female body might provoke anger in some men who are used to 'seeing' in the public space.

> We are very different to the average non-Muslim woman. We are doing everything that the media tells us we shouldn't be doing in terms of how women should dress.
>
> *(Roukia, 27 years old)*

In Western societies men are used to seeing women in all their glory really, aren't they? I think men appreciate the fact that they can see a woman's face and that they can see her figure. They probably feel deprived of this opportunity because they can't assess a Muslim woman in the same way that they can assess a Christian, Sikh or Hindu woman.

(Aleena, 28 years old)

In this sense, the face and body of a woman is an object of sexual attraction and when these are covered it disrupts public expectations of how women should behave and dress in public in order to visually 'please' men. This emphasises the 'appropriate' feminine sexuality, which ensures that the behaviour and attire of women are strictly monitored (Dwyer 1999). This was evident in incidents where veiled Muslim women in this study were subjected to remarks of a sexual nature, which were often accompanied by menacing staring, sexual gestures, whistling and kissing noises made by (mostly white young) men on the street.

Give us a flash!

(Alima, 20 years old)

Show me what you're wearing under there!

(Ruqiia, 17 years old)

This form of sexual harassment is motivated by a male gaze that desires possession of women's bodies and 'wants to see' (Al-Saji 2010). As a solution to this 'problem', perpetrators often demanded that participants uncovered their face and body by shouting 'Take it off' and 'Show me your face'. These findings lend weight to the view that there is a male desire to uncover the female Muslim body, which is covered in public (Dwyer 1999). This was also evident in the following comments made exclusively by white young men:

Why don't you take it off? Are you not hot in that?

(Jahidah, 22 years old)

What's that on your face? Why are you covering it?

(Sarah, 31 years old)

Take that shit off your face!
    Why do you have a mask on? Are you really ugly under there?

(Focus group participants)

Furthermore, participants reported that they were used as a form of entertainment. For example, they were called names such as 'Ninja', 'Catwoman', 'Batman', 'Darth Vader', 'Ghost woman', 'Bin bag', 'Letterbox', 'Postbox', 'Witch', and

50 Gendered Islamophobia

'Walking coffin'. Moreover, participants noted that they had been subjected to swearing such as 'Fucking freak', 'Muslim bitch', and 'Muslim whore'. In addition, a couple of participants reported that people on the street sometimes took photographs of them (without asking their permission) whilst others revealed that they had been followed and/or stalked. Though alarming enough when taken in isolation, these examples of intimidation, hostility, and abuse were made all the more harrowing by the fact that they were sometimes accompanied by physical abuse.

Physical attacks

Participants in Zempi's (2014) study also reported that incidents of physical abuse involved attempted and actual physical assaults (including taking the veil off), pushing, shoving, being spat at, and even incidents where passing vehicles had attempted to run them over.

> Taking the veil off and getting slapped in the face.
>
> *(Iman, 37 years old)*

> I was six months pregnant with my first baby and a white man elbowed me in the stomach when I was in the queue at Boots.
>
> *(Kalila, 29 years old)*

> I was beaten up in the park. Nobody stepped in to help me.
>
> *(Salimah, 22 years old)*

Participants also described incidents where people on the street or from moving cars had thrown eggs, stones, alcohol, water bombs, bottles, take-away food, and rubbish at them. The following quotations are just some of the many examples from participants' accounts that help to illustrate this point:

> I've had cups of tea thrown at me from a van. There was a building firm on my street and I was going to the mosque and the man looked out of his window, had his cup of tea and threw it on me. When I complained he started swearing at me. He said "Don't make it a big deal, fuck off".
>
> *(Yasmine, 28 years old)*

> I was waiting at the bus stop and some lads threw a lit cigarette on my jilbab.
>
> *(Nadia, 29 years old)*

Additionally, some participants had experienced some serious incidents of criminal damage such as graffiti, eggs thrown at the property, alcohol or petrol poured through the letterbox, as well as bacon, pork, ham, and dog excrement put through the letterbox or sent via post. Bowling (2009) argues that persistent attacks on property are also attacks on those inside the dwelling (whether or not they are present at the time of the incident). Some participants reported being targeted with threatening or abusive hate mail, which often involved death threats:

> We had a letter come through the post. It had a white powder in there and it said 'We hate Muslims' and also there was a razor blade in the letter.
>
> *(Raja, 40 years old)*

With respect to both verbal and physical abuse, participants were convinced that it was their distinctive Muslim appearance that made them a target. Participants also felt more vulnerable in comparison to Muslim men on the basis of their gender.

> The more you dress as a Muslim, the more you are going to be seen as a threat because you are personifying what they see as evil.
>
> *(Shelina, 36 years old)*

> On the news they portray women who wear a veil as oppressed but I am not oppressed. If you ask my husband he'll say I wear the trousers in the house. What I don't understand is if people think we are oppressed and we're forced to wear it, why do they attack us about it? They don't attack Muslim men. They attack Muslim women in veil.
>
> *(Zafirah, 33 years old)*

> We stand out so much, when we walk into town everyone knows we are Muslims. As women we are more vulnerable as well. It is easier to attack a woman in niqab rather than attacking a Muslim man with the beard.
>
> *(Focus group participant)*

The criminalisation of the niqab in Europe

Several European countries such as France, Belgium, Denmark, and Austria have enforced legislation, which makes it illegal for Muslim women to wear the niqab in public. In 2011, France became the first country in Europe to introduce a law banning the wearing of the niqab in public places. That said, it is important to point out that in 2004, France enacted a law banning the hijab for students in public schools. In particular, the legislation prohibited the display of 'conspicuous' religious symbols such as the Jewish skullcap, the Christian crucifix, and the Sikh turban by the students of public elementary and high schools. This law appeared to deal with religious symbols *per se*, although the public debate was mostly concerned with the Muslim headscarf (Lyon and Spini 2004). In 2016, France introduced a controversial ban on women's full-body swimsuits, known as 'burkinis'. Prime Minister Manuel Valls called the swimsuits "the affirmation of political Islam in the public space" (Chrisafis 2016). The burkini ban, imposed by French Riviera mayors, was later lifted in seaside resorts after France's top administrative court overruled the law.

52 Gendered Islamophobia

Belgium was the second European country after France to enforce a niqab ban, which came into effect in July 2011. In December 2012, Belgium's Constitutional Court rejected appeals for the ban to be annulled, ruling that it did not violate human rights. The European Court of Human Rights in its judgment in S.A.S v. France (No. 43835/11, 2014), and subsequent judgments in Belcacemi and Oussar v. Belgium (No. 37798/13, 2017) and Dakir v. Belgium (No. 4619/12, 2017), held that the French and Belgian laws and decrees banning the wearing of clothing that fully or partially conceals the face in public places are not in breach of the European Convention on Human Rights.

Grillo and Shah (2012) point out that while local in origin, policies to ban the niqab are usually followed by other countries. Indeed, following the example set by France and Belgium, the Dutch Government has introduced a ban on face covering in public in November 2016. The ban reflected the influence of populist politician Geert Wilders, of the anti-immigration Freedom Party, who wants tougher policies on Islam. In October 2017, legislation has gone into effect in Austria banning the niqab in public spaces. The ban was an attempt to protect Austrian values on the basis that the wearing of the niqab stands in the way of 'open communication', which is fundamental to an 'open society'.

In Italy, several towns have local bans on the wearing of the niqab. The north-western town of Novara is one of several local authorities to have already brought in rules to deter public use of the niqab whilst in the Lombardy region of Italy, a niqab ban came into effect in January 2016. A parliamentary commission has approved a draft law banning women from wearing the niqab in public whilst an old anti-terrorist law against concealing the face for security reasons has already been used by some local Italian authorities to fine Muslim women who wear it. Some mayors from the anti-immigrant Northern League have also banned the use of Islamic swimsuits. In Spain, the city of Barcelona has announced a niqab ban in some public spaces such as municipal offices, public markets, and libraries, whilst at least two smaller towns in Catalonia, the north-eastern region that includes Barcelona, have already imposed veil bans. A ban in the town of Lleida was overturned by Spain's Supreme Court in February 2013. It ruled that it was an infringement of religious liberties.

Although there are no national laws restricting the wearing of veils in Germany, there have been proposals for banning the niqab. In 2016, Chancellor Angela Merkel stated the wearing of the niqab should be prohibited in Germany "wherever it is legally possible" (BBC 2017). These comments were made following the proposals of Interior Minister Thomas de Maiziere to ban the niqab in public buildings in Germany. In September 2003, the federal Constitutional Court ruled in favour of a teacher who wanted to wear the hijab (headscarf) to school. However, it said that states could change their laws locally if they wanted to. At least half of Germany's 16 states went on to ban teachers from wearing headscarves and in the state of Hesse the ban included civil servants (BBC 2017).

As such, there exists a cross-national interweaving of media, political, and public discourses against the 'Islamisation' of Europe and in favour of restrictions on the practice of Islam in the West. The Council of Europe Parliamentary Assembly (2010, n.p.) legitimises the ban on the basis that the wearing of the niqab is seen as a 'threat' to gender equality, public safety, and national cohesion:

> The veiling of women, especially full veiling through the burqa or the niqab, is often perceived as a symbol of the subjugation of women to men, restricting the role of women within society, limiting their professional life and impeding their social and economic activities … Article 9 of the Convention includes the right of individuals to choose freely to wear or not to wear religious clothing in private or in public. Legal restrictions to this freedom may be justified where necessary in a democratic society, in particular for security purposes or where public or professional functions of individuals require their religious neutrality or that their face can be seen.

Although it acknowledges that Muslim women have the right to freedom of religious expression, the Council of Europe justifies the implementation of legal restrictions upon the wearing of the niqab in public in Europe. Indeed, justifications in favour of the ban in public generally take three forms: covering the face is incompatible with Western values including gender equality; wearing the niqab impedes communication and integration; and wearing the niqab poses a security risk.

The British Government has not entertained a veil ban so far. In this regard, there are no legislative or administrative provisions that forbid the wearing of the niqab at the national or local level. However, although the UK does not have any legislative prohibitions in place, there are calls for such legislation to be introduced. In 2010, the Conservative MP Philip Hollobone sought to introduce a Private Members' Bill, entitled the Face Coverings Regulations Bill, which would make it illegal for people to cover their faces in public. The Bill, which received its second reading in the House of Commons in December 2011, was rejected. The British National Party and the UK Independence Party both supported a veil ban in their election manifestos in 2010, while extreme protest movements such as the English Defence League have staged a number of violent anti-Muslim protests against elements of Islam, namely Sharia law, mosques, and the wearing of the niqab. Former UKIP leader Nigel Farage has said that full veils are a symbol of an "increasingly divided Britain" (BBC 2010), that they 'oppress' women, and are a potential security threat. Although there is no official policy on the Muslim code of dress in the UK, there has been considerable debate. A YouGov (2016) poll showed that 57 per cent of the British public support a burka ban in the UK.

Tourkochoriti (2012) points out that the veil ban, like the hijab ban in public schools in France, is justified by the need to protect Muslim girls and women from being forced to wear it by their families or local community. It also aims to protect them from themselves when wearing the veil happens to be an authentic choice of the women concerned. In this regard, Muslim women are denied the possibility to be active agents capable of rational choices because they are considered to be alienated and 'blind' to their own oppression. Although religions in general may

54 Gendered Islamophobia

provide the means and justification for the subjection of women, a distorted view of Islam denies recognition of Muslim women's autonomy.

Clearly, the veil debate has not translated into a sophisticated understanding of the ways in which veiled Muslim women's lived experiences are mediated by factors such as gender, age, race, ethnicity, education, socio-economic status, and space, to name but some. Rather, the gradual mutation of the veil from a symbol of religious identity to a contentious marker of 'difference' paves the way for further contamination of the veil as a visible sign of Muslim 'Otherness'. Ultimately, the veil ban – including support for state veil bans – prevents veiled Muslim women from full participation in society by exacerbating their multiple and intersectional discrimination on the grounds of both religion and gender, thereby increasing (rather than decreasing) social exclusion by pushing these women to the margins of society.

Islamophobia as a result of the veil ban

The veil ban stigmatises veiled Muslim women as 'criminals', thereby potentially 'legitimising' acts of violence towards them when they are seen in public. In this sense, the law increases the sense of vulnerability of veiled Muslim women in the public sphere. Even if not explicitly inciting hate-motivated violence, the law in its application contributes to a climate of intolerance and to mounting tensions between Islam and the West (Chakraborti and Zempi 2012). Veiled Muslim women who took part in Zempi's (2014) study reported that hostility towards them had increased significantly since the French veil ban:

> The French veil ban is a form of Islamophobia. We are attacked verbally and physically and through the ideology that the media and politicians are promoting.
>
> *(Hasna, 43 years old)*

> My friends in France tell me that they don't go out. They continue to wear it because they don't want to take it off. For them it feels like stripping off if they don't wear it, so they stay inside the house and they don't go out. The law started in April 2010 and one of my friends told me on the phone that she has not been out of the house since then. My husband and I decided to leave France when the debate started there.
>
> *(Kamil, 30 years old)*

> It has given people an excuse to attack women in niqab. I read blogs about banning the veil and most comments are like 'They should ban it here as well'. I think it's getting worse now anyway. I don't think it's safe for us anymore to walk on the street. As time goes by it will get worse.

France's action has given British people the right to say things that they wouldn't have said before. So whereas before they'd keep it quiet because they know that British values are different, that we are tolerant and very pro-multicultural, the moment France banned the veil, suddenly these people thought 'Right, now we've got a voice, now we've got justification, now we can talk because if the government in France thinks this is illegal, it's ok for us to raise our racist opinions'.

(Focus group participants)

Accordingly, research in Belgium (Brems et al. 2012) and France (Bouteldja 2013) shows that the veil ban has emboldened ordinary citizens to show aggressive behaviour towards veiled Muslim women. Drawing on research with 35 veiled Muslim women in France, Bouteldja (2013) examined the effects of the French veil ban on their lives. Participants in Bouteldja's (2013) study emphasised their personal religious commitment to continue wearing the niqab. The implementation of the French veil ban had not stopped women from wearing it. All of the participants argued that the law had significant negative effects on their lives, and that it had neither empowered nor liberated them (Bouteldja 2013). They compared their lives in France after the veil ban to being held in a prison. Some participants continued to wear the niqab in France after the implementation of the ban but argued that the fear of being stopped by the police or abused by members of the public prevented them from leaving their house (Bouteldja 2013). It is important to point out that no participants reported experiencing empowerment or liberation as the law was intended; rather, all the participants reported socialising less, and reducing their outdoor activities to the strictest minimum (Bouteldja 2013). However, the constraints on their movements and lack of physical exercise had taken a toll on the physical and mental health of many participants. They reported suffering depression and anxiety attacks when leaving their house, and an overall deterioration of their health (Bouteldja 2013). The veil ban had also affected their family life, increasing their dependence on their partners, relatives, and friends, and negatively affecting their relationship with their children. Participants noted that since they could no longer perform everyday activities, the burden of most outdoor activities fell on their partners, relatives, and friends; as a result, several participants reported feeling deprived of their motherhood roles (Bouteldja 2013). This shows that veiled Muslim women in France might experience a serious decline in their social life and their mobility because of the veil ban.

Participants in Bouteldja's (2013) study also reported that verbal abuse and harassment by members of the public was a common experience for women who continued to wear the niqab after the ban was introduced in France. Participants reported physical assaults, including having their veil pulled off, being violently pushed, and being spat on (Bouteldja 2013). Many participants described incidents in which members of the public abusively confronted them, in some cases using their mobile phones to report them to the police or situations where angry groups gathered around them (Bouteldja 2013). Participants felt that the law has given the

56 Gendered Islamophobia

green light for people to be abusive and discriminate against them. When discriminated against or abused, participants felt there was no legal recourse with which to seek justice (Bouteldja 2013).

Brems (2011) conducted semi-structured, in-depth interviews and two focus group interviews with 27 veiled Muslim women in Belgium. Some participants were interviewed before and some were interviewed after the veil ban in Belgium. All the participants reported that it was their autonomous choice to wear the niqab (Brems 2011). They experienced the veil ban as a denial of their autonomy and as anti-emancipatory. Participants in Brems' (2011) study continued to wear it despite the ban, yet avoided going out. A strong sense of danger was prevalent amongst participants whilst they reported that verbal abuse and occasional physical abuse was a common aspect of their lives (Brems 2011). In some cases, they reported being refused to be served, for example at the hospital, school, or the market, because of their niqab. This discussion shows the implications of the veil ban for Muslim women who continue to wear it in the West.

Key questions

- How does Orientalism portray Muslim women in veil?
- What is the nature and scope of the targeted victimisation of Muslim women who wear the niqab?
- What are the implications of the veil ban for Muslim women in the West?

Further reading

- Brems, E. 2014. *The Experiences of Face Veil Wearers in Europe and the Law*. Cambridge: Cambridge University Press.
- Meer, N., Dwyer, C., and Modood, T. 2010. Embodying nationhood? Conceptions of British national identity, citizenship and gender in the 'veil affair'. *The Sociological Review*, 58(1): 84–111.
- Said, E. 1981. *Covering Islam: How the Media and the Experts Determine How We See the Rest of the World*. New York: Pantheon.

References

Ahmad, F. 2010. The London bombings of 7/7 and Muslim women in Britain – media representations, mediated realities. In: F. Shirazi (ed.) *Images of Muslim Women in War and Crisis*. Austin, TX: University of Texas Press.

Ahmed, L. 1992. *Women and Gender in Islam*. London: Yale University.

Al-Saji, A. 2010. The racialisation of Muslim veils: A philosophical analysis. *Philosophy and Social Criticism*, 36(8): 875–902.

Ameli, S. R., Elahi, M., and Merali, A. 2004. *British Muslims' Expectations of Government – Social Discrimination: Across the Muslim Divide*. London: Islamic Human Rights Commission.

BBC. 2010. UKIP chief Nigel Farage calls for burka ban. *BBC*. 17 January. Available at: http://news.bbc.co.uk/2/hi/8464124.stm

BBC. 2017. *The Islamic Veil Across Europe*. Available at: www.bbc.co.uk/news/world-europe-13038095

Bouteldja, N. 2013. *After the Ban: the Experiences of 35 Women of the Full-Face Veil in France*. York: Open Society Foundations.

Bowling, B. 2009. Violent racism: Victimisation, policing and social context. In: B. Williams and H. Goodman-Chong (eds) *Victims and Victimisation: A Reader*. Maidenhead: Open University Press.

Bradford, V. 1999. The veil and the visible. *Western Journal of Communication*, 63(2): 115–139.

Brems, E. 2011. *Human Rights: Universality and Diversity*. Hague: Martinus Nijhoff.

Brems, E., Janssens, Y., Lecoyer, K., Ouald Chaib, S., and Vandersteen, V. 2012. *Wearing the Face Veil in Belgium; Views and Experiences of 27 Women Living in Belgium concerning the Islamic Full Face Veil and the Belgian Ban on Face Covering*. Available at: www.ugent.be/re/publiekrecht/en/research/human-rights/faceveil.pdf

Cantle, T. 2001. *Community Cohesion – A Report of the Independent Review Team*. London: Home Office.

Chakraborti, N. and Zempi, I. 2012. The veil under attack: Gendered dimensions of Islamophobic victimisation. *International Review of Victimology*, 18(3): 269–284.

Chrisafis, A. 2016. French mayors refuse to lift burkini ban despite court ruling. *The Guardian*. 28 August. Available at: www.theguardian.com/world/2016/aug/28/french-mayors-burkini-ban-court-ruling

Choudhury, T. 2010. *Muslims in Europe: A Report on 11 EU Cities*. New York: Open Society Institute.

Council of Europe Parliamentary Assembly. 2010. *Islam, Islamism and Islamophobia in Europe*. Available at: www.assembly.coe.int/ASP/XRef/X2H-DW-XSL.asp?fileid=17880&lang=EN.

Dwyer, C. 1999. Veiled meanings: Young British Muslim women and the negotiation of difference. *Gender, Place and Culture*, 6(1): 5–26.

Garner, R. 2005. Imperial College bans students from wearing hoodies and veils. *The Independent*. Available at: www.independent.co.uk/news/education/education-news/imperial-college-bans-students-from-wearing-hoodies-and-veils-516547.html.

Ghumman, S. and Ryan, A. M. 2013. Not welcome here: Discrimination towards women who wear the Muslim headscarf. *Human Relations*, 66(5): 671–698.

Githens-Mazer, J. and Lambert, R. 2010. *Islamophobia and Anti-Muslim Hate Crime: A London Case Study*. London: European Muslim Research Centre.

Grillo, R. and Shah, P. 2012. *Reasons to Ban? The Anti-Burqa Movement in Western Europe*. Göttingen: Max Planck Institute.

Hughes, L. 2016. David Cameron: More Muslim women should "learn English" to help tackle extremism. *The Telegraph*. 7 January.

Kapur, R. 2002. The tragedy of victimisation rhetoric: Resurrecting the 'native' subject in international/post-colonial feminist legal politics. *Harvard Human Rights Journal*, 15(1): 1–38.

Khan, F. 2007. *Islamophobia – The Impact on London*. London: Muslim Safety Forum.

Khiabany, G. and Williamson, M. 2008. Veiled bodies – Naked racism: Culture, politics and race in the sun. *Race and Class*, 50(1): 69–88.

Klaus, E. and Kassel, S. 2005. The veil as a means of legitimisation: An analysis of the interconnectedness of gender, media and war. *Journalism*, 6(3): 335–355.

Kumar, D. 2012. *Islamophobia and the Politics of Empire*. Chicago: Haymarket Books.

Leggatt, J., Dixon, C., and Milland, G. 2006. The veil is banned in hospitals. *The Express*. Available at: www.express.co.uk/news/uk/1345/The-veil-is-banned-in-hospitals

Lyon, D. and Spini, D. 2004. Unveiling the headscarf debate. *Feminist Legal Studies*, 12(3): 333–345.

58 Gendered Islamophobia

Mancini, L. 2013. Burka, niqab and women's rights. In: A. Ferrari and S. Pastorelli (eds) *The Burka Affair Across Europe*. Surrey: Ashgate.

Meer, N., Dwyer, C., and Modood, T. 2010. Embodying nationhood? Conceptions of British national identity, citizenship and gender in the 'veil affair'. *The Sociological Review*, 58(1): 84–111.

Rashid, N. 2017. 'Everyone is a feminist when it comes to Muslim women': Gender and Islamophobia. In: Runnymede Trust (ed.) *Islamophobia: Still a Challenge for us All*. London: Runnymede Trust, pp. 61–65.

Robert, N. 2005. *My Sisters' Lips: A Unique Celebration of Muslim Womanhood*. London: Bantam Press.

Runnymede Trust. 1997. *Islamophobia: A Challenge For Us All*. London: Runnymede Trust.

Said, E. 1981. *Covering Islam: How the Media and the Experts Determine How We See the Rest of the World*. New York: Pantheon, New York.

Sallah, M. 2010. *The Ummah and Ethnicity: Listening to the Voices of African Heritage Muslims in Leicester*. Leicester: Leicester City Council.

Sheridan, L. and Gillett, R. 2005. Major world events and discrimination. *Asian Journal of Social Psychology*, 8(2): 191–197.

Stott, R. 1992. *The Fabrication of the Late Victorian Femme Fatal*. Basingstoke, Hants: Macmillan.

The Guardian. 2013. Birmingham college makes U-turn on face veil ban. *The Guardian*. 13 September. Available at: www.theguardian.com/uk-news/2013/sep/13/birmingham-col lege-uturn-veil-ban

Tissot, S. 2011. Excluding Muslim women: From hijab to niqab, from school to public space. *Public Culture*, 23(1): 39–46.

Tourkochoriti, I. 2012. The burka ban: Divergent approaches to freedom of religion in France and in the U.S.A. *William and Mary Bill of Rights Journal*, 20, 791–852.

YouGov. 2016. Ban the burka, says majority of the British public. Available at: https://yougov.co.uk/news/2016/08/31/majority-public-backs-burka-ban/

Zempi, I. 2014. *Uncovering Islamophobia: The Victimisation of Veiled Muslim Women*. Leicester: University of Leicester.

5

ISLAMOPHOBIA AND PERCEIVED MUSLIM IDENTITY

Introduction

The body of Islamophobic hate crime scholarship has grown significantly over the past decade. Existing research on Islamophobic hate crime focuses on the verbal, physical, and emotional attacks against Muslims. However, the experiences of non-Muslim men who suffer Islamophobic hate crime because they look Muslim remain 'invisible' in both official statistics and empirical research. In order to address this gap in the literature, we conducted 20 semi-structured interviews with a diverse sample of non-Muslim men who had experienced Islamophobic hate crime online and/or offline (Awan and Zempi 2019). This chapter outlines the study's key findings. As discussed later in this chapter, participants described being verbally and physically attacked, threatened, and harassed as well as their property being damaged. 'Trigger' events included the Brexit vote, Donald Trump's presidency, as well as ISIS-inspired terrorist attacks in European countries such as France, Germany, Sweden, and the UK. The impacts upon victims included physical, emotional, psychological, and economic damage. These experiences were also damaging to community cohesion and led to polarisation between different communities in the UK. Before examining the findings in more detail, it is important to briefly outline the methodology of this study.

Research methods

This was a qualitative study, which set out to record the experiences of non-Muslim men who suffer Islamophobic hate crime because they look Muslim. Participation to the study was voluntary. The study involved individual, in-depth interviews with 20 non-Muslim men. Participants were recruited through engagement with (non-Muslim) religious and secular organisations in the UK. The main aims of the research were to: (a) examine the nature of Islamophobic hate

60 Islamophobia and perceived Muslim identity

crime directed towards non-Muslim men who are perceived to be Muslim; (b) consider the impact of Islamophobic hate crime upon victims and wider communities; (c) examine the coping strategies, which are used by victims in response to their experiences of such hostility; (d) offer recommendations on preventing and responding to this problem.

The interview guide contained a series of open-ended questions related to these research questions. Interviews typically ranged from one to two hours, with an average interview length of one hour. Interviews were undertaken by the authors. All interviews were digitally recorded, transcribed verbatim, and then analysed thematically. In order to ensure participants' anonymity, their real names have been replaced by pseudonyms whilst any personal information that could identify them has been removed. The sample was diverse in terms of age, race/ethnicity, and religion. Participants' ages ranged from 19 to 59. In terms of race/ethnicity, participants included those from Asian heritage (14), Black (three), White Other (two), and White British (one). In terms of faith/belief, participants included those of Christian faith (six), Sikh (nine), Hindu (three), and Atheist (two). However, it is useful to note the limitations of the study. First, the small victims sample means that it is not possible to generalise the findings. Second, we did not interview hate crime perpetrators, and therefore it is not possible to identify their motivations for these attacks; rather we focus on victims' perspectives. Another limitation of the study is the focus only on male perspectives. Despite these limitations, these findings strongly support a greater focus on cases of mistaken identity with respect to Islamophobic hate crimes.

Urban Islamophobic hate crime and public transport

Islamophobia has affected people in a range of different ways. The current discourse around Muslims has obfuscated the narrative around Islam and the conflation between race, ethnicity, religion, and terrorism. This study shows that Islamophobia impacts upon the daily activities of non-Muslims in the UK who use the urban environment and public space to get on with their daily lives. Increasingly, crime is being viewed within spatial and geographical locations, including hot spots areas where specific communities are targeted (Sherman, Gartin and Buerger 1989; Horwitz and Wheeler 1989). Sherman (1995) describes these events as repeat occurrences that lead to victimisation within locations and within a hot spot concentration area.

Merton's (1968) anomie theory of societies and Shaw and McKay's (1942) ecological perspective on neighbourhoods describe how such instances act as a trigger point for further macro-level crimes that target individuals and communities. With respect to Islamophobic hate crime, forms of power, social control, and situational crime prevention can lead to repeat offences (Clarke 1992). Cohen and Felson (1979) go a step further and describe spatial differences and routine activities as being a key part of a perpetrator's crime pattern. Sherman (1995, p. 38) states that: "Places are analogous to oxygen: unless heat and fuel are brought together with oxygen, combustion cannot take place". Participants in this study highlighted how normal routine activities had become more difficult for them because of their perceived Muslim identity and being in the wrong place at the wrong time. For example, some participants noted how travelling at airports had become more problematic following recent ISIS-inspired terrorist attacks.

> I was travelling to America and they even asked us to take our shirts off. We asked for a room but they refused. I was scared, I did not know what would happen next.
>
> *(Ramandeep, 21, Indian, Sikh)*

> Being held at the airport consistently and being treated as a suspect. Because I'm mixed race and I look Muslim, I always get stopped and get abuse at airports. The association of looking like a Muslim is the problem for me. Someone actually asked me 'why do you look like a Muslim?'
>
> *(Samuel, 58, African-Caribbean, Christian)*

The geographical context in which hate crimes occur vary too, for example, in the context of routine activities, crime is socially constructed. The focus and settings of crime tell us a lot about the scope of Islamophobic hate crime suffered by victims. In the context of the present study, this directly relates to public spaces and places such as schools, hospitals, businesses, airports, and car parks. Cornish and Clarke (1986, p. 44) argue that the rational choice perspective lends itself to particular structures and situations that allow offenders to target people by space and location. Sherman (1995, p. 44) states that "To the extent that place features enhance the ability of offenders to commit some crimes, but not any crime, in theory, places should display crime specialization". Therefore, hate crimes are not solely manifested in terms of physical abuse directed against the victim. In some instances, hate crimes move beyond the victim and in fact target the individual's home, place of work, or location where they are. In this study, participants described how the places where they lived were targeted because they were perceived to be Muslim:

> I live on a rough estate. I had dog excrement shoved through the mailbox. They also threw paint over my door.
>
> *(Paul, 37, White, Atheist)*

> Slogans including 'Muzzies out' were painted across the exterior walls of my house. The graffiti was in large white letters. A week later, I received anti-Muslim hate letter in the post. My parents were concerned for my safety, given the threats made on the letter.
>
> *(Joshua, 21, Pakistani, Christian Catholic)*

As well as properties being targeted, the nature of abuse also related back to the place of work. For example, Paul (37, White, Atheist) went for a job interview and he was asked if he was a Muslim. Paul stated 'How was that relevant to the job description?' The research data illustrate how people's education was impacted by their perceived Muslim identity. For example, Ranveer (21, Indian, Sikh) described an experience where his teacher had asked him to perform the role of a terrorist for a play in college. Whilst the rest of his group were not Muslim, Ranveer, who is in fact Sikh, felt very uncomfortable on the basis that he was singled out and asked to play the role of a terrorist:

> I've had incidents in college where as part of a group presentation I had to play a particular actor who had the label of a terrorist. The teacher said 'we need a terrorist for the role play', the group was all white and I'm brown. The teacher asked me if I'm comfortable to play the terrorist. I felt pressured to play this role.
>
> *(Ranveer, 21, Indian, Sikh)*

Ranveer experienced a similar incident at university when he was called a 'terrorist' by one of his fellow students:

> There was a guy from London on our course. He kept calling me a 'terrorist'. When I told him "I am a Sikh, I'm not a terrorist" he said "it doesn't matter if you're a Sikh or whatever, you're all terrorists."
>
> *(Ranveer, 21, Indian, Sikh)*

According to Newton (2014), the reporting and recording of crime and disorder on public transport remains problematic. Smith and Cornish (2006) argue that crimes on public transport can include assault and anti-social behaviour. They also argue that route crimes between stations and stops rely upon spatial patterns of crime, which are more likely to occur on the public transport network. This lends itself to opportunities for offenders who are able to target people because of their movements and predicted travel arrangements on public transport. Garland and Hodkinson (2014) found that public transport was a frequent place of abuse in their study. This often manifested into participants being spat at from behind or out of a window. Places of abuse included city centres, nightclubs, public parks, subways, and on the bus or when waiting for a taxi. In terms of gender, Garland and Hodkinson (2014) found that male participants provided more examples of being violently attacked than female participants. In another similarity with recognised forms of hate crime, the most common locations for the participants in the present study to be targeted were public parks or on public transport, or in 'risky' locations such as town and city centres at night, when they were most vulnerable to drink-fuelled hostility. Similarly, while greater research is still needed on the identity and motivations of offenders, participants' descriptions of those responsible for targeting them was consistent with existing evidence with respect to the profile of the offenders:

> I am stared at constantly. People stare at me as if I am an alien. In a recent incident, a man yelled 'terrorist' as I got on the train. I've had things like people refusing to sit next to me on the bus and being avoided in the shops.
>
> *(Dalbir, 30, Indian, Sikh)*

> This week, I went to supermarket and I was verbally abused in the car park. In another incident, I was on the train, and I was working on my laptop. Another passenger told me to get off the train as I was using my laptop suspiciously. I switched off my laptop and got off at the next stop to calm down the situation.
>
> *(Vinesh, 32, Indian, Hindu)*

The Department for Transport (2010) has found that between 2008–2009, there were 12 crimes per million passengers on the bus network and 13 crimes per million on the underground and overground services. This would indicate that it remains a popular choice for offenders. Newton (2014) argues that when evaluating the types of crime committed on public transport, we should be assessing three components of the transport journey: the walking, waiting, and en route settings. This would include crime committed at stops and stations (Tompson, Partridge, and Shepherd 2009). These types of incidents do vary as crimes on public transport can lead to people feeling a sense of fear that they will be targeted. Vilalta (2011) used data from the 2007 Survey Victimisation and found that in the Mexico City Metropolitan area, the fear of crime on public transport was higher amongst young users including those who used public transport for work purposes. According to Hale (1996), victimisation is shaped by both direct and indirect forms of victimisation. Whilst direct victimisation correlates to physical abuse on public transport, indirect victimisation can lead to a sense of fear and insecurity. In the context of social vulnerability, this is likely to have a damaging effect on actual and potential victims (Chadee and Ditton 2003).

> I was walking late at night, and someone came from behind. I had a rucksack on my back. I felt a knock on my back, and when I looked back, I saw that a knife had gone through it. Luckily, I had some clothes in the rucksack so they had stopped it going any further.
>
> *(Parminder, 59, Indian, Sikh)*

> I was walking home back from the shop and the bus was passing by. Some boys opened the window and shouted 'P★★i Terrorist'. It happened so fast that I did not have time to react. I was shocked. I just stood there trying to take it all in.
>
> *(Ramandeep, 21, Indian, Sikh)*

64 Islamophobia and perceived Muslim identity

> It has happened multiple times, verbal abuse on the street and on the train. Specifically I've been called 'P★★★' and 'Terrorist'. People often say 'Go back'. People call me a 'bastard'. The other day some people threw bottles at me.
>
> *(Dalvinder, 22, Indian, Sikh)*

Two theoretical perspectives that can be applied to the public transport network are the crime pattern and routine activity theories. Crime pattern theory defines people's activity spaces in terms of three main components: nodes, paths, and edges (Clarke and Eck 2005). The term node is used to describe where people (both offenders and victims) travel to and from, and the idea of personal activity nodes closely resembles the ideas of a person's routine activities. These nodes are linked by paths, which would include roads or other transport routes. According to the crime pattern theory, crimes are more likely to concentrate where offender routine activity spaces intersect with those of suitable targets of crime.

> I am regularly subjected to verbal anti-Muslim abuse on public transport. I was on the bus and a group of young girls slurred abuse at me. They said they 'voted for Muslims to be kicked out'. I've also suffered verbal abuse from a motorist who drove by while I was waiting at the bus stop.
>
> *(Mark, 40, White, Christian Orthodox)*

> I suffer hate crime whenever I'm travelling on public transport. Once I was getting on the train and someone just shouted at me 'f★★k off you P★★★ Muslim' and I told him I was not a Muslim and he started laughing saying 'you all look the same'.
>
> *(Govinda, 42, Indian, Hindu)*

'Triggers' of Islamophobic hate crimes

Islamophobic language used by offenders was the most common reported indicator for participants that their victimisation was motivated by the offenders' hostility towards Islam and Muslims. Specifically, participants differentiated between 'external' and 'personal' factors that contributed to their experiences of Islamophobic hate crime. External factors included issues unrelated to them (such as Brexit, Trump, and ISIS-inspired terrorist events) whereas personal factors entailed aspects of their appearance that contributed to them being perceived as Muslim. Awan and Zempi (2015) note how 'trigger' events of local, national, and international significance can influence the prevalence and severity of hate incidents both in the online and offline world, thereby heightening the vulnerability of 'other' groups and communities. In June 2016, the British public took part in a historic vote to decide on whether the UK should remain in the EU. The vote, which was held on Thursday 23 June 2016, resulted in England voting in favour of Brexit, by 53.4 per cent to 46.6 per cent. At the same time as England voted to leave, the UK witnessed a sudden surge in hate crimes. This led to an increase of 42 per cent in England and Wales since the Brexit result was announced. Participants reported that they experienced a spike in Islamophobic hate crimes following the Brexit vote.

I have seen a spike in abuse since the UK voted to leave the EU last year.

(Paul, 37, White, Atheist)

On Facebook, someone wrote on my timeline 'Shouldn't you be on a plane back to Pakistan? We voted for you being out.'

(Joshua, 21, Pakistani, Christian Catholic)

Two weeks before the EU Referendum vote, I received messages on WhatsApp like 'Vote out. Kick out the Muslims'.

(Dalbir, 30, Indian, Sikh)

Indeed, evidence shows that the EU referendum result of June 2016 was a catalyst for an unprecedented surge in reports of hate crime (BBC News 2017). The majority of police forces in England and Wales saw record levels of hate crimes in the first full three months following the EU referendum. More than 14,000 hate crimes were recorded between July and September 2016 whilst in ten forces, the number of suspected hate crimes increased by more than 50 per cent, compared to the previous three months. Similarly, the 2016 Presidential Election in the US has resulted in worrying spikes in hate crime, especially towards (actual and perceived) Muslims (Southern Poverty Law Centre 2016). Along similar lines, participants also noted how the Trump administration and its stance towards Muslims had promoted Islamophobic sentiments both nationally and globally:

I've noticed that abuse has increased on social media after Trump coming into power. People are now very open on social media about their hatred. Before Trump, people were more reserved. I'm on a lot of sites having discussions with people, and I find that racism and Islamophobia are very prevalent. Trump's views are very extreme like banning Muslims to enter US.

(Richard, 28, White, Atheist)

Trump really changed everything, didn't he? He is so blatantly racist and anti-Muslim that he changed the climate completely. Brexit added to that and then you have the rise of Marie Le Pen and far-right groups everywhere in Europe like France, Germany, Netherlands and Austria. The rise of the far-right is now a global thing, their voices are heard more and more, and acted upon, which is really worrying.

(Paul, 37, White, Atheist)

Participants also noted how ISIS-inspired terrorist events in European countries such as France, Germany, Sweden, and the UK have led to an increase in Islamophobic hate crime attacks:

66 Islamophobia and perceived Muslim identity

I've noticed a rise in abuse when there is a terrorist attack. Sadly the overall situation is deteriorating. Islamophobia is having an increasing impact on the lives of Asian men who look Muslim. The hatred that lies behind Islamophobia is spreading.

(Deepak, 45, Indian, Sikh)

I've experienced a rise in hostility after the Manchester terrorist bombings and the London Bridge attack. I've witnessed the same trend after the Lee Rigby murder and the Charlie Hebdo terrorist attacks.

(Raj, 39, Indian, Hindu)

With respect to personal factors, some participants argued that their beard and/or turban (for Sikh men) were key aspects of their appearance that led to being perceived to be Muslim:

On a daily basis, I get people on the streets calling me 'traitor' and 'Ginger Terrorist' because of my beard. They think that I'm Muslim, a convert to Islam but I'm not, I'm an atheist. Having a beard is part of my style, not for any religious reasons.

(Paul, 37, White, Atheist)

Because of being a Sikh man with a beard and turban, people see me as a terrorist.

(Dalvinder, 22, Indian, Sikh)

Asian men who wear the turban and have a beard suffer more abuse because they are more visible.

(Dalbir, 30, Indian, Sikh)

Some participants also felt that their skin colour and/or gender also contributed to being perceived as Muslim:

Whenever people see a terrorist attack in the media, if the terrorist is black, then they assume all blacks must be terrorists. I have a small beard, people see my beard and my colour, and think 'he's one of those lot' and that's about it.

(Cameron, 19, Afro-Caribbean, Christian)

It's my skin colour and also because I have a little beard and look like a Muslim. That's why they think 'he must be a Muslim'. As I am a male, and all these terrorists are males too, that's probably why they look at me and target me too.

(Nick, 24, Afro-Caribbean, Christian)

Having explored the motivations of these attacks, the following section highlights the multiple layers of harm associated with Islamophobic hate crimes including emotional damage, psychological scars, physical violence as well as the escalation of social tensions between different religious communities.

Impacts upon individual victims

Hate crimes cause greater harm than equivalent crimes without bias intent (Iganski 2001). Hate crimes send a message to the victim and the victim's group members that they are neither safe nor welcome in the community (Perry 2014). The research data illustrate the emotional, psychological, behavioural, physical, and financial impacts of experiencing Islamophobic hate crime upon our participants. For example, individuals reported that they suffered anxiety and panic attacks, depression, difficulty sleeping, fear, loss of confidence and feelings of vulnerability, physical illness, loss of income and employment. Participants unanimously reported feeling fearful for their personal safety in public:

> I've experienced more attacks and intimidation after the terror attacks in London and Manchester […] I don't feel secure in the UK anymore. The UK has become a much scarier place.
>
> *(Joshua, 21, Pakistani, Christian Catholic)*

> People have been calling me names on Twitter like 'You're a p★★i c★★t'. I have also been threatened on Facebook like 'Today is the day we get rid of the likes of you!' I fear for my safety when I read this.
>
> *(Vinesh, 32, Indian, Hindu)*

In some cases, participants had to leave their job (particularly those working in the night-time economy) as they feared for their safety. This had implications for them financially:

> The most horrific incident was when a group of white lads punched me and broke my teeth on my way back from work. While they were punching me, they shouted 'all Muslims should be killed'. I was working in a chip shop at the time. I have now left my job since this incident happened.
>
> *(Richard, 28, White, Atheist)*

Clearly, participants feared for their safety although this sense of vulnerability depended upon the geographical area in which they were located. For example, some participants argued that they felt safer in diverse cities in the UK such as Birmingham, Luton, and Leicester. In contrast, in less diverse areas, the sense of vulnerability as well as the risk of attack was perceived to be significantly higher. Participants argued that they avoided

68 Islamophobia and perceived Muslim identity

going to 'white' places. This infers that the impact of fear of future attacks had restricted participants' freedom of movement:

> Whenever I consider going to a place where there are less people of colour, I feel literally very scared. That's why I love Birmingham. You see people from all over the world here. I feel safer here.
>
> *(Dalvinder, 22, Indian, Sikh)*

At the same time though, the geographical area where participants lived was also a factor that identified them as Muslims and thus enhanced their vulnerability to both online and offline attacks. For example, one of our participants, Richard (28, White, Atheist), argued that people thought that he was a Muslim convert because he lived in a Muslim neighbourhood. He noted that people could see his location on his profile on social media, and this meant that he was targeted (both online and offline) because of his perceived affiliation to Islam. Richard moved out of this area to prevent being targeted in the future. Other participants also referred to examples of behavioural changes. They argued that they tried to be aware of their surroundings, minimise the time they were in public, and/or avoid certain areas.

> It worried me when someone tried to stab me. But I can't let this affect me. I minimise how much I go out but if it's going to happen, it's going to happen. But I try not to let it affect me. I do what I want to do but I try to be aware of my surroundings, more now than I used to.
>
> *(Parminder, 59, Indian, Sikh)*

Other participants changed their appearance in order to protect themselves from future abuse. For some individuals, shaving their beard and/or taking their turban off seemed to be a promising strategy for helping them to erase the perceived source of their vulnerability, and therefore reduce the risk of future attacks. But despite taking measures to prevent future victimisation, feelings of insecurity were exacerbated by the fact that these incidents usually took place in public places in view of people passing-by who did not intervene to help them. Considering the serious limitations of official data on hate crimes, bystanders could be an important source of information on the level of hate crime occurring in the community (Wickes et al. 2017). However, the fact that no one would normally intervene to help victims had culminated in feelings of loneliness and isolation, as indicated in the following quotes:

> I was verbally abused by another passenger on the bus who branded me an 'ISIS terrorist' while passengers looked on without intervening. In another incident, I had 'Brexit' yelled in my face. I feel very lonely. No one has come to my assistance or even console me.
>
> *(Mark, 40, White, Christian Orthodox)*

Islamophobia and perceived Muslim identity **69**

> When I was younger, I was chased by a gang of skinheads. I was beaten up. I had stones thrown at me. I had incidents where people tried to knock my turban off. No one has ever come to my defense.
>
> *(Parminder, 59, Indian, Sikh)*

Furthermore, a key finding amongst our participants was the fact that they constantly felt the need to prove their identity, and differentiate themselves from Islam and Muslims. They explained that this was an attempt to prevent future victimisation; however, this was also emotionally draining for our participants. As the following quotes indicate, the need to constantly 'prove their identity' had resulted in a cumulative experience of emotional burnout over time:

> We [Sikhs and Muslims] are different people. People see us through eyes of Muslims but we are not. Because of my beard, I need to explain why I have this and that I'm not Muslim. I think 'why do I need to prove who I am?' Every second, every minute, every day I have to prove myself.
>
> *(Dalvinder, 22, Indian, Sikh)*

Some participants argued that they suffered from depression, eating disorders, and sleep pattern disturbances:

> After the latest incident I went into depression. I didn't want to talk to anybody for a few days. In addition to depression, my sleeping pattern changed. Sometimes eating is a problem, I don't normally eat that much [obesity]. I didn't realise I was having a problem with my diet.
>
> *(Ranveer, 21, Indian, Sikh)*

Iganski and Lagou (2014) note that, compared with victims of parallel crimes, victims of hate crime are more likely to report experiencing: higher levels of depression (McDevitt et al. 2001) and withdrawal (Ehrlich 1992); anxiety (Ehrlich 1992) and nervousness (McDevitt et al. 2001); loss of confidence (Ehrlich 1992); anger (Herek et al. 1997); increased sleep difficulties (Ehrlich, 1992); difficulty concentrating (McDevitt et al. 2001); fear and reduced feelings of safety (McDevitt et al. 2001). On the strength of this evidence, it is clear that Islamophobic hate crimes caused damage to the emotional, psychological, and physical well-being of participants, and reinforced the sense of isolation and powerlessness typically felt within groups who encounter targeted hostility as a routine feature of being 'different'.

Impacts upon wider communities

Each hate crime has many victims in respect of the vicarious, or terroristic, impacts it can have upon targeted communities (Iganski 2001). The harms of hate crime

70 Islamophobia and perceived Muslim identity

extend beyond the immediate victim to negatively impact the victim's reference community. This is a problem that affects not only the victim but the wider community to which victims belong. Hate crimes are more harmful to the community than non-hate crimes on the basis that they undermine tolerance and social inclusion by conveying an 'outsider' status of the victim and fellow group members to the broader community (Wickes et al. 2017). As mentioned in Chapter 2, hate crime is a unique form of offending. The aim of the offender is to send a message to the victim and the victim's group members that they are not welcome in the community (King, Messner, and Baller 2009; Perry 2014). Correspondingly, the impact of hate crime extends even further, affecting all members of the community in question. Therefore, hate crimes are considered more damaging to the social fabric of society than parallel crimes as they attack collective values, disrupt social harmony, and fuel intolerance for diversity (Wickes et al. 2017). Indeed, participants in the present study noted that fellow members of their communities were also fearful for their safety; they knew that they themselves were equally vulnerable to verbal and physical abuse as (perceived) Muslims. Some participants argued that some individuals were angry, upset, and frustrated as they felt it was unfair to be targeted because of their perceived affiliation with Islam. This had led to feelings of polarisation and hostility between the Muslim community and other religious groups, particularly Sikhs and Hindus. In the words of one of our participants: 'Communities are polarised'. Similar views were expressed in the following:

> This is a divided society. Some Sikhs blame Muslims for the abuse they get. We are facing a huge challenge which is cohesion in our communities. Local councils need to do more to bring the Muslim community and the Sikh community together.
>
> *(Parminder, 59, Indian, Sikh)*

> People think that Muslims are the same as ISIS. I know that the Muslim community are doing the best they can internally to fight ISIS but it's not enough.
>
> *(Mark, 40, White, Christian Orthodox)*

Reporting incidents, responses and barriers to Islamophobic hate

Victims of hate crime can often minimise their experiences because of their everyday experiences of suffering hate crimes. The normalisation of targeted harassment and violence can also lead to non-reporting of such incidents to the police. For example, where victims suffer a hate crime, they are unlikely to report this to the police. Under-reporting of hate crime is also a common factor when taking into account official statistics. Victims of hate crime are less likely to report incidents for a variety of reasons, such as anxiety, mental health related problems, fear that they will not be taken seriously, previous unsatisfactory experiences, a lack of confidence in the police, and fear that they will be become the victims of repeat offences (Berzins, Petch, and Atkinson 2003). Clement et al. (2011) argue that victims do not report hate crimes because of the overall trauma of the incident and the fact that they fear being humiliated or targeted again because of the power relationship perpetrators often have over their victims.

In instances of Islamophobic hate crimes, a number of third party reporting centres have now emerged, which provide an alternative system for victims to report incidents. The use of a third party reporting mechanism is meant to make things easier for victims of hate crime. However, a key finding in the study was that participants were not aware of the range of these resources. For victims, better signage and visible posters displayed across public platforms could have a direct and indirect impact on helping dismantle some of the barriers towards reporting hate crimes. In 2015, the then British Prime Minister, Theresa May, announced that all police forces in England and Wales must record Islamophobic hate crimes as a separate category within their central recording systems. It was envisaged that this would mean a more accurate picture could be ascertained in regards to Islamophobic hate crimes. In this study, as the victims were not Muslim, questions about how the police might record such incidents were less clear. For example, some participants noted how they would like the incident to be recorded as a religious hate crime and not necessarily as an Islamophobic incident. This does, therefore, raise further questions about reporting and recording incidents of hate crime. Some participants who had experienced online abuse decided to take action and report their abusers to social media providers, namely Twitter and Facebook. However, they unanimously reported that 'nothing happens' when they report their abusers to the social media providers:

> On Twitter I just report the accounts that verbally abuse me but I still see those people on there so I'm confused why Twitter fails to remove people.
>
> *(Govinda, 42, Indian, Hindu)*

> My profile on Facebook is open. Other users downloaded my pictures, wrote 'Ginger Terrorist' on them and then reposted them on Facebook tagging me along. I reported these accounts to Facebook but nothing happened. I have now made my account private.
>
> *(Paul, 37, White, Atheist)*

Some participants argued that when they reported their experiences to the police, they did not feel satisfied:

> The last incident included being verbally abused by a taxi driver in Oxford. When I got into the car, he said 'Get out! I don't put Muslims in my car'. I said I'm not Muslim but then he came out and dragged me out the car. I reported it to the police but they said that the CCTV outside the train station did not work so it was my word against his. They did not believe me and the case was closed.
>
> *(Mark, 40, White, Christian Orthodox)*

72 Islamophobia and perceived Muslim identity

Some participants argued that they would not normally report their experiences to the police. Lack of confidence in the police was prevalent amongst our participants:

> I didn't call the police because I was too afraid and embarrassed. Because I'm a professional, I don't think that looks good and sometimes I get worried the police will think I'm making it up.
>
> *(Govinda, 42, Indian, Hindu)*

> Friends and family are like 'you should tell the police' but I'm stuck because I think the police will just laugh at me. Don't forget, the police haven't really helped black people so I don't trust them.
>
> *(Cameron, 19, Afro-Caribbean, Christian)*

> I don't have confidence in local police. I don't think I will be listened to, I don't think I will be taken seriously. Offenders will not be brought to justice.
>
> *(Raj, 39, Indian, Hindu)*

> Once I punched a man who called me a 'Muslim child groomer'. I didn't report it to the police but the man who I punched did (laughing). The police were rubbish. They said it was my fault for punching him.
>
> *(Paul, 37, White, Atheist)*

When considering Islamophobic hate crimes, a number of barriers remain difficult to dismantle. For example, these include fear of being stereotyped, fear of prejudice, fear of mistreatment, and issues around mistrust and cultural barriers (Qulsoom 2007). One of the ways barriers can be challenged is through better awareness and knowledge from a cultural and religious perspective of victimisation. In understanding the reporting mechanisms of hate crime, far too often is the emphasis placed on the victims. However, a multiagency approach requires the police and other stakeholders to empower a multicultural and open dialogue with different communities. Diversity cultural units should be helping build relationships with those seeking assistance and support. Multicultural training programmes can also promote a sense of awareness and skills and can be important in giving confidence to different people.

Key questions

- What does Islamophobia in cases of mistaken identity entail?
- How can crime pattern and routine activity theories explain Islamophobic hate crime?
- What are the implications of Islamophobic hate crimes towards non-Muslim men?
- What challenges do non-Muslim men face as victims of Islamophobic hate crime when it comes to reporting their experiences to the authorities?

Further reading

- Clarke, R. V. 1992. (ed.) *Situational Crime Prevention: Successful Case Studies*. Albany, NY: Harrow and Heston.
- Cohen, L. E. and Felson, M. 1979. Social change and crime rate trends: A routine activity approach. *American Sociological Review*, 44: 588–605.
- Iganski, P. 2001. Hate crimes hurt more. *American Behavioural Scientist*, 45(4): 626–638.

References

Awan, I. and Zempi, I. 2015. 'I will blow your face off'—Virtual and physical world anti-Muslim hate crime. *British Journal of Criminology*. doi:10.1093/bjc/azv122

Awan, I. and Zempi, I. 2019. 'You all look the same': Non-Muslim men who suffer Islamophobic hate crime in the post-Brexit era. *European Journal of Criminology*. doi:10.1177/1477370818812735

BBC News. 2017. Record hate crimes after EU referendum. Available at: www.bbc.co.uk/news/amp/38976087.

Berzins, K. M., Petch, A., and Atkinson, J. M. 2003. Prevalence and experience of harassment of people with mental health problems living in the community. *British Journal of Psychiatry*, 183, 526–533.

Chadee, D. and Ditton, J. 2003. Are older people most afraid of crime? *British Journal of Criminology*, 43(2): 417–433.

Clarke, R. V. 1992. (ed.) *Situational Crime Prevention: Successful Case Studies*. Albany, NY: Harrow and Heston.

Clarke, R. and Eck, J. 2005. *Crime Analysis for Problem Solvers in 60 Small Steps*. Washington, D. C.: Office of Community Oriented Policing Services. United States Department of Justice.

Clement, S., Brohan, E., Sayce, L., Pool, J., and Thornicroft, G., 2011. Disability hate crime and targeted violence and hostility: A mental health and discrimination perspective. *Journal of Mental Health*, 20(3): 219–225.

Cohen, L. E. and Felson, M. 1979. Social change and crime rate trends: A routine activity approach. *American Sociological Review*, 44: 588–605.

Cornish, D. and Clarke, R. (eds) 1986. *The Reasoning Criminal: Rational Choice Perspectives on Offending*. New York, NY: Springer-Verlag.

Department for Transport. 2010. *Estimated Costs to Society of Crime on Public Transport in England in 2006/07: Final Report on Findings*. London: Department for Transport.

Ehrlich, H. 1992. The ecology of anti-gay violence. In: G. M. Herek and K. T. Berrill (eds) *Hate Crimes. Confronting Violence Against Lesbians and Gay Men*. Newbury Park, CA: Sage, pp. 105–112.

Garland, J. and Hodkinson, P. 2014. F**king freak! What the hell do you think you look like? Experiences of targeted victimisation among goths and developing notions of hate crime. *British Journal of Criminology*, 54(4): 613–631.

Hale, C. 1996. Fear of crime; A review of the literature. *International Review of Victimology*, 4: 79–150.

Herek, G. M., Gillis, J. R, Cogan, J. C., and Glunt, E. K., 1997. Hate crime victimization among lesbian, gay, and bisexual adults: Prevalence, psychological correlates, and methodological issues. *Journal of Interpersonal Violence*, 12(2): 195–215.

Horwitz, S. and Wheeler, L. 1989. Drug market intensifies violence on Drake Place. *Washington Post*. 17 February, p. Dl.

Iganski, P. 2001. Hate crimes hurt more. *American Behavioural Scientist*, 45(4): 626–638.

74 Islamophobia and perceived Muslim identity

Iganski, P. and Lagou, S. 2014. The personal injuries of hate crime. In: N. Hall, A. Corb, P. Giannasi, and J. Grieve (eds) *The Routledge International Handbook on Hate Crime*. New York, NY: Routledge, pp. 34–46.

King, R., Messner, S., and Baller, R. 2009. Contemporary hate crimes, law enforcement, and the legacy of racial violence. *American Sociological Review*, 74: 291–315.

McDevitt, J., Balboni, J., Garcia, L., and Gu, J. 2001. Consequences for victims a comparison of bias- and non-bias-motivated assaults. *American Behavioral Scientist*, 45: 697–713.

Merton, R. K. 1968. *Social Theory and Social Structure*. New York, NY: Free Press.

Newton, A. D. 2014. Crime on public transport. In: G. Bruinsma and D. Weisburd (eds) *Encyclopedia of Criminology and Criminal Justice*. London: Springer, pp. 709–720.

Perry, B. 2014. Exploring the community impacts of hate crime. In: N. Hall, A. Corb, P. Giannasi, and J. Grieve (eds) *The Routledge International Handbook on Hate Crime*. New York, NY: Routledge, pp. 47–57.

Qulsoom, I. 2007. Islamophobia and the therapeutic dialogue: Some reflections. *Counselling Psychology Quarterly*, 20(3): 287–293.

Shaw, C. R. and McKay, H. D. 1942. *Juvenile Delinquency and Urban Areas*. Chicago, IL: University of Chicago Press.

Sherman, L. 1995. Hot spots of crime and criminal careers of places. In: J. Eck and D. Weisburd (eds) *Crime and Place: Crime Prevention Studies 4*. Monsey, NY: Willow Tree Press.

Sherman, L. W., Gartin, P. R., and Buerger, M. E. 1989. Hot spots of predatory crime: Routine activities and the criminology of place. *Criminology*, 27, 27–55.

Smith, M. and Cornish, B. 2006. *Secure and Tranquil Travel: Preventing Crime and Disorder on Public Transport*. London: UCL Jill Dando Institute of Crime Science.

Social Mobility Commission. 2017. *The Social Mobility Challenges Faced by Young Muslims*. London: Social Mobility Commission.

Southern Poverty Law Centre. 2016. *The Trump Effect: The Impact of the 2016 Presidential Election on our Nation's Schools*. Available at: www.splcenter.org/20161128/trump-effectimpact-2016-presidential-election-our-nations-schools.

Tompson, L., Partridge, H., and Shepherd, N. 2009. Hot routes: Developing a new technique for the spatial analysis of crime. *Crime Mapping: A Journal of Research and Practice*, 1(1): 77–96.

Vilalta, C. 2011. Fear of crime in public transport: Research in Mexico City. *Crime Prevention and Community Safety*, 13: 171–186.

Wickes, R., Sydes, M., Benier, K., and Higginson, A. 2017. 'Seeing' hate crime in the community: Do resident perceptions of hate crime align with self-reported victimization? *Crime and Delinquency*, 63(7): 875–896.

6

USING AUTOETHNOGRAPHY FOR ISLAMOPHOBIC HATE CRIMES

Introduction

Following the 9/11 and 7/7 terrorist attacks, and more recently the ISIS-inspired terrorist attacks in the UK, France, Belgium, and Germany, there has been a significant increase in anti-Muslim attacks in the West. The hostile rhetoric of US President Donald Trump and the Brexit vote in Britain have also contributed to the sharp increase in Islamophobic hate crimes. Against this background, the aim of the present chapter is to consider the advantages and limitations of using auto-ethnography in order to research religion and specifically the victimisation of Muslims in a post-9/11 climate. We use our two independent research projects as case studies (Zempi and Awan 2017), whereby we refer to our distinct experiences of employing autoethnography when researching Islamophobic hate crime. In particular, we reflect upon our experiences of suffering Islamophobic hate crime as a result of being 'visibly' Muslim in public spaces in the UK. The chapter concludes with the advantages, challenges, and limitations of using autoethnography to research Islamophobic hate crime.

What is autoethnography?

As Chang (2016) notes, autoethnography is a qualitative research method that uses the researcher's personal experiences as empirical data. Grounded on postmodernism, autoethnography rejects the paradigm of positivism. By and large, positivism is seen as the scientific approach to research, which promotes the objective measurement of social issues (Charmaz 2006). However, the terms that are commonly used to demonstrate rigour in quantitative research – such as validity, reliability, representativeness, generalisability, and objectivity – are problematic for qualitative research and specifically for autoethnography (Payne 2004). Autoethnography

76 Using autoethnography

focuses on the researcher's experiences, feelings, and emotions, and uses self-reflexivity to connect the 'self' with the 'social' (Campbell 2016). To put it differently, autoethnography employs self-reflexivity and emotionality in order to understand the researcher's lived experiences and extend sociological understanding (Sparkes 2000).

Historically, it is important to note that the term autoethnography was coined by anthropologist Karl Heider in the 1970s in order to describe the way in which members of a culture could provide accounts about their own experiences (Heider 1975). Hayano (1979) then used the term to refer to anthropological studies conducted by individuals of their own culture. From this perspective, autoethnography was understood as 'insider ethnography'. In the 1980s, autoethnography emerged as a distinct research method (Campbell 2016). Nevertheless, as Ellingson and Ellis (2008, p. 449) point out, "the meanings and applications of autoethnography have evolved in a manner that makes precise definition difficult". It could be argued that although the exact definition of autoethnography is elusive, autoethnography relies on using and analysing the researcher's own experiences.

Ellis and Bochner (2000) observe that autoethnography ranges from studies in which the researcher's experiences are explored alongside those of the participants, through to stories in which the researcher's experiences become the sole focus of investigation. According to Denshire and Lee (2013), there are two key strands of autoethnography: 'evocative' and 'analytic' autoethnography. The evocative approach relies on the researcher's personal stories. In this case, autoethnographers focus more on the self rather than the social world (Denzin 2006). Analytic autoethnography uses empirical data – that is, the insider's perspective – to gain insight into some broader set of social phenomena than those provided by the data themselves (Wakeman 2014). Denshire and Lee (2013) argue that this dichotomy of 'evocative' and 'analytic' autoethnography is useful on the basis that it demonstrates the variation in how autoethnographic writers integrate the strands of self and culture in their writing. Relatedly, the two independent research projects that we use as case studies in the present chapter employ the analytic approach. This means that we both used our personal experiences as empirical data in order to gain insight into the role of Muslims' visible religious identity with respect to 'triggering' Islamophobic hate crime in public in the UK.

Case studies

Case study 1

Irene's research project examined the experiences of Muslim women who wear the niqab (face veil) as victims of Islamophobic hate crime in the UK (Zempi 2014). This was a qualitative study that included 60 in-depth interviews and 20 focus groups with niqab-wearing women in Leicester, UK, between 2011 and 2012. In addition to interviews and focus groups with veiled Muslim women, the study also included autoethnography whereby Irene wore the full veil – including jilbab (long dress), hijab (headscarf), and niqab (face veil) – for prolonged periods of time in public. However, it is important to point out that employing autoethnography was not part of Irene's original research methodology. In other words, when Irene was initially developing her research project, her plan was to only use individual and focus group interviews with veiled Muslim women. However, while she was doing the pilot interviews, some participants suggested that Irene should wear the niqab. Irene's religious identity (Greek Orthodox Christian) meant that she was perceived as an 'outsider' by her participants. By wearing the niqab, the aim was for Irene to become an 'insider' and thus feel part of veiled Muslim women's 'reality' despite her non-Muslim identity. Some participants actually insisted that Irene should wear the niqab in order to accurately interpret their stories and represent their 'voices' regarding the nature, extent, and impact of anti-Muslim hate crime. In light of this, Irene decided to wear the niqab as part of her daily routine in public places in Leicester. The main research question was: "How does Irene's perceived identity as a (perceived) veiled Muslim woman render her vulnerable to suffering Islamo-phobic hate crime in public?" Throughout the fieldwork, Irene kept a personal diary in order to write her reflections.

As a result of being perceived to be Muslim (on the basis of wearing the niqab), Irene suffered hostility, harassment, and intimidation such as name-calling, swear-ing, and threats of physical violence. Underlying these forms of verbal abuse was a clear sense of anti-Muslim hatred and hostility, which was made apparent through the language used by the perpetrators. For instance, typical examples of the name-calling Irene suffered included: 'Muslim terrorist', 'suicide bomber', and 'You lot are terrorists', which indicated the perpetrators' perceptions of veiled Muslim women as a terrorist 'threat'. Although verbal abuse was usually momentary when walking on the street or waiting for public transport, in some cases Irene suffered sustained periods of 'low-level' hostility, particularly when stuck within a confined space, such as on the bus or train, and in a shop. For instance, persistent staring, dirty looks, being ignored, or being refused to be served were common examples of 'low-level', everyday hostility throughout Irene's experiences behind the niqab. Physical attacks were much less common than verbal forms of abuse with the exception of a passing car that threw eggs at Irene.

Research shows that 'visible' Muslims and veiled Muslim women in particular are targeted because their abusers perceive all Muslims to be terrorists or terrorist sympathisers (Allen, Isakjee, and Young 2013; Githens-Mazer and Lambert 2010). Grillo and Shah (2012) suggest that the wearing of the Muslim veil marks an unwelcome religious, cultural, and racial presence. In the eyes of their abusers, veiled Muslim women are seen as 'other' who 'don't belong' and therefore, 'they are not welcome' in the UK. As already indicated elsewhere in this book, Islamo-phobic hostility can be seen as a 'message' which is designed to tell the wider Muslim community that they are 'unwelcome' and 'don't belong', thereby extending the impact of this victimisation beyond the actual, immediate victim to instil fear in the whole of the targeted community. Qualitative research into the experiences of Muslim women who wear the niqab has been conducted in five

78 Using autoethnography

European countries: Belgium, Denmark, France, the Netherlands, and the UK (Brems 2014). The data from qualitative interviews in these five countries show very strong similarities, namely, harassment and abuse of veiled Muslim women by strangers in public. For example, veiled Muslim women in the Netherlands reported regularly being confronted with people who scolded, insulted, or spat at them on the street (Moors 2009; 2014). Some also mentioned being physically threatened, with cars attempting to hit them, people throwing things at them, or trying to pull off the niqab (Moors 2009; 2014). Echoing these experiences, veiled Muslim women in the UK and France described a stream of violent insults in public places including being violently pushed, spat on, and having their niqabs pulled off (Bouteldja 2011).

As might be expected, employing autoethnography to research Islamophobic hate crime had emotional, psychological, and physiological impacts upon Irene's well-being. According to Denshire and Lee (2013, p. 224), "putting the self into the picture at all is challenging enough in this context, but putting the very notion of a self at risk opens up places of vulnerability". Indeed, experiences of Islamophobic hate crime affected Irene emotionally, including feeling afraid, shocked, and/or upset. Such feelings were particularly pronounced immediately after an incident, but they seemed to develop into longer-term anxieties. Irene gradually developed sleep problems and lost her appetite. Moreover, there were days when Irene felt reluctant to leave her house. She started to feel cautious, nervous, suspicious, and distrustful of people that she encountered within public spaces. She gradually became more insular and wary of other people walking by on the street. The possibility of verbal and physical violence meant that Irene felt anxious, vulnerable, and exposed when walking on the street or travelling on public transport. Eventually Irene became isolated and withdrawn.

Case study 2

Imran is Muslim but his religious identity is not visible in terms of his physical appearance. To illustrate this, he does not have a beard and does not dress in traditional Islamic clothing. In 2015, Imran was interviewing Muslim individuals as part of a qualitative study on anti-Muslim hate crime. All the participants in this study were individuals who were visibly identifiable Muslims in public due to their physical appearance. During the interviews, Imran's status as a non-visible Muslim was challenged by one of the male participants, Mohammed. Mohammed had a beard and wore the Islamic cap as well as traditional Islamic clothing. Mohammed challenged Imran about the lack of his visibility as a Muslim, and his ability to understand Mohammed's experiences of anti-Muslim hate crime. Specifically, Mohammed stated: "Look Imran, you don't dress as a Muslim, you simply don't know how it feels like". Although Imran has suffered abuse on social media for researching anti-Muslim hate crime, he has never experienced anti-Muslim hostility in public as he is not identifiable as a Muslim. In light of Mohammed's comments, Imran took the decision to employ autoethnography in order to research anti-Muslim hate crime through adopting a visible Muslim identity in public. Specifically, Imran grew a beard and wore the jubba (male Islamic dress) and Islamic cap as part of his daily routine in Birmingham, UK. The main research question was: "How does Imran's perceived identity as a Muslim man render him vulnerable to Islamophobic hate crime in public?" The fieldwork took place between August and September 2015. Throughout the fieldwork, Imran kept a personal diary in order to write his reflections.

Research indicates the vulnerability of 'visible' Muslim men as victims of Islamophobic hate crime in public places (Abbas 2004; Hopkins 2007; Mac an Ghaill and Haywood 2014). Cole and Maisuria (2007) assert that Muslims who are visibly identifiable are more likely to suffer abuse because of their appearance. They state that: "People who appear to be of Islamic faith (wearing a veil, sporting a beard, or even carrying a backpack) are immediately identified as potential terrorists" (Cole and Maisuria 2007, p. 104). In light of his visible Muslim identity in public, Imran's experiences of Islamophobic hate crime included hostility, harassment, and intimidation such as name-calling, swearing, and threats of physical violence. Additionally, persistent staring, being ignored, being sneered and sworn at, and called a 'F★★★★★★ terrorist' were part of his daily experiences in public in Birmingham. Because of his Asian background, Imran also suffered verbal abuse such as 'P★★★ terrorist', which revealed both racist and anti-Muslim attitudes on the part of the offenders. This shows the link between religion and race whereby anti-Muslim hate can be seen as a 'new' form of racism (Law 2010). Cole and Maisuria (2007, p. 103) state that, similar to other forms of racism, Islamophobia can be cultural, biological, or both: "The racist term, 'Paki' co-exists with the racist term of abuse, 'Bin Laden'" (Cole and Maisuria 2007, p. 103).

Imran portrayed himself as a 'visible' Muslim man in public in Birmingham for four weeks, but he felt relieved when autoethnography was over. Birmingham is a diverse and multicultural city, and the place where Imran lives and works. For Imran, Birmingham is 'home' but experiences of anti-Muslim hostility made him question his sense of 'belonging'. On reflection, Imran felt that he should have reported these incidents to the police but, similar to most victims of hate crime, he felt that the police would not take it seriously. Research by Githens-Mazer and Lambert (2010) shows that most Muslim Londoners who had been victims of anti-Muslim hate crimes after the 9/11 terrorist attacks did not report their experiences to the authorities. In the words of Githens-Mazer and Lambert (2010, p. 38): "While some of the more serious attacks of the kind we have illustrated have been reported to police, the overwhelming majority of Muslim victims of hate crimes appear not to have reported the incidents to police". During the fieldwork, the impact of the abuse that Imran experienced as a visible Muslim man was immense. Because of these experiences, he felt embarrassed, humiliated, 'not wanted', and in some cases he started questioning whether he was really accepted in Britain as a British Muslim. Moreover, he felt fearful, humiliated, and emotionally bruised although he was not physically attacked. Writing down his feelings and experiences in the diary helped him to cope with it. However, he gradually became isolated

80 Using autoethnography

and withdrawn; he even kept his distance from his family and friends. There were days that he would not enter into conversation with his family, and he would avoid having dinner with them or talking to them. Ultimately, he felt 'guilty' about his Muslim identity and its visibility.

Advantages, ethical challenges and limitations

The key research question in the aforementioned case studies was "How does the researchers' (perceived) visible Muslim identity render them vulnerable to suffering Islamophobic hate crime in public?" We both employed autoethnography in order to examine Islamophobic hate crime through the lens of victims. Using auto-ethnography gave us 'insider' knowledge of Islamophobic hate crime. Indeed, employing autoethnography provided us with a unique insight into visible Muslims' vulnerability to Islamophobic hostility in public. The fact that we do not normally wear Muslim clothes allowed us to see the difference in people's behaviour in public spaces. As such, using autoethnography helped us identify the role of the 'visibility' of our (perceived) Muslim identity in 'triggering' Islamophobic hostility in public spaces. Imran would not have been abused had he not worn the jubba and grown a beard. Along similar lines, gaining 'insider' knowledge is something that Irene would not have learnt from the interviews alone, especially as a non-Muslim woman researching Islamophobic hate crime.

Insider research refers to when the researcher conducts research with a group of which he or she is a member, based on characteristics such as religion, race/ethnicity, gender and sexual identity (Asselin 2003; Kanuha 2000). It is argued that being of an insider position provides the study with specific advantages including promoting a more balanced understanding of the research population and the transference of information from the participant to the researcher (Labaree 2002). This can be particularly useful in research with groups that could be seen as underrepresented, oppressed, or 'hard-to-reach'. Relatedly, it is argued that outsider researchers fail to understand or represent accurately participants' experiences (Savvides et al. 2014). This is particularly important when research is conducted with stigmatised, marginalised communities (Hayfield and Huxley 2015).

That said, it is important to acknowledge that although employing auto-ethnography helped us to see the world through the eyes of our participants we were not fully insiders. Rather, using autoethnography enabled us to acquire an 'outsider within' status (Hill Collins 1986). According to Mohanty (2003), the 'outsider within status' provides researchers with a unique standpoint. In other words, we developed a particular way of seeing reality. As Hooks (1984, p. vii) points out, "we looked from the outside and in from the inside outside … we understood both". For Hill Collins (1986), researchers can benefit from the 'outsider within' status. Hill Collins (1986) highlights the ability of the 'outsider within' researcher to see patterns that may be more difficult for those immersed in the situation to see. Our 'outsider within' status enabled us to deepen our understanding of Islamophobic hate crime and as a result, accurately interpret participants' stories, and represent their 'voices' regarding the nature, extent, and impact of Islamophobic hate crime. However, we acknowledge that it is not possible for 'outsiders within', no matter how skilled in autoethnographic technique, to ever fully grasp the experience of being visibly Muslim on the basis that visible Muslims live in a context where they are vulnerable 24/7. Their experiences of Islamophobic hate crime will always be more 'authentic'.

Another important issue to highlight is that both case studies evoked strong emotions and demanded emotion management (Hochschild 2003). Hochschild (2003, p. 7) defined emotional labour as "the management of feeling to create a publicly observable facial and bodily display". As such, emotion management is the active process whereby social agents manage their emotional responses to correspond to a social situation. Hochschild (2003, p. 7) stated that qualitative research often involves a form of 'emotional labour', a situation where one is required "to induce or suppress feeling in order to sustain the outward countenance that produces the proper state of mind in others". Indeed, we both undertook a significant amount of emotional labour. Hochschild (2003) refers to the 'human costs' of emotional labour, from 'burnout' to feeling 'guilt' and 'self-blame'. In both case studies, there were certain 'costs' in relation to 'emotional labour'. To illustrate this, feelings of emotional exhaustion and physical distress emerged because of the intimidation, abuse, and hostility we experienced from members of the public. To this end, using autoethnography enabled us to experience many of the emotions that victims of Islamophobic hate crime feel such as depression, sadness, fear, anxiety, suspicion, anger, helplessness, and isolation. In both case studies, the aim was to see the world through the eyes of Muslims, using ourselves as research instruments. However, this does not mean that one needs to turn oneself into a victim in order to research Islamophobic hate crime. Unarguably, this would be ethically problematic. Rather, our approach was a process of exploration, employing autoethnography to research Islamophobic hate crime.

Finally, using autoethnography to research Islamophobic hate crime entailed certain ethical issues in both case studies. With respect to traditional research, obtaining informed consent from the study participants is a requirement. In autoethnographical research projects, it could be argued that informed consent is implicit as the only participant is the researcher; however, as Sikes (2006) points out, autoethnographical accounts put the researcher on 'dodgy ground'. For example, it is inevitable that other people will be (in)direct participants in autoethnographic research, yet their consent is not obtained (Campbell 2016). In some cases, it is not possible to obtain consent from people when it is not clear if and how they will be part of the story. Indeed, Campbell (2016, p. 103) explains that it is not practically feasible to say to people 'I am an autoethnographer and I might write something which may or may not have a connection to you one day'. In both case studies, although it was not possible to obtain the consent of the public, we made sure that we maintained complete anonymity for members of the public including those who abused us. Also, we did not engage in activities such as audio or video recording, which could have potentially revealed their identity.

82 Using autoethnography

Furthermore, the fact that we used autoethnography in the form of covert research was ethically challenging. In both case studies, withholding our true identity meant that we adopted a covert role and did not disclose to members of the public that we were researching Islamophobic hate crime. Unarguably, employing autoethnography in the form of covert research is ethically dubious due to there being a level of deception involved. We both developed feelings of emotional distress as a result of this. Lofland and Lofland (1995) state that researchers may feel uncomfortable if they deceive the people being observed when they do not totally reveal the true nature of their study. Nevertheless, covert research can uncover issues that would otherwise remain 'invisible'. It could be argued that assuming a covert role was key to the success of the research projects. According to this line of argument, people's awareness of our real status as researchers would influence how they behaved towards us. Ultimately, although there are important ethical questions here, the fact remains that in our case studies, 'going undercover' was ethically defensible.

Conclusion

In this chapter, we have used two case studies in order to discuss the advantages and limitations of undertaking autoethnography when researching anti-Muslim hate crime. Despite our 'outsider' status (as a Greek Orthodox Christian researcher for Irene, and a non-visible British Muslim researcher for Imran), we employed autoethnography in order to research the experiences of victimised 'others'. A key advantage of using autoethnography provided us with 'insider' knowledge. This helped us to understand visible Muslims' experiences of anti-Muslim hate crime in public. However, there were ethical as well as moral issues involved such as putting ourselves at risk and employing covert research. Taber (2010, p. 5) asserts that "researchers must continually push methodological boundaries in order to address research questions that cannot be explored with traditional methods". However, the risks presented by autoethnographic research should be balanced against the opportunities to produce useful empirical data. We argue that researchers within the field of hate crime studies should employ autoethnography methods in order to gain insights into the impacts of hate crimes. However, we also add caution by stating that such research is sensitive and requires considerable ethical considerations.

Key questions

- What is the meaning of autoethnography?
- How can research be used to shape perceptions of Islamophobia?
- Do you think academics should engage in 'risky' research?
- What impact has this study had upon you?
- How important is reflexivity in academic work?

Further reading

- Carolyn, E. and Bochner, A. 2000. Autoethnography, personal narrative, reflexivity: researcher as subject. *Communication Faculty Publications*, 91.
- Ellis, C., Adams, T., and Bochner, A. 2011. Conventions and institutions from a historical perspective / Konventionen und institutionen in historischer perspektive. *Historical Social Research / Historische Sozialforschung*, 36(4) (138): 273–290.

References

Abbas, T. 2004. After 9/11: British South Asian Muslims, Islamophobia, multiculturalism, and the state. *American Journal of Islamic Social Sciences*, 21(3): 26–38.

Allen, C., Isakjee, A., and Young, O. 2013. *Understanding the Impact of Anti-Muslim Hate on Muslim Women*. Birmingham: University of Birmingham.

Asselin, M. E. 2003. Insider research: Issues to consider when doing qualitative research in your own setting. *Journal for Nurses in Staff Development*, 19: 99–103.

Bouteldja, N. 2011. *Unveiling the Truth: Why 32 Muslim Women Wear the Full Face Veil in France*. London: Open Society Foundations.

Brems, E. 2014. Introduction to the volume. In: E. Brems (ed.) *The Experiences of Face Veil Wearers in Europe and the Law*. Cambridge: Cambridge University Press, pp. 1–17.

Campbell, E. 2016. Exploring autoethnography as a method and methodology in legal education research. *Asian Journal of Legal Education*, 3(1): 95–105.

Chang, H. 2016. Autoethnography in health research: Growing pains? *Qualitative Health Research*, 26(4): 443–451.

Charmaz, K. 2006. *Constructing Grounded Theory: A Practice Guide through Qualitative Analysis*. London: Sage.

Cole, M. and Maisuria, A. 2007. 'Shut the f★★★ up', 'you have no rights here': Critical race theory and racialisation in post-7/7 racist Britain. *Journal for Critical Education Policy Studies*, 5(1): 94–120.

Denshire, S. and Lee, A. 2013. Conceptualizing autoethnography as assemblage: Accounts of occupational therapy practice. *International Journal of Qualitative Methods*, 12: 221–236.

Denzin, N. K. 2006. Analytic autoethnography, or de ja vu all over again. *Journal of Contemporary Ethnography*, 35(4): 419–428.

Ellis, C. and Bochner, A. P. 2000. Autoethnography, personal narrative, reflexivity. In: N. K. Denzin and Y. S. Lincoln (eds) *Handbook of Qualitative Research*. Thousand Oaks, CA: Sage, pp. 733–768.

Ellingson, L. and Ellis, C. 2008. Autoethnography as constructionist project. In: J. A. Holstein and J. F. Gubrium (eds) *Handbook of Constructionist Research*. New York: Guilford Press, pp. 445–465.

Githens-Mazer, J. and Lambert, R. 2010. *Islamophobia and Anti-Muslim Hate Crime: A London Case Study*. London: European Muslim Research Centre.

Grillo, R. and Shah, P. 2012. *Reasons to Ban? The Anti-Burqa Movement in Western Europe*. Göttingen: Max Planck Institute.

Hayano, D. M. 1979. Auto-ethnography: Paradigms, problems, and prospects. *Human Organization*, 38: 113–120.

Hayfield, N. and Huxley, C. 2015. Insider and outsider perspectives: Reflections on researcher identities in research with lesbian and bisexual women. *Qualitative Research in Psychology*, 12(2): 91–106.

Heider, H. 1975. What do people do? Dani auto-ethnography. *Journal of Anthropological Research*, 31(1): 3–17.

84 Using autoethnography

Hill Collins, P. 1986. Learning from the outsider within. *Social Problems*, 33(6): S14–S32.

Hochschild, A. 2003. *The Managed Heart: Commercialization of Human Feeling*. Los Angeles: University of California Press.

Hooks, B. 1984. *Feminist Theory: From Margin to Center*. Boston: South End Press. Hopkins, P. E. 2007. Global events, national politics, local lives: Young Muslim men in Scotland. *Environment and Planning*, 39(5): 1119–1133.

Kanuha, V. K. 2000. Being native versus "going native": Conducting social work research as an insider. *Social Work*, 45(5): 439–447.

Labaree, R. V. 2002. The risk of 'going observationalist': Negotiating the hidden dilemmas of being an insider participant observer. *Qualitative Research*, 2(1): 97–122.

Law, I. 2010. *Racism and Ethnicity: Global Debates, Dilemmas, Directions*. London: Pearson Education.

Lofland, J. and Lofland, L. 1995. *Analysing Social Settings*. California: Wadsworth Publications Company.

Mac an Ghaill, M. and Haywood, C. 2014. Pakistani and Bangladeshi young men: Re-racialization, class and masculinity within the neo-liberal school. *British Journal of Sociology of Education*, 35(5): 753–776.

Mohanty, C. T. 2003. 'Under Western Eyes' revisited: Feminist solidarity through anticapitalist struggles. *Signs: Journal of Women in Culture and Society*, 28(2): 499–535.

Moors, A. 2009. The Dutch and the face-veil: The politics of discomfort. *Social Anthropology*, 17(4): 393–408.

Moors, A. 2014. Face veiling in the Netherlands: Public debates and women's narratives. In: E. Brems (ed.) *The Experiences of Face Veil Wearers in Europe and the Law*. Cambridge: Cambridge University Press, pp. 19–41.

Payne, S. 2004. Designing and conducting qualitative studies. In: S. Michie and C. Abraham (eds) *Health Psychology in Practice*. London: Routledge, pp. 126–149.

Savvides, N., Al-Youssef, J., Colin, M., and Garrido, C. 2014. Journeys into inner/outer space: Reflections on the methodological challenges of negotiating insider/outsider status in international educational research. *Research in Comparative and International Education*, 9 (4): 412–425.

Sikes, P. 2006. On dodgy ground? Problematics and ethics in educational research? *International Journal of Research & Method in Education*, 29(1): 105–117.

Sparkes, A. C. 2000. Autoethnography and narratives of self: Reflections on criteria in action. *Sociology of Sport Journal*, 17: 21–43.

Taber, N. 2010. Institutional ethnography, autoethnography, and narrative: An argument for incorporating multiple methodologies. *Qualitative Research*, 10(5): 5–25.

Wakeman, S. 2014. Fieldwork, biography and emotion: Doing criminological autoethnography. *British Journal of Criminology*, 54(5): 705–721.

Zempi, I. 2014. *Uncovering Islamophobia: The Victimisation of Veiled Muslim Women*. Leicester: University of Leicester.

Zempi, I. and Awan, I., 2017. Doing 'dangerous' autoethnography on Islamophobic victimisation ethnography. DOI: doi:10.1177/1466138117697996

7

INSTITUTIONAL ISLAMOPHOBIA

Policing, profiling, and hate

Introduction

A relatively new phenomena in relation to Islamophobia is the construct of how institutions, government policies, legislation, and agents of the state can perpetuate Islamophobia. Specifically, we argue that Islamophobia has moved from personal physical attacks to institutions – such as prisons, the police, the workplace, education, and wider criminal justice system – that respond to Muslims through the lens of fear, security, and Islamophobia. Such practices of discrimination and prejudice have now also led to calls for a public inquiry into political parties in Britain and the specific problems in relation to tackling Islamophobia. Institutional Islamophobia therefore cuts across all parts of society and can also be viewed in terms of integration strategies. As discussed in detail in Chapter 2, according to the Social Mobility Commission young Muslims are less likely to succeed in the workplace because they experience Islamophobia. Specifically, they found that young Muslims reported discrimination in the workplace because they had ethnic-sounding names. Alan Milburn, chair of the Social Mobility Commission (2017) stated that:

> The British social mobility promise is that hard work will be rewarded. Unfortunately, for many young Muslims in Britain today, this promise is being broken … Young Muslims themselves identify cultural barriers in their communities and discrimination in the education system and labour market as some of the principal obstacles that stand in their way.

As noted earlier, institutional Islamophobia goes beyond actual physical hate crimes and becomes part of the everyday experiences of Muslims, both in the workplace and when they are getting on with their daily lives. Whilst some forms of

86 Institutional Islamophobia

institutional Islamophobia are covert in nature, increasingly institutional Islamo-phobia has moved into places where Muslims are targeted simply because of who they are and how they look. One of those key institutions responsible for the hard-line strategies of Islamophobia is the police force, which has been responsible for using processes, such as stop and search powers, to profile Muslims because of their appearance. This chapter draws on research evidence regarding policing and securitisation of Muslims and makes the case that institutions such as the police must address parts of the organisation, which are institutionally Islamophobic in nature.

Policing Muslims and Islamophobia

Historically, police and minority relations in the UK have been problematic since the early 1970s and 1980s when tensions grew over policing methods of public order in the UK (Gordon and Rowe 2007; Waddington 1999). This notion of policing was based on hard-line strategies with regards to minority communities and manifested because of extensive police autonomy (Hall et al. 1978). In the 1980s this sense of animosity between the police and minority groups in the UK was based fundamentally on the treatment of minority communities by police officers (Spalek 2010). This damning critique of minorities was further developed by Kenneth Newman, the then Commissioner of the Metropolitan Police, and in a provocative speech he gave the UK a 'new' conceptualised view of policing and security. He stated that:

> Throughout London there are locations where unemployed youth – often black youths – congregate; where the sale and purchase of drugs, the exchange of stolen property and illegal drinking and gaming is not unknown. The youths regard these symbolic locations as their territory. Police are viewed as intruders.
>
> *(McConville and Shephard 1992, p. 229)*

Newman's statement was controversial since it did not deal with the contributing factors of why Black Afro-Caribbean men were getting involved in street crime; such as age, socio-economic factors, underclass, relative deprivation, sub-culture, and marginalisation (Graef 1989). As a result, policing in the UK went through a series of reforms beginning with the Scarman Report following the Brixton riots in 1981 which recommended new innovative ways of policing and included more active work in recruitment of ethnic minorities, enacting new legislation in the Police and Criminal Evidence Act 1984 (PACE) and developing new ideas of community liaison and anti-racism campaigns.

Following the racist murder of Stephen Lawrence in 1993, the Macpherson report was commissioned in 1997 and its findings were reported in 1999; it described the police as an 'institutionally racist' organisation. The Macpherson report concluded that:

> Unwitting racism can arise because of a lack of understanding ignorance or mistaken beliefs. It can arise from well-intentioned but patronising words or actions…. from unfamiliarity with the behaviour or cultural traditions of people or families from minority ethnic communities … from racial stereotyping of black people as potential criminals.
>
> *(Macpherson Inquiry 1999, 6.17)*

One of the major issues that has crept into modern-day policing since then is institutional Islamophobia, whereby racial profiling can single out Muslims because of their appearance. Historically, the policing of Muslim communities has often been tainted by allegations of policing by stereotypes that include racial prejudice and racial discrimination. If we are to apply our definition of Islamophobia (see Chapter 1) being a new form of racism, we argue that the police therefore through the securitisation of Muslim communities are becoming an institutionally Islamophobic organisation. Bowling (1999) argues that such practises can be traced back to historical issues such as the 1981 Brixton riots which has led to a legacy of mistrust between BAME (Black, Asian, and Minority Ethnic) communities and the police. However, following the 9/11 attacks the risk is that those stereotypes have re-emerged with 'over policing' of Muslim communities, who are increasingly viewed with suspicion. This intensified with cases such as Rizwaan Sabir. Sabir, who was a student at the University of Nottingham, was arrested by the police for downloading an al-Qaeda training manual but released without charge. After winning damages of £20,000 from Nottinghamshire police, Sabir said: "I was very, very lucky in the sense that I was released without charge because I was innocent in the first place…" (cited in *The Guardian* by Jones 2011).

The Sabir case highlighted how, post-9/11, the police need to be very careful about how they deal with counter-terrorism arrests, because old stereotypes may re-emerge and may have a wider impact upon how Muslim communities report abuse. Indeed, Awan, Blakemore, and Simpson (2013) also found that policing and Muslim community relations had broken because the participants in their study would describe the police as being 'racist', 'heavy-handed', 'unprofessional', and having a 'lack of communication skills'. This in turn resulted in the Muslim community not reporting crime to the police because they felt a sense of mistrust (Awan, Blakemore, and Simpson 2013).

Furthermore, victims' lack trust and confidence in the police could be due to racist stereotyping at the hands of police and also traumatic events that may have occurred. Awan, Blakemore, and Simpson's (2013) study of Muslim community perceptions of the police found real issues of a lack of trust of the police service and also the view that individual experiences with the police shaped that mistrust and were some of the reasons why they felt not comfortable reporting hate crimes to the police. In 2009, West Midlands police sent counter-terrorism officers to visit a local nursery in the area of Birmingham (UK) where it was perceived children may have been radicalised (Casciani 2009). This might have been because of the Association of Chief Police Officers (ACPO) statistics of Channel (the radicalisation

88 Institutional Islamophobia

interventions programme) from the period April 2007 to the end of December 2010, which showed that the majority of referrals were males aged between 13 and 25. Despite these statistics, the initiative sparked a wider debate amongst policy-makers about the rationale of policing Muslim communities who are increasingly being viewed as suspects.

The importance of such a case also is that it reveals how a top down approach towards extremism can often lead to police officers having to enforce fear about Muslims. The impact of such an incident is that it could have a detrimental effect upon police and community relations and reveals how Islamophobia can become mainstream and normalised. What was increasingly problematic was the language reported and used by one of the officers. In an email one of the officers states that:

> I am a police officer and therefore it will always be part of my role to gather intelligence and I will report back any information or intelligence which may suggest someone is a terrorist, or is planning to be one or to support others.

He adds that: "And I do hope that you will tell me about persons, of whatever age, you think may have been radicalised or be vulnerable to radicalisation" (cited in BBC article by Casciani 2009).

The language used in this email does raise important questions about police and community relations as regards policing Muslim communities. Police and minority community relations in 2003 became further strained following a BBC Panorama investigation called 'The Secret Policeman'. The programme which was broadcast in October 2003 involved an undercover journalist acting as a secret policeman in Manchester. Although the programme was broadcast in 2003, it revealed how a particular police force could emerge as an ineffective organisation in its way of engagement with communities. Such conduct had at the time formed a basis of poor police and community relations. In particular, following the Macpherson report the programme highlighted the fact that lessons had not been learnt and that in particular there was still inadequate training of police officers when dealing, in this case, with Muslim communities. Moreover, the programme showed a graphic image of racist police officers who were part of a law enforcement agency of whom the public should be able to trust.

Case study: *Project Champion*, surveillance, and Islamophobia

In Birmingham (UK), the impact of institutional Islamophobia and its operation on the Muslim community has led to a heightened atmosphere between Muslims and the police (Home Office 2004). This was intensified after a local policing initiative, known as *Project Champion* (run by West Midlands Police (WMP), Safer Birmingham Partnership and Birmingham City Council), which used surveillance to target a Muslim community in the suburbs of Birmingham. The CCTV cameras were installed in predominately Muslim areas with a network of 218 cameras, including 72 hidden ones (Thornton 2010). The police described *Project Champion* as a 'community-led' initiative for tackling violent crime and anti-social behaviour. However, the cameras were paid for by the Terrorism and Allied Matters fund, administered by the ACPO, and implicitly in this measure viewed the Muslim community as potentially vulnerable to extremism in some way (HM Government 2006). Indeed, Fenwick and Choudhury (2011, p. 36) state that:

> Reducing crime and anti-social behaviour appears to have been highlighted as the main reason for the cameras … Protests from local residents, MPs and councillors erupted after it was discovered that the money for these cameras came out of a counterterrorism funding stream.

To understand *Project Champion* better, there needs to be a critique of the landscape post-9/11, 7/7, and the numerous terror plots, as it was anticipated that by selectively targeting the Muslim community the police could help prevent and foil a major terrorist attack. In actual fact what happened was a failure by the police to carry out any significant community development and consultation before installing the cameras, which the police thought would provide intelligence in the fight against terrorism (Goldsmith 2005). This also resulted in policing methods being used through the lens of security that viewed Muslims with suspicion and profiled them as 'would be terrorists'. Since the terrorist attacks of 7 July 2005, the UK has been on high alert, thus making counter-terrorism policy shift towards tackling home-grown terrorism. Within this context, the police service and Muslim communities have had to work together in preventing extremism, becoming 'the new police partners' (Spalek and Lambert 2008). However, for a partnership to exist, there needs to be a level of trust and confidence between both parties, something that Spalek (2010) argues much of the broader literature in this area does not adequately examine. She observes: "discussion concerning what constitutes trust in this context is almost completely absent" (Spalek 2010, p. 790).

Clearly, there are problems for the police when dealing with ethnic minorities; apart from police culture, there is a historical sense of mistrust (Virta 2008). However, community policing therefore becomes essential in negotiating and understanding social groups and the cultural barriers that exist between the police service and minority communities. The image of community policing has suffered as a result of the 'war on terror' and Pickering, McCulloch, and Wright-Neville (2008) refer to an important strength of community policing over counter-terrorism policing in a case study adopted by Victoria police in Australia. In this case study the local police were responding to a conflict amongst minority communities by using recreational activities to bring together the local community and the police. This emphasis on a community-led approach increased social cohesion and allowed the police to engage in a meaningful manner by reaching out to an otherwise 'hard to reach' group.

There is no universal definition of community policing; instead there are a myriad of interpretations by both academics and policy-makers. For Trojanowicz and Bucqueroux (1990), community policing is a concept where police officers

90 Institutional Islamophobia

and citizens work together for the good of the neighbourhood and eradicate the 'decay' of that area. According to Spalek (2010, p. 793), however, "Community policing is not something that can be easily defined". For Skogan and Hartnett (1997), community policing is defined by relationships that consist of communication between both the police and public. They state that: "community policing relies upon organizational decentralization" (Skogan and Hartnett 1997, p. 5; Spalek, 2010). However, Spalek (2010) criticises this interpretation of community policing on the basis that the word 'trust' is absent. Critics argue that community policing models have been replaced by counter-terrorism-led policing initiatives that target Muslim communities (Virta 2008). For Innes (2006), a far better approach to counter-terrorism policing is the community-led intelligence approach (i.e. the Neighbourhood Policing Model) which, he argues, does include trust as a mechanism for community engagement. Leichtman (2008, p. 69) takes a similar view; he states that: "[I]t is now acknowledged that it is difficult to stop crime without the help of the neighbourhoods".

After the 11 September 2001 terror attacks, community policing suffered a huge blow in its role of working with communities and gave new impetus to the military model for policing (MPM). Apart from the concept of counter-terror policing being legitimised as a justification for community-led policing, critics have argued that we are steadily moving towards MPM in the UK (Shearing and Johnston 2010). Leichtman (2008) refers to three models of policing: the urban policing model; the pre-reform (or machine) policing model; and the professional and military policing model (Kraska 1999). The MPM has evolved to shape a philosophy of authoritarianism and control of communities through state-centred measures that do not use engagement with communities as a source of policing but instead suppress them (Douglas and Atherton 2007). The MPM is thus both heavy handed in nature and detrimental to community-led policing. As Pickering, McCulloch, and Wright-Neville (2008, p. 20) note: "[t]here is evidence that replacing the community-policing model with one based on the excessive use of hard power is likely to spread rather than shrink the threat". Therefore, the urban policing model remains the best method for policing in the 21st century as it uses engagement rather than fear to promote community relations (Leichtman 2008).

There is evidence to suggest that the MPM will only alienate and stigmatise members of the Muslim community, driving them away from constructive dialogue and partnership work with the police (Dupont 2006). Rigakos (2005) argues that contemporary typologies of policing are based on five fundamental processes: polemic; sentry-dataveillant; investigative; patrol; and civic sumptuary. The polemic standard is where the police use subjective tactics such as lethal force or oppressive tactics against citizens (such as in the 'Arab Spring' of 2010). Rigakos (2005, p. 273) states that: "[t]he more divided or unequal the society, the more likely type one policing will be deployed". This policing notion is by its very nature a more subversive form of policing and uses counter-terror measures in many cases to tackle dissent. On the other hand, sentry-dataveillant policing is associated with what Rigakos (2005, p. 283) calls "keeping watch". Therefore,

Institutional Islamophobia 91

sentry-dataveillant policing is much more about monitoring people through surveillance, and is increasingly becoming less passive and more proactive in its use of technology as a vehicle for gathering information (O'Connor et al. 2008).

According to Hier and Greenberg (2009), surveillance has led to political and social problems within society, such as over-policing, suspicion, and fear. Surveillance in this context can be understood to be an activity whereby law enforcement agencies gather factual information and evidence about criminals, and now terrorists (Hier 2003). This image of surveillance invokes an Orwellian picture of a surveillance society and, since the 'war on terror', police forces across Britain have been given greater powers of surveillance (Dupont 2006). The problem with the increasing use of surveillance is the conflict between civil liberties and national security. As noted earlier, threats of terrorism have been used to justify government social power and control (Sheptycki 1997). This can amplify itself into future terrorist attacks and violent extremism amongst vulnerable people within the community who feel that the police have unfairly labelled them as 'radicals' (Haggerty and Ericson 2000). This element is best described through the #FlyingwhilstMuslim which showed a series of cases where Muslims have been stopped at airports or whilst they have been on public transport revealing the nature of Islamophobia.

Airports and flying whilst Muslim

In 2013, *The Guardian* journalist Glenn Greenwald's partner, David Miranda, was detained at Heathrow airport, in London, under Schedule 7 of the Terrorism Act 2000. Greenwald, famous for exposing the National Security Agency's mass surveillance project, described the treatment to Miranda as both "despotic" and an attack against journalism. "It's bad enough to prosecute and imprison sources," he stated. "It's worse still to imprison journalists who report the truth" (Greenwald 2013). Unwarranted detention is something ethnic minority communities and, in particular, Muslim communities have also experienced with Schedule 7. For example, statistics show that between April 2011 and March 2012 almost 70,000 people were questioned by officers at British ports and airports and 45 per cent of these detainees were of Asian or Asian British origin (Liberty 2012).

The case has caused anger and outrage in the UK, as the chairman of the Home Affairs Select Committee, Yvette Cooper, said the police needed to explain why they used terrorism powers in this case. Indeed, the then independent reviewer of counter-terrorism legislation, David Anderson, had asked the Home Office and the Metropolitan Police to explain why anti-terrorism laws were used.

Schedule 7 gives the police the power to stop and detain an individual and search passengers both at ports and airports to try to determine whether they are terrorists or not. They can also be detained, as in Miranda's case, for up to nine hours and their possessions can be examined. The problem, however, with this statute is that it assumes someone is guilty of being a terrorist without actual evidence of criminality in the first instance. This is why Greenwald, himself, described

92 Institutional Islamophobia

the incident as a means to "intimidate" and "bully" him because of his writings and revelations regarding the NSA. Greenwald stated:

> They never asked him about a single question at all about terrorism or anything relating to a terrorist organisation ... They spent the entire day asking about the reporting I was doing and other Guardian journalists were doing on the NSA stories.
>
> *(Greenwald 2013)*

In this case, and like many others, there is a deprivation of both liberty and an intrusion of privacy. For example, a case brought before the European Court of Human Rights, by Sabure Malik, a British national, also shows that Schedule 7 can have a long-lasting effect on an individual. After being detained under Schedule 7 following a trip to Hajj, he was marched through the terminal by police officers and bundled in the back of a police van. Malik would later describe the incident as a humiliating experience and, like Miranda, he had his possessions examined. In his case, the detective inspector noted that an officer under Schedule 7 "does not require any reasonable grounds to stop a person and conduct any such examination" (cited in Malik 2013).

It is because of this intrusion of privacy and an absence of reasonable suspicion that a consultation took place between September and December of 2012 to examine the implications of Schedule 7 (Home Office 2013). It found that many respondents were concerned with the disproportionate use of Schedule 7 against ethnic minority communities. For example, questions such as "which Mosque do you attend?" or "how often do you pray?" were viewed as negative and Islamophobic. The Terrorism Act of 2000 was enacted in order to combat the international threat. However, this case has again highlighted the problem with such laws when exercised for spurious reasons. The Terrorism Act allows the police to act in this way because in many cases they do not need evidence to justify detaining someone. As long as the court has evidence that they are carrying out their investigations diligently and expeditiously, this will suffice.

This undermines these due process rights, undercutting the right to liberty, the right to silence, the right to be promptly informed of any charges, and the right to be free from detention. It can also pave the way to abusive practices, which might result in detainees making involuntary statements and confessions. Further, it is an unnecessary curtailment of a suspect's freedom for the sake of prolonged and speculative investigations by the police. In this case, it was a heavy-handed decision to hold someone who clearly was not a terrorist or a threat to British national security, but merely for his association with Greenwald, Miranda had to suffer at the hands of the UK authorities. Surely, now, people must recognise that the golden thread that runs back to the Magna Carta of justice, due process, and the principle of habeas corpus are being undermined by anti-terrorism laws that target innocent people like Miranda.

Islamophobia and the 'war on terror'

As well as institutions becoming part of the problem in relation to Islamophobia, the controversial terrorism legislation and powers which have enabled them to do so can form part of our understanding of institutional Islamophobia. For example, following the 'war on terror', Muslim communities have been viewed in much the same way as the Black Afro-Caribbean and Irish communities who were treated as a 'suspect group' (Pantazis and Pemberton 2009). The UK Government has enacted a number of counter-terrorism legislation, namely: the Terrorism Act 2000, the Prevention of Terrorism Act 2005, the Terrorism Act 2006, the Counter-Terrorism Act 2018, and the Counter Terrorism and Security Act 2015 which have given the police wider powers of stop and search, pre-charge detention, and collecting and downloading material deemed to be useful for a terrorist purpose.

One of the more contentious pieces of legislation that has changed following the UK Government's review of counter-terrorism legislation is the police use of stop and search powers (HM Government 2011). Section 44 of the Terrorism Act 2000 allowed the police to stop and search anyone without the need for 'reasonable suspicion' provided the powers were authorised by a senior police officer and confirmed by the Home Secretary. Controversially, under ss44–47 of the Terrorism Act 2000, the police used blanket stop and search powers that were not dependant on 'reasonable suspicion' but were operated by the police with a free reign (Bowling 1999).

A broad power of this type is deeply worrying as in essence, it created an arbitrary piece of legislation that gave the police the ability to abuse their position and in many cases, inevitably, stop and search innocent people (including Muslims). There is evidence that an increase in stop and search has not necessarily led to more terrorism related convictions and as such the powers have been used disproportionately against members of the Muslim community in the UK. Fenwick and Choudhury's (2011) research, which examined the impact of counter-terrorism legislation upon Muslim and non-Muslim families, found that 283 terrorism related arrests have been made by the police but not a single person has been convicted of a s44 stop and search offence. Fenwick and Choudhury (2011, p. 34) state that:

> Among Muslim participants, the strongest negative feelings arose from perceptions that individuals were being stopped because of their religion or race ... the absence of the need for the police to provide any reason for stopping a person, combined with individual experiences and accounts of stops from friends and family, led most Muslim participants to feel that they are stopped because of their ethnicity or religion.

Moreover, if legislation provides a power that can be exercised by the police without a requirement for any need to show 'reasonable suspicion' then it is crucial for the criminal justice system to ensure that such powers are not exercised without due care and diligence. As noted earlier, following the events of 7 July 2005, the

94 Institutional Islamophobia

UK Government and police had to act as the main threat of terrorism began to emerge from al-Qaeda-inspired terrorism. However, such threats do not mean a justification in stigmatising a whole community (Kundnani 2009). These are policies which heighten Islamophobia and provide a nuanced viewpoint on extremism (Githens-Mazer and Lambert 2010). The UK Government needs to begin to try and understand the causes and drivers of extremism and, at the same time, value the British Muslim contribution to the wider British society (Spalek 2010).

Debate: what is a suspect community?

The 'suspect' community and Islamophobia

The problem with current counter-terrorism policies is that it has the potential of profiling Muslims as extremists and indeed 'suspects'. As a result, law enforcement agencies have begun a dangerous process of trying to identify extremists based on a person's characteristics, age, background, ethnicity, and faith. This has led to a wave of issues and policies that have left Muslims feeling as though they are suspect communities. Pickering, McCulloch, and Wright-Neville (2008) argue that "Profiles based on race, ethnicity or religion are ineffective as law enforcement tools and ethically indefensible". Critics argue that the problem with using terms such as 'suspect community' to describe Muslims is that in actual fact it will lead to an unnecessary climate of fear. According to Greer (2010), this is because there is no universal interpretation of what is a 'suspect' community: "the assumption that Muslims in the United Kingdom constitute a single national community, and the lack of clarity about what constitutes 'official suspicion', how and why it is formed, and the circumstances in which it might be objectionable" (Greer 2010, p. 1177).

Muslims are, however, divided by different religious entities and sects and critics argue this can lead to a problem in defining who is a 'Muslim'. Therefore, before understanding the nature of whether such legislation and policies disproportionately impact upon Muslim communities, the overall definition of the word 'Muslim' needs to be broadened. This project also found that overall communities who were considered as suspects did not feel that sense of victimisation or stigma as a result. In contrast, in a report by Hickman et al. (2011) entitled 'Suspect communities: Counter-terrorism policy, the press and the impact on Irish and Muslim communities in Britain', the authors recommended that the UK Government have greater awareness and understanding of Muslim communities and the impact of counter-terrorism policies which have led to them being viewed as suspects.

As shown earlier, counter-terrorism policies are being perceived as being discriminatory against Muslim communities; however, critics argue that in actual fact anti-discrimination laws in Britain such as the Racial and Religious Hatred Act 2006 and the Equality Act 2010 give Muslims greater equality and fairness. Indeed, they point to the study by Innes et al. (2011) which found that Muslims overall did trust their police forces when it came to delivering Prevent programmes although the study found that young British Muslims did not trust the police. The study used evidence and statistics from the British Crime Survey and found overall that young British Muslim men's attitudes towards the policing of Prevent (which is part of the UK Government's counter-terrorism strategy known as CONTEST) were negative (Innes et al. 2011).

Conclusion

Institutional Islamophobia is a complex problem and impacts a whole range of different institutions and organisations. It does appear that where there are issues of mistrust between the police and communities, then Muslims are less likely to report incidents to the police. Currently, the new guidance operational policing guidelines on policing hate crime is welcomed and it is hoped that this will give police forces a clearer and stronger direction with regards to Islamophobic hate. Whilst policing Islamophobic hate crime has come a long way, there are still clearly questions about how relationships between the police and Muslim communities can be better understood. Furthermore, countering terrorism has led to a wave of policies, which now mean that Muslims are viewed with suspicion and therefore are a suspect community.

Key questions

- What is the difference between institutional Islamophobia and hate crime?
- How does racial inequality lead to Islamophobia?
- Are the police an institutionally racist organisation?
- What is the significance of flying as a Muslim in the context of Islamophobia?
- Do you think Muslims are a suspect community?

Further reading

- Chakraborti, N. and Garland, J. 2014. (eds) *Responding to Hate Crime: The Case for Connecting Policy and Research*. Bristol: The Policy Press.
- Jewkes, Y. 2010. Public policing and the Internet. In: Y. Jewkes and M. Yar (eds) *Handbook of Internet Crime*. Cullompton: Willan.
- Jewkes, Y. and Leukfeldt, R. 2012. Policing cyber crime. In: R. Leukfeldt and W. Stol (eds) *Cyber Safety: An Introduction*. Eleven Publishing.
- Jewkes, Y. and Yar, M. 2010. The Internet, cybercrime, and the challenges of the 21st century. In: Y. Jewkes and M. Yar (eds) *Handbook of Internet Crime*. Cullompton: Willan.

References

Awan, I., Blakemore, B., and Simpson, K. 2013. Muslim communities attitudes towards and recruitment into the British Police Service. *International Journal of Law, Crime and Justice*, 41 (4): 421–437.

96 Institutional Islamophobia

Bowling, B. 1999. *Violent Racism: Victimisation, Policing and Social Context*. Revised Edition. Oxford: Oxford University Press.

Casciani, D. 2009. Nursery visited by counter-terrorism police officer. *BBC News*. Available at: www.news.bbc.co.uk/1/hi/uk/8408305.stm

Douglas, S. and Atherton, S. 2007. To serve and protect? The experiences of policing in the community of young people from black and other ethnic minority groups. *British Journal of Criminology*, 47(5): 746–763.

Dupont, B. 2006. Delivering security through networks: Surveying the relational landscape of security managers in an urban setting. *Crime, Law & Social Change*, 46(2): 165–184.

Fenwick, H. and Choudhury, T. 2011. The impact of counter-terrorism measures on Muslim communities (Equality and Human Rights Commission Research Report 72). Available at: www.equalityhumanrights.com/uploaded_files/research/counter-terrorism_research_report_72.pdf

Githens-Mazer, J. and Lambert, R. 2010. Islamophobia and anti-Muslim hate crimes: A London case study. *European Muslim Research Centre*. Available at: http://centres.exeter.ac.uk/emrc/publications/IAMHC_revised_11Feb11.pdf

Goldsmith, A. 2005. Police reform and the problem of trust. *Theoretical Criminology*, 9(4): 443–470.

Gordon, H. and Rowe, M. 2007. Neighbourhood policing and community safety: Researching the instabilities of the local governance of crime, disorder and security in contemporary UK. *Criminology & Criminal Justice*, 7(4): 317–346.

Graef, R. 1989. *Talking Blues: The Police in their Own Words*. London: Collins Harvill.

Greer, S. 2010. Anti-terrorist laws and the United Kingdom's 'suspect Muslim community': A reply to Pantazis and Pemberton. *British Journal of Criminology*, 50: 1171–1190.

Greenwald, G. 2013. Glenn Greenwald: Detaining my partner was a failed attempt at intimidation. *The Guardian*. Available at: www.theguardian.com/commentisfree/2013/aug/18/david-miranda-detained-uk-nsa

Haggerty, K. and Ericson, R. 2000. The surveillant assemblage. *British Journal of Sociology*, 51 (4): 605–622.

Hall, S., Critcher, C., Jefferson, T., Clarke, J. and Roberts, B. 1978. *Policing the Crisis: Mugging, the State, and Law and Order*. London: Macmillan.

Hickman, Mary J., Thomas, L., Silvestri, S., and Nickels, H. 2011. 'Suspect communities'? Counter-terrorism policy, the press and the impact on Irish and Muslim communities in Britain. *City University London*. Available at www.city.ac.uk/__data/assets/pdf_file/0005/96287/suspect-communities-report-july2011.pdf

Hier, S. 2003. Probing the surveillant assemblage: On the dialectics of surveillance practices as processes of social control. *Surveillance & Society*, 1(3): 399–411.

Hier, S. and Greenberg, J. 2009. The politics of surveillance: Power, paradigms, and the field of visibility. In: S. Hier and J. Greenberg (eds) *Surveillance: Power, Problems, and Politics*. Vancouver: University of British Columbia Press.

HM Government. 2006. Countering international terrorism: The United Kingdom's strategy. Available at: www.fco.gov.uk/resources/en/pdf/contest-report

HM Government. 2011. Prevent strategy. Available at: www.homeoffice.gov.uk/publications/counter-terrorism/prevent/prevent-strategy/prevent-strategy-review?view-_Binary

Home Office. 2004. Counter terrorism powers: Reconciling security and liberty in an open society (Discussion Paper Cm6147). Available at: www.statewatch.org/news/2004/feb/uk-CT-discussion-paper.pdf

Home Office. 2013. Review of the operation of Schedule 7: A public consultation. Available at: www.gov.uk/government/uploads/system/uploads/attachment_data/file/212548/WEB_-_2013_07_15_Review_of_the_operation_of_Schedule_7_A_Public_Consulta___.pdf

Innes, M. 2006. Policing uncertainty: Countering terror through community intelligence and democratic policing. *Annals of APSS*, 605(May): 1–20.

Innes, M., Roberts, C., Innes, H., Trudy, L., and Lakhani, S. 2011. Assessing the effects of prevent policing: A report to the Association of Chief Police Officers. *Online Research @ Cardiff*. Available at: http://orca.cf.ac.uk/23060

Jones, S. 2011. Student in Al Qaida raid paid £20,000 by police. *The Guardian*. Available at: www.theguardian.com/uk/2011/sep/14/police-pay-student-damages-al-qaida

Kraska, P. 1999. Militarizing criminal justice: Exploring the possibilities. *Journal of Political and Military Sociology*, 27(Winter): 205–215.

Kundnani, A. 2009. Spooked! How not to prevent violent extremism. *Institute of Race Relations*. Available at: www.irr.org.uk/pdf2/spooked.pdf

Leichtman, E. 2008. Complex harmony: The military and professional models of policing. *Critical Criminology*, 16(1): 53–73.

Liberty. 2012. Liberty's response to the Home Office's review of the operation of Schedule 7, December. Available at: www.liberty-human-rights.org.uk/pdfs/policy12/liberty-s-resp onse-to-the-consultation-on-the-operation-of-schedule-7-dec-20.pdf

Macpherson Inquiry. 1999. *The Stephen Lawrence Inquiry (Report of an Inquiry by Sir William Macpherson of Cluny, Cm 4262-I)*. London: Stationery Office.

Malik, S. 2013. Malik v United Kingdom, Fourth Section Decision, European Court of Human Rights. Available at: https://hudoc.echr.coe.int/eng?i=001-121698#%20.

McConville, M. and Shepherd, D. 1992. *Watching Police, Watching Communities*. London: Routledge.

O'Connor, D., Lippert, R., Smylie, L., and Spencer, D. 2008. Seeing private security like a state. *Criminology and Criminal Justice*, 8: 203–226.

Pantazis, C. and Pemberton, S. 2009. From the 'old' to the 'new suspect' community: Examining the impacts of recent UK counter-terrorist legislation. *British Journal of Criminology*, 49(5): 646–666.

Pickering, S., McCulloch, J., and Wright-Neville, D. 2008. *Counter-Terrorism Policing: Community, Cohesion and Security*. New York, NY: Springer.

Rigakos, G. 2005. Beyond public private: Towards a new typology of policing. In D. Cooley (ed.) *Re-Imagining Policing in Canada*. Toronto: University of Toronto Press.

Shearing, C. and Johnston, L. 2010. Nodal wars and network fallacies: A genealogical analysis of global insecurities. *Theoretical Criminology*, 14(4): 495–514.

Sheptycki, J. 1997. Insecurity, risk suppression and segregation: Some reflections on policing in the transnational age. *Theoretical Criminology*, 1(3): 303–315.

Skogan, W. and Hartnett, S. 1997. *Community Policing Chicago Style*. Oxford: Oxford University Press.

Social Mobility Commission. 2017. Young Muslims in the UK face enormous social mobility barriers. Available at: www.gov.uk/government/news/young-muslims-in-the-uk-fa ce-enormous-social-mobility-barriers

Spalek, B. 2010. Community policing, trust, and Muslim communities in relation to new terrorism. *Politics & Policy*, 38(4): 789–815.

Spalek, B. and Lambert, R. 2008. Muslim communities, counter-terrorism and de-radicalisation: A reflective approach to engagement. *International Journal of Law. Crime and Justice*, 36(4): 257–270.

Thornton, S. 2010. Project Champion review. West Midlands Police. Available at: www. west-midlands.police.uk/latestnews/docs/Champion_Review_FINAL_30_09_10.pdf

Trojanowicz, R. and Bucqueroux, B. 1990. *Community Policing: A Contemporary Perspective*. Cincinnati: Anderson.

Virta, S. 2008. Community policing meets new challenges. In: S. Virta (Ed.) *Policing Meets New Challenges: Preventing Radicalization and Recruitment*. Tampere, Finland: University of Tampere Department of Management Studies, European Police College.

Waddington, P. A. J. 1999. *Policing Citizens*. UCL Press Ltd.

8

ISLAMOPHOBIA, TERRORISM, AND THE MEDIA

Introduction

This chapter explores the role of Islamophobia in the media and the impact this has had upon Muslims. Previous studies looking at media coverage of Muslims in particular post-9/11 have often stereotyped Muslims in a negative light. For example, Moore, Mason, and Lewis' (2008) study from 2001–2008 examined over 974 newspaper articles and found that the majority of news coverage post-9/11 about Muslims was negative. Their research into media coverage of British Muslims involved a content analysis of 974 newspaper articles about British Muslims in the British press and an analysis of visual images. Using statistical analysis of stories and language they found that at least two thirds of newspaper articles were focused around stories on terrorism. These stories had used the words such as 'militancy' and 'radicalism' to depict Muslims in an overtly negative fashion and were a product of a wider anti-Muslim prejudice, which they found across British newspapers.

They also found that the language, news coverage, headlines, and stories used regarding British Muslims were overall negative and often coupled British Muslims with a narrative that they were a 'problem group', a 'threat', or indeed Islam was deemed to be 'dangerous' and an 'irrational religion'. They also found that the common nouns used in relation to British Muslims were the words 'extremist', 'Islamist', 'suicide bomber', 'militant'; and the common adjectives used included the words 'radical', 'fanatical', and 'fundamentalist'. The research by Moore, Mason, and Lewis (2008) found that 36 per cent of stories about British Muslims between those periods were exclusively about terrorism. They also found that news coverage of stories in more recent times had been focused around religious and cultural barriers between Islam, Muslims, and British culture and around the implementation of Sharia law. Indeed, their study found that the print media stories were often based around societal and political experiences of Muslims in the UK.

100 Islamophobia, terrorism, and the media

Furthermore, a study conducted by Baker, Costas and McEnery (2013), which provided an analysis of stories regarding Islam and Muslims in British newspapers, found that overall stories concerning Islam were negative. Using a critical discourse analysis which sought to address some key questions from over 200,000 media articles on Islam they examined the use of language, which they found represented Muslims and Islam in a prejudicial manner. Similarly, Poole's (2002, p. 2006) research found a clear link between Muslims being associated with terms such as 'terrorists', 'politics', and 'reactions to the war in Iraq'. We argue that such reporting and representation of British Muslims also helps create the framework for the 'othering' of communities and in particular may influence people's perceptions of Muslims because of the type of headlines and stories they read.

What is 'Othering'?

Othering is when communities or individuals are negatively stereotyped groups who are viewed as a despised social group. This can have consequences which can lead to separateness and formulation of 'in-' and 'out-groups', and over-policing of minorities.

The moral panic syndrome

Tabloid newspapers have consistently been part of a wider push to demonise Muslims through the consistent nature of stories surrounding Islam and Muslims. As per the Cohen model of moral panic, Muslims are now depicted as the new folk devils and Muslim women wearing the niqab pose a national security threat, or the amount of Muslim babies being born in Britain as being the problem. For example, a series of articles have now emerged that have depicted Muslims in a negative light. This includes a number of journalists who have now used false assumptions and poor journalism by describing all Muslims as terrorists. For example, the headline 'Jolly Jihadi boy's outing to Legoland' in the *Daily Mail* in 2014 characterised all Muslims as being part of the problem. The author of the article, Richard Littlejohn, continued his attack on Muslims by using the word, Family 'Fun' Day to mean 'Fun' as in 'Fundamentalism'. Indeed, the high-profile Leveson inquiry, which was set up by the British Government to examine the culture, practices, and ethics of the Press, would have been appalled at the lack of ethics in regards to this article. Sadly, it is because of newspapers such as the *Daily Mail* that there is an atmosphere which has demonised Muslims and fuelled an anti-Muslim narrative.

The media, including newspapers such as the *Daily Mail*, must provide a more responsible, objective, and proportionate way of reporting on stories. Unfortunately, this article and many others like it, including the one in *The Sun* entitled 'Ramadan a ding-dong' in 2013, provide a sensationalised and biased viewpoint that seeks to undermine all Muslims and portray Islam in a negative light. As a result, we are seeing that British Muslims as a group suffer from very bad journalism and media reporting that actually fuels attention to extremist and far-right fringe groups such as Anjem Choudary and Muslims for Crusades that do not represent Muslims.

These stories are often coupled with poor journalism that does not actually examine the true facts of each case. It is important to bear in mind the story from 2010, when windows at a Black Country leisure centre were being covered up because, according to the *Daily Mail*, 'Swimmers plunged into dark after council covers swimming pool windows to protect Muslim women's modesty'. This apparently was because all Muslim women had demanded the windows be blacked out. However, that did not appear to be the case, and the council revealed later that the requests to black out the windows had not come solely from the Muslim community.

The case of a Muslim woman and the Westminster attack

The image of a Muslim woman walking and checking her phone may seem harmless. However, this incident caused a public outrage after a Twitter account noted that the anonymous Muslim woman was: "[paying] no mind to the terror attack, casually [walking] by a dying man while checking [her] phone" (Mortimer 2017).

The image received hundreds of retweets and was shared across a number of international platforms including from those individuals linked to the American alt-right movement. However, the account which appeared to be sent by Russian hackers just revealed how quickly individuals can use the media to direct negative perceptions of Muslims. The image was significant because it not only showed this Muslim woman ignoring victims of the Westminster terror attack but also tried to quickly further exacerbate the hate and abuse Muslims suffer.

The media is oxygen for the far-right

In the 1980s, Margaret Thatcher, the former British Prime Minister, famously coined the phrase that media publicity is like oxygen for terrorists. By this she meant that terrorists seek change through the use of fear and intimidation and in particular specific terrorist attacks can often be employed in a manner that allows them to maximise the impact of their activities. If we extend this definition, we see that the media can also act as oxygen for the far-right who perpetuate Islamopho-bia. This is often amplified by the use of the media in how they display and send their message. Bozarth (2005) argues that the impact of terrorist attacks can there-fore be measured by how terrorists specifically use the media to propagate their cause. For Bozarth (2005) this type of impact could be measured with the pre-valence of media coverage, the number of media sources who report the incident, the duration of coverage of an attack, and the details of the coverage.

Clearly, there is a fine line between reporting a news story and portraying a negative version of the story or simply acting as a sound piece for a terrorist. For

102 Islamophobia, terrorism, and the media

example, *The New York Times* and *The Washington Post* both published the political manifesto of Ted Kaczynski, the Unabomber, in 1995. At the time, he made a declaration that he would cease the bombings if newspapers would publish his manifesto and as a result both *The New York Times* and *The Washington Post* published his manifesto called 'Industrial Society and Its Future' (The Washington Post 2013). Indeed, more recently Al Jazeera, the Qatari-based media news channel, has received criticism for its close links with the al-Qaeda leadership. For example, a number of videos of Osama bin Laden and Ayman Az-Zawarhi have been broadcast directly through Al Jazeera.

Similarly, as noted earlier, a number of British media news channels were heavily criticised for their reporting of the Woolwich attack. ITV News and Sky News were amongst the groups that were criticised for effectively broadcasting the Adebolajo statement after the murder of Lee Rigby in 2013. Terrorists do look to the media to amplify their actions and spread their message to a wider audience. Ultimately this forms a 'signal' by which they disseminate their cause for violence and terrorism to a wider audience. This in turn can help provide an impetus for terrorists to use the media as a means to broadcast their message and thereby create a theatre of fear. Nacos (2002), for example, argues that this forms a triangle of political communication, which is used by terrorists to identify the news media and the public as a means to disseminate their ideological reasons for their crime.

In each section of the triangle the media allows the flow of messages to the general public. This is particularly important in Woolwich because the individuals had the urge and impetus to communicate their causes and grievances to a wider audience. For example, both the print and news media, therefore, in effect allowed the Woolwich attackers the platform to magnify and maximise publicity by broadcasting Adebolajo's reasons for committing this murder. Critics would argue that British newspapers, therefore, may also have been complicit in this act as they used the pictures and his words to create news headlines that caused controversy. More specifically, the media can act as gatekeepers in communicating wider messages of counter-terrorism issues. We argue, therefore, that they have to take a socially responsible decision in how they report such events because, as we have found out, this can have implications for the communities and faith groups they target.

The Leveson inquiry

The dilemma between what to report and how to report a big news story is a key consideration when examining what is in the 'public interest'. Indeed, the high-profile Leveson inquiry in the UK revealed serious concerns about media corruption following the *News of the World*'s closure after it had admitted it had hacked into Milly Dowler's mobile phone and voicemail after her death. The Leveson inquiry was set up by the British Government to try and create better government oversight and press regulation. As noted earlier, evidence is needed for a much more balanced and nuanced way of reporting stories by the media concerning Islam, and this could be achieved if a system of self-regulation was introduced because it would allow a process that challenges inaccuracies in reporting stories. Moreover, the Leveson inquiry did make a number of recommendations that included tighter monitoring of Internet sites and blogs where there was evidence of anti-Muslim prejudice emerging.

Case study: Mohammed Saleem and Woolwich

In 2013, the Muslim grandfather Mohammed Saleem, who was 82, was murdered by a far-right Ukranian student, Pavlo Lapshyn. The following case study aimed to examine the media response in relation to the murder of Lee Rigby in 2013 and the murder of Mohammed Saleem (Awan and Rahman 2016). Rigby's shocking murder in May 2013 at the hands of Michael Adebolajo and Michael Adebowale was repeatedly described by both police and media as an act of terrorism, while the killing of Saleem we found was labelled as 'racially motivated', despite Pavlo Lapshyn being found guilty under the Terrorism Act. The research findings showed that from the three-week period when the Woolwich attack took place, similar notions of terrorism were being linked to Islam and Muslims. This was evidenced by negative stories that were portrayed by a number of British newspapers. Furthermore, the findings seemed to mirror the work of Allen (2012, p. 8) who found that 91 per cent of British newspapers' coverage of British Muslims was deemed negative. Utilising the principle of grounded theory, the following case study examined the role of the print media and its use of news headlines and news coverage of the Woolwich incident by observing a three-week data set (Awan and Rahman 2016). Using grounded theory and content analysis is important because it allowed for a more useful method for examining wider trends and patterns, and helped provide a robust empirical basis for understanding the language within the print newspapers. The sample for the content analysis was then gathered from the Nexis database examining British broadsheet and regional newspapers. The three-week period was used because the aim was to capture only the initial reporting of the incident as we felt it would provide us with a starting point for further research in this area and also shed light on how the print media reacted to the Woolwich incident in its immediate aftermath.

We then used NVivo, an electronic software system, which allowed us to analyse and collect themes that emerged from the newspaper articles (Awan and Rahman 2016). This also meant we were able to create coded themes and use the word-frequency generator within the program which generated the 75 most frequent words that emerged from both regional and broadsheet newspapers. We found the most common words within the top 75 most frequent terms that appeared were 'Muslim', 'terrorist', 'terror', and 'Islamic'. This was not surprising since previous studies have shown links between the words 'Islam' and 'terrorism'. For example, Akbarzadeh and Smith (2005, p. 23) state that the identification of Islam with acts of terrorism, or terrorism in the name of Islam, is commonly known as 'Islamic terrorism' and therefore is likely to appear simultaneously. Through both Nexis and NVivo we captured some of the key stories and

104 Islamophobia, terrorism, and the media

headlines, which yielded over 1,022 articles. Out of the total results, only a selected volume of broadsheet (four) and regional (five) newspapers were used for the research, as we found that these daily newspapers provided extensive coverage of the Woolwich attack during the three-week period and more importantly they were the key themes emerging from NVivo (see Tables 8.1 and 8.2). The data set of three weeks post-Woolwich was utilised because we felt it would capture the scene at the time and therefore provide important data with regards the way in which the print media were reporting this incident from the beginning.

The term 'Muslim' in the British newspapers following Woolwich

We found that a number of British broadsheet newspapers initially reported the Woolwich incident based around comments from within the Muslim community. For example, *The Times* and *The Telegraph* reported how the Muslim Council of Britain within hours of the attack was quick to distance Islam from the incident. The Muslim Council of Britain is a national organisation which represents news and stories about the Muslim community in Britain. However, it is important to note that when acts of terrorism do occur, such as Woolwich, 9/11, and 7/7, then it does appear that public outrage can lead to a sense that community leaders are encouraged or need to come out and distance themselves from such acts of terrorism. Following the Woolwich attack, it was visible that many Muslim organisations and Muslim community leaders were interviewed across British Television screens and via print media condemning the attack in a manner, we argue, is an attempt to alleviate any fears communities may be experiencing about reprisal attacks.

TABLE 8.1 Reference made to Woolwich in broadsheet newspapers

Broadsheet newspapers	Articles in relation to Woolwich attack
The Telegraph	244
The Times	150
The Independent	137
The Guardian	66

TABLE 8.2 Reference made to Woolwich in regional newspapers

Regional newspapers	Articles in relation to Woolwich attack
Scotsman	38
Scotland on Sunday	25
Yorkshire Post	23
Belfast Telegraph	22
Evening Standard	21

This was noted by the *London Evening Standard*, which a day after the Woolwich attack used the headline: 'The threat from lone wolf terrorism'. Interestingly, their coverage revealed how they felt Muslim groups were perhaps too quick to come out and condemn the incident without obtaining all the facts. Terrorism incidents can obscure and conflate arguments that sometimes lead to counter-productive assertions embedded within the narrative that some people are sympathetic to terrorism causes, if they try to rationalise terrorist behaviour and do not condemn certain actions.

The use of such language does seem to relate to a wider international problem of how Islam and Muslims are viewed. For example, Akbarzedah and Smith (2005, p. 21) outline in their analysis of newspaper articles the use of common adjectives such as: 'Muslim fanatics', 'radical Islamic group', and 'Islamic fundamentalism' as being frequently used by Australian newspapers to "describe Muslims and Islam in connection to terrorism in both international and domestic cases". We also argue that this can be seen as problematic in particular when the public may not be aware of what Islam stands for. Indeed, Allen (2012) found that 64 per cent of the British public claim that what they do know about Muslims is 'acquired through the media'. The following case study will now examine the news coverage of the term 'Muslim' via British regional newspapers.

The term 'Muslim' in regional newspapers following Woolwich

Similar to British broadsheet newspapers, the British regional newspapers also adopted a position of stories that were heavily focused initially around Muslim community leaders expressing their anger at what had happened and crystallising the view that Islam and Muslims were not to blame. This amounted to, for example, 36 per cent of stories in the *Scotland on Sunday* in comparison with Broadsheets, such as *The Telegraph*, which was 45 per cent. This was also personified by responsible reporting from many local regional newspapers, which made a strong case for using references from Muslim councillors and Muslim Members of Parliament to show the visible outrage etched across Muslim communities after Woolwich. The *Burton Mail* (2013), for example, used the headline 'The British people will not accept this – Burton MP speaks out on Woolwich attack'.

We feel that this type of narrative was used in particular across smaller local regional newspapers as a means to stop the potential of problems escalating within tight knit communities. Clearly, the role of all communities is vital when confronting issues of this nature and the British print media did make an attempt to highlight how Muslim community leaders were expressing their outrage and anger over Woolwich. We can only speculate that this might affect their readership that would view this either in a positive or negative manner. However, within the first three weeks after Woolwich the impact seemed to show a polarised viewpoint about Muslim communities in Britain. For example, a YouGov survey of over 1,839 adults conducted following Woolwich showed there was clear evidence people felt Muslims were a threat to democracy. Furthermore, two thirds of those

106 Islamophobia, terrorism, and the media

people believed that Britain was facing a clash of civilisation between British Muslims and White Britons.

Indeed, in a survey conducted later in September 2013, by BBC Radio 1 Newsbeat, of 18–24-year-olds they found that from the 1,000 people questioned, 28 per cent of young people believed Britain would be a safer place with fewer Muslims and 44 per cent of people felt Muslims did not share the same values as the rest of Britain. Interestingly, the people questioned did state that Islamophobia existed in mainstream politics and within the media. They also blamed terrorist groups abroad for this image (26 per cent), and the media was second place at 23 per cent for depicting Muslims in a negative light and finally, UK Muslims who had committed acts of terrorism were ranked at 21 per cent.

We find those results worrying because it does tend to point towards a wider endemic problem of anti-Muslim reporting and prejudice. Moreover, in a Unitas Report, which was submitted to the Leveson inquiry, it did suggest that the British Press had continued to report negative stories about Muslim communities since 9/11. They found that there was a serious problem of racism within the British Press and anti-Muslim reporting of stories continued to shape news items. The following case study will provide a comparative analysis of the media portrayal of the Woolwich attack and the case of Mohammed Saleem who was murdered in April 2013 and why one incident was categorised as an act of terrorism whilst another was categorised as a racial hate crime.

British newspapers: the Print Media portrayal of the word 'terrorist' in Woolwich and in the case of Mohammed Saleem

We found that in almost all the articles we reviewed regarding Woolwich, the term 'terrorism' was used to describe the attack. The British Prime Minister David Cameron argued that Muslim leaders should help: "challenge the poisonous narrative of extremism on which this violence feeds" (Watson 2013). However, this is in stark contrast to what happened three weeks prior on 29 April 2013 when Mohammed Saleem, an 82-year-old grandfather, was stabbed to death while on his way home from evening prayers at a mosque in Birmingham. The attack was immediately labelled as 'racially motivated' by the police but it was later revealed that the person who murdered Mohammed Saleem was in actual fact a Ukrainian man named Pavlo Lapshyn, who would be characterised not as a 'terrorist' but as a 'white supremacist' by a number of newspapers. Lapshyn was also involved in planting a number of bombs outside mosques in Birmingham. The most serious was at the Aisha mosque in Walsall but no one was injured.

In a statement after the Cobra meeting, following Woolwich, the Prime Minister said: "the nation should come together to stand against those who sought to divide us" (Watson 2013). Comments of such were supported by the Muslim community; however, further headlines by *The Telegraph* (2013), which stated that 'Woolwich shows that Muslim leaders have learned how to respond to terrorism', were headlines that associated the general Muslim community with acts of terrorism and potentially fuelled far-right groups like the English Defence League and Britain First to stage demonstrations against Muslims. Allen (2012, p. 10) argues that such tactics can increase feelings of insecurity, suspicion, and anxiety amongst non-Muslims.

We also believe that such statements made in newspapers like *The Telegraph* (2013), which stated that: 'Muslims have had to embark on this learning curve without any help from the media' showed a clear sense of negativity which implied that all Muslims must condemn acts of terrorism. For instance, *The Independent* partially headlined one of its articles on the night of the attack as a 'suspected Islamic terrorist attack'. The following morning, *The Telegraph* headline was: 'Woolwich attack: terrorist proclaimed "an eye for an eye" after attack'; "A British soldier has been butchered on a busy London street by two Islamist terrorists, one of whom proclaimed afterwards: 'An eye for an eye and a tooth for a tooth'." Both newspapers went on to use the term 'terrorist' to headline additional articles relating to the attack as days went by.

However, in the case of Mohammed Saleem, our findings from the database revealed how *The Telegraph* did not use the term 'terrorist' initially to describe the attack or attackers. Moreover, the term 'terrorist' was not used as a headline even when Pavlo Lapshyn was found guilty of the murder of Mohammed Saleem and the three mosque bombings under the Terrorism Act 2006. Instead *The Telegraph* chose the headline: 'Ukrainian white supremacist avoids life sentence over murder and mosque bombings' (Whitehead 2013). On the other hand, *The Guardian* headline after the conviction did use the words: 'Mosque bombing suspect arrested over "terrorist" murder of pensioner.'

Furthermore, *The Guardian* did make the case for a responsible manner for reporting the term 'terrorist' for the second time with the headline: 'Ukrainian man charged with "terrorist-related murder" of Mohammed Saleem' (Dodd 2013). It seems odd that even after Lapshyn was charged under the Terrorism Act 2006 for the murder of Mohammed Saleem and three mosque explosions, *The Times* also appeared as one of the few newspapers who used the word 'terrorist' in their headlines. On 26 October 2013, *The Times* stated: '"Lone wolf" terrorist jailed for minimum 40 years for killing Muslim man'.

British regional newspapers: use of the word 'terrorist'

In the case of regional articles, the term 'terrorist' was primarily used in headlines as well as within articles to condemn the Woolwich murder. Nonetheless its usage was loaded with over-generalising statements. We believe that the way in which the news was reported in this story was crucial in creating a 'them versus us' mentality. This was depicted by many of the images of the news showing the victim wearing a Help for Heroes t-shirt. This also helped create a coup for far-right groups such as the EDL who were quick to take note of 'Britishness' and argue the 'them versus us' narrative. In relation to Mohammed Saleem the term was limited in use by the regional newspapers. This does leave the question of

108 Islamophobia, terrorism, and the media

whether Pavlo Lapshyn, who was convicted of a terrorism offence under the Terrorism Act 2006, is in actual fact a terrorist. In the view of some parts of the British print media it can be argued that he is not. It should be noted that Lapshyn's label as a terrorist in the print media was relatively low in comparison to the perpetrators in the Woolwich attack, as the average usage of the term 'terrorist' was 11 in broadsheet newspapers in comparison to 155 for the Woolwich attack.

British newspapers: use of the word 'terror' in Woolwich, and the Mohammed Saleem case

As has been highlighted, the word 'terrorist' was consistently used in newspaper headlines and within articles after Woolwich by both formats; its sub-branch of the word 'terror' was also consistently used in article headlines by both regional and broadsheet newspapers. Through the content analysis of article headlines, it is noticeable that the word 'terror', which also means fear, horror, shock, panic, and fright, was used repetitively along with the word 'attack'. Immediately after the murder, regional articles used headlines such as a 'terror attack' yet again without proper clarity and transparency of the overall incident. On the day of the murder, articles from *The Guardian* and *The Independent* also declared the attack as a 'terror attack'. However, like the word 'terrorism' the word 'terror' was also used in a limited capacity by both broadsheets and regional newspapers after Lapshyn was charged.

Attention should also be paid as to why the expression 'terror attack' was used repeatedly by both newspaper formats, and in a sense why it became a reoccurring theme when addressing the story. This article headline in fact was to some extent misleading, as it was immediately clarified through media and the recording of the shocking footage by ITV that there was no 'Terror attack', and the attack actually occurred on a London street, outside the 'barracks' as opposed to the inner parts of the barracks, which is what *The Independent* seemed to depict. The headline could also illustrate the problems around misrepresentation of stories as in this case, which assumed that there was more than one victim. Nevertheless, this was then rectified by the newspaper, as they used the headline: 'Sickening deluded and unforgivable: Horrific attack brings terror to London streets' the following day (Sengupa et al. 2013).

Whilst the term 'terror attack' was used for Woolwich it is surprising that both broadsheet and regional newspapers did not use the same headline for the killing of Mohammed Saleem or even the three mosque explosions. For instance, in relation to Mohammed Saleem, the term 'terror' was first used by *The Guardian* three months after the murder, when Pavlo Lapshyn was charged with the murder and further offences related to mosque explosions.

British newspapers: use of the terms 'Islam' and 'Islamic' to address Woolwich attack

As noted earlier, following the Woolwich attack the British media made some imbalanced assumptions with Islam and terrorism. For example, the former Prime

Minister, Tony Blair, argued that "there is a problem within Islam" and the attack on the soldier was "profound and dangerous" (Dominiczak 2013).

It was further revealed in a separate article by *The Telegraph* that Robinson went on to say:

> They're [Muslims] chopping our heads off. This is Islam. That's what we've seen today. They've cut one of our Army's heads off on the streets of London. Our next generation are being taught through schools that Islam is a religion of peace. It's not. It never has been. What you saw today is Islam.
>
> *(Dixon and Hall 2013)*

Moreover, generalisations were made by *The Independent*, which partially labelled one of its articles in relation to the Woolwich murder as an "Islamic terrorist attack" (Sengupa et al. 2013). Similar headlines were also printed on regional newspapers such as *The Daily Mail* which stated: "'You and your children will be next': Islamic fanatics wielding meat cleavers butcher and try to behead a British soldier, taking their war on the West to a new level of horror" (Martin et al. 2013).

The evidence does suggest that the term was used without due diligence in headlines, which was coupled with 'extreme' words such as 'terror' and 'terrorists', which provided the adequate influence to discriminate against wider Muslim communities. Moreover, newspaper articles by *The Telegraph* used the term 'Islamic' over 46 per cent of times within many of their articles. For example, stating that: 'A soldier was hacked to death in a south London street on Wednesday by two men shouting Islamic slogans' (Dixon and Hall 2013). Yet it was not stated that the attackers in fact cited various political dogmas for their actions in a video recording, which was released by ITV.

The term 'Islamic' was also displayed in the top hits of news coverage. The terms presented as a main theme in this research, as it depicts a certain religion and its followers, and links them directly with the attack on Lee Rigby. Thus, the use of 'Islamic' or 'Muslim' as adjectives implies that Islam sanctions terrorism. This is also informed through the work of Said (1981, p. 56) who in his book 'Covering Islam' states that the definitions of Islam today are predominately negative. The findings revealed that the term 'Islamic' was used over 57 per cent by *The Telegraph* and 36 per cent by the *Scotland on Sunday*, which showed the divide in comparison and the coverage of those stories which was overtly negative.

British Muslims in the media

News headlines:

- 1 in 5 Brit Muslims' Sympathy for Jihadis – *The Sun*, 23 November 2015
- Christmas is Banned: It offends Muslims – *The Daily Express*, 2 November 2005
- Now Muslims get their own Laws in Britain – *The Daily Express*, 30 April 2007
- 3,000 Jihadists on the streets of Britain, *The Daily Mail*, 24 May 2017

110 Islamophobia, terrorism, and the media

Please consider the following questions:

1. What do you think about the content of these articles generally?
2. Can you see anything wrong with these articles (think written content and images)? If yes, use specific examples to provide evidence.
3. What is wrong with these representations of minority groups in the media?
4. How might these representations contribute to prejudicial attitudes?
5. What might the societal implications be of publishing these types of stories?
6. Is it possible that these articles might exacerbate or mitigate some of the motivations for why some individuals exhibit prejudicial behaviour?
7. In your view, are these stories examples of 'hate speech'? If yes, can they be prosecuted as such?
8. Should we be looking to 'censor' the media? What can be done about media representations?

ANSWERS:

Theme 1: Coverage

- Coverage of British Muslims has increased significantly since 2000, peaking in 2006, and remaining high in 2007 and 2008.
- Increasing prevalence of stories that focus on religious and cultural differences between Islam and British culture.
- In 2008, the volume of stories about religious/cultural differences overtook terrorism related stories.
- BUT, coverage of attacks on/problems faced by Muslims has steadily declined.
- Therefore, the bulk of coverage of Muslims (around two-thirds) focuses on British Muslims as a threat, a problem or both.

(Moore, Mason, and Lewis 2008)

Theme 2: Language

- The language used about British Muslims reflects the negative or problematic contexts i.e. Muslims as a threat, a problem, or in opposition to British values.
- Common nouns used: terrorist, extremist, Islamist, suicide bomber, militant.
- Common adjectives used were: radical, fanatical, fundamentalist, extremist, militant.
- Muslims much more likely than non-Muslims to be identified simply as 'Muslim' rather than as individuals e.g. job title or profession.
- Also much more likely than non-Muslims to be unnamed or unidentified.

(Moore, Mason, and Lewis 2008)

Theme 3: Images

- Widespread use of police mugshots used to portray Muslim men.
- Muslim women viewed as the embodiment of oppression.
- Most common venues used for images of Muslim men were outside police stations and law courts.
- Other images focused on cultural/religious differences e.g. Muslims seen engaged in religious practices in a way non-Muslims rarely are.

(Moore, Mason, and Lewis 2008)

Theme 4: Summary

- Stories in the context of the 'war on terror', cultural/religious differences, and Muslim extremism.
- Framed within the perceived threat and fear of Islam.
- Articles played up these newsworthy angles at the expense of objectivity, balance, and context.

Conclusion

The media depiction of Muslim women has often been stereotyped as being oppressed or described as being fundamentalists. For example, in the BBC drama called *The Bodyguard*, which across 28 days was viewed by over 17.1 million people, the prominent Muslim female character called Nadia was depicted as being both oppressed and as a terrorist. The problem with such a view of Muslims in the media is that it can mean that over 17.1 million people who viewed this negative portrayal will also hold such views about Muslims. The prominent Muslim actor Riz Ahmed who has starred in a number of Hollywood movies has described what he calls the Riz Test. According to the test, if one of the following criteria is met this means that the Muslim character is being stereotyped. The test is as follows:

1. Talking about, the victim of, or the perpetrator of Islamist terrorism.
2. Presented as irrationally angry.
3. Presented as superstitious, culturally backwards, or anti-modern.
4. Presented as a threat to a Western way of life.
5. If the character is male, is he presented as misogynistic? Or if female, is she presented as oppressed by her male counterparts?

If any of these criteria are met, then the film/show fails the test. Simple.

The previous case study also reveals how the print media has depicted Muslims in a negative light. For example, the Woolwich attack in the summer of 2013 caused public outrage and continues to make the news headlines as the two men, Adebolajo and Adebowale, were sentenced to life imprisonment for the murder of

112 Islamophobia, terrorism, and the media

drummer Lee Rigby. Research suggests that following Woolwich, the print newspaper coverage of Muslim communities in the immediate aftermath provided a lens by which the terms 'Islam' and 'Muslims' were used alongside 'terrorism' in an overtly negative manner (Awan and Rahman 2016). Sadly, we believe this is a trend within the British Press that has often negatively termed Muslims as 'fanatics', 'extremists', and indeed 'terrorists'. We argue by using the comparison of Mohammed Saleem, who was also a victim of a terrorist attack, that a more balanced viewpoint of reporting terrorism is required otherwise we risk as a society stoking up further anti-Muslim prejudice and also exacerbating the potential for unfair treatment of Muslim communities.

Key questions

- Do you think the media has impacted upon the way Muslims are viewed?
- Why is the case of Mohammed Saleem and Woolwich so significant?
- What is the role of the media in reporting Islamophobic hate crime attacks?
- Is the media biased against Muslims?
- What should IPSO do to regulate the media?

Further reading

- Davis, A. 2003. Whither mass media and power? Evidence for a critical elite theory. *Media, Culture Society*, 25(5): 669–690.
- Edward, S. 1981. *Covering Islam*. London: Routledge.
- Gross, B., Kerry, M., and Threadgold, T. 2007. *Broadcast News Coverage of Asylum April to October 2006: Caught Between Human Rights and Public Safety*. Cardiff: Cardiff School of Journalism, Media and Cultural Studies, Cardiff University.
- Jewkes, Y. 2011. *Media and Crime*, Revised 2nd Edition. Sage.

References

Allen, C. 2012. *A Review of the Evidence Relating to the Representation of Muslims and Islam in the British Media*. Birmingham: University of Birmingham, Institute of Applied Social Studies, School of Social Policy.

Akbarzedah, S. and Smith, B. 2005. *The Representation of Islam and Muslims in the Media*. Monash University: School of Political and Social Inquiry.

Awan, I. and Rahman, M. 2016. A content analysis of British Muslims in UK newspapers. *Journal of Muslim Minority Affairs*, 36(1): 16–31.

Baker, P., Costas, G., and McEnery, T. 2013. *Discourse Analysis and Media Attitudes: The Representation of Islam in the British Press*. Cambridge: Cambridge University Press.

Bozarth, M. 2005. Terrorism and the media: Amplifying the terrorist's impact: The media as unwilling allies to the terrorists agenda. Available at: www.ferndalek12.org/fhs/teachers/lemmon/Terrorism-Media__2_.pdf

Burton Mail. 2013. The British people will not accept this—Burton MP speaks out on Woolwich attack. *Burton Mail*. Available at: www.burtonmail.co.uk/News/The-British-peop

le-will-not-accept-this-Burton-MPspeaks-out-on-Woolwich-attack-20130523171901.
htm#ixzz2mKyrV8MS

Dixon, H. and Hall, M. 2013. Woolwich attack: As it happened May 23. *The Telegraph*. 24
May. Available at: www.telegraph.co.uk/news/uknews/terrorism-in-the-uk/10077616/
Woolwich-attack-soldier-terror-live.html

Dodd, V. 2013. Ukranian man charged with 'terrorist-related murder' of Mohammed
Saleem. *The Guardian*. 22 July. Available at: www.theguardian.com/uk-news/2013/jul/
22/ukranian-man-charged-murder-mohammed-saleem

Dominiczak, P. 2013. Tony Blair: Woolwich attack shows there is a problem 'within Islam'.
The Telegraph. 2 June. Available at: www.telegraph.co.uk/news/uknews/terrorism
-in-the-uk/10094007/Tony-Blair-Woolwich-attack-shows-there-is-a-problem-with
in-Islam.html

Martin, A., Greenhill, S., Greenwood, C., and Cooper, R. 2013. 'You and your children
will be next': Islamic fanatics wielding meat cleavers butcher and try to behead a British
soldier, taking their war on the West to a new level of horror. *The Daily Mail*. 23 May.
Available at: www.dailymail.co.uk/news/article-2329089/Woolwich-attack-Two-m
en-hack-soldier-wearing-Help-Heroes-T-shirt-death-machetes-suspected-terror-attack.
html#ixzz3LySuJOYV

Moore, K., Mason, P., and Lewis, J. 2008. The representation of British Muslims in the
National Print News Media 2000–2008. *Cardiff School of Journalism, Media and Cultural Studies*. Available at: www.channel4.com/news/media/pdfs/Cardiff%20Final%20Report.pdf

Mortimer, C. 2017. Man who posted image of Muslim woman 'ignoring Westminster terror
victims' was a Russian troll. *The Independent*. Available at: www.independent.co.uk/news/
uk/politics/man-muslim-woman-london-terror-attack-phone-russian-troll-identity-a
8052961.html

Nacos, B. 2002. *Mass-Mediated Terrorism: The Central Role of Media in Terrorism and Counter-
terrorism*. Oxford: Rowman & Littlefield.

Poole, E. 2002. *Reporting Islam: Media Representations of British Muslims*. London: I. B. Tauris.
Also see Poole, E. (2006) The effects of September 11 and the War in Iraq on British
newspaper coverage. In: E. Poole and J. Richardson (eds) *Muslims and the News Media*.
London & New York: I. B. Tauris, pp. 89–102.

Said, E. 1981. *Covering Islam*. London: Routledge.

Sengupta, K., Peachey, P., Manning, S., and Morris, N. 2013. 'Sickening, deluded and
unforgivable': Horrific attack brings terror to London's streets. *The Independent*. 23 May.
Available at: www.independent.co.uk/news/uk/crime/sickening-deluded-and-unforgiva
ble-horrific-attack-brings-terror-to-london-s-streets-8627647.html

The Telegraph. 2013. Woolwich shows that Muslim leaders have learned how to respond to
terrorism. *The Telegraph*. Available at: http://blogs.telegraph.co.uk/news/cristinaodone/
100218622/woolwichshows-that-muslim-leaders-have-learned-how-to-resp
ond-to-terrorism

The Washington Post. 2013. The Unabomber Trial: The Manifesto 1995. *The Washington
Post*. Available at: www.washingtonpost.com/wp-srv/national/longterm/unabomber/ma
nifesto.text.htm [accessed: 14 November 2013].

Watson, R. 2013. Cameron urges Muslim leaders to confront extremism after Woolwich
attack. *The Times*. 23 May. Available at: www.thetimes.co.uk/article/cameron-urges-m
uslim-leaders-to-confront-extremism-after-woolwich-attack-87z6m5zfnnr

Whitehead, T. 2013. Ukranian white supremacist avoids life sentence over murder and
mosque bombings. *The Telegraph*. 25 October. Available at: www.telegraph.co.uk/news/
uknews/terrorism-in-the-uk/10405268/Ukranian-white-supremacist-avoids-life-
sentence-over-murder-and-mosque-bombings.html

9

IMPACTS OF ISLAMOPHOBIC HATE CRIME

Introduction

Similar to other forms of hate crime, the impact of Islamophobia is felt at a variety of levels: by the direct victim, the wider community to which the victim belongs, and society as a whole (Iganski 2001). As such, the following discussion operates on three broad levels: individual, community, and societal impacts.

Individual impacts

Generally speaking, being a victim of any kind of crime can have devastating and long-term impacts upon individuals including emotional, psychological, behavioural, physical, and financial effects. However, victims who have been targeted on the basis of their perceived 'difference' are likely to experience a host of negative emotions that are qualitatively distinct from those experienced following victimisation; that is, not motivated by hate or fear towards the 'Other' (Craig-Henderson and Sloan 2003). The significance of hate crime is premised on the fact that verbal and physical attacks upon victims 'hurt' more than ordinary crimes as they are seen as an attack upon the victims' core identity.

Analysis of the Crime Survey for England and Wales by the Home Office demonstrated that victims of hate crime were more likely than non-hate crime victims to say that they were emotionally affected by the incident (92 per cent and 81 per cent respectively) whilst 36 per cent of hate crime victims stated they were "very much" affected compared with 13 per cent for victims of crime overall (Corcoran, Lader, and Smith 2015). The emotional impacts of hate crime can be especially severe, with 39 per cent of hate crime victims suffering a loss of confidence or feelings of vulnerability after the incident compared with 17 per cent for victims of non-hate crime. Hate crime victims were also more than "twice as likely to experience

Impacts of Islamophobic hate crime **115**

fear, difficulty sleeping, anxiety or panic attacks or depression compared with victims of overall CSEW crime" (Corcoran, Lader, and Smith 2015, p. 22).

Along similar lines, empirical studies of hate crime emphasise the more severe impact for victims of hate crime when compared to non-hate victims. Ehrlich (1992) and Garofalo (1997) compared the victimisation experiences of hate crime victims to victims of non-hate motivated offences. They found that victims of hate crimes generally suffered more traumatic effects such as anger, fear, and vulnerability following victimisation than did victims of other crimes. This is in line with the research findings of Herek et al. (1997) who examined victims' experiences in cases of homophobic hate crime in the US. They found that in some cases hate crime victims needed as many as five years to overcome the effects of their victimisation, and this time period was more than twice that necessary for victims of non-hate crimes to overcome their victimisation experience (Herek et al. 1997). In a subsequent larger study of US-based homophobic hate crime, Herek, Cogan, and Gillis (2002) found that even 'minor' expressions of hostility towards members of minority groups can be traumatic, given that minority groups are aware of the extreme violence that has been perpetrated on other members of their group. McDevitt et al. (2001) surveyed a sample of victims of hate and non-hate motivated aggravated assaults in the US city of Boston. Similarly with previous studies, McDevitt et al. (2001) found significant differences between hate and non-hate victims with respect to their psychological reactions. They found that hate crime victims were more likely to lose their jobs, suffer health problems, experience post-incident traumatic stress, and have greater difficulty in overcoming the incident.

In the context of Islamophobic hate crime, both virtual and physical world attacks upon Muslims 'hurt' more than 'normal' crimes as they are seen as an attack upon the victims' Muslim identity (Awan and Zempi 2015). From this perspective, the impact of Islamophobic hate crime may exceed that of 'normal' crime because of victims' perceived and actual vulnerability due to their affiliation to Islam. As mentioned in Chapter 2, a key feature of hate crime is that single incidents tend to be part of a long-term pattern of victimisation, a recurring and, in some cases, constant feature of one's everyday life. This suggests that Islamophobia – similar to other forms of hate crimes – is not a static problem, but instead should be seen as a dynamic social process involving context, structure, and agency (Chakraborti 2010; Bowling 1999; Kelly 1987). For Rowe (2004), the fact that this victimisation is part of the routine of the victim's daily experience makes the victimisation more, rather than less, serious. Consequently, Islamophobic hate crime can place a potentially huge emotional burden on actual and potential victims.

In some cases, Islamophobic hate crime can result in serious injury or even death. In August 2016, a 34-year-old woman was verbally abused in a Co-op supermarket in Milton Keynes before being followed to her car by the attacker. He swore at her and said: "You come here with your clown outfit on…" She was kicked in the torso, knocking her to the ground. The woman lost her unborn child as a result of the assault. Her husband was also attacked during the incident. He was hit over the head with a bag of ice and a bottle, and needed hospital treatment.

116 Impacts of Islamophobic hate crime

The attacker, David Gallacher, was later jailed for nearly four years in May 2017. Another high-profile news story includes the case of 82-year-old Mohammed Saleem, who was stabbed to death as he walked the few hundred yards from a Birmingham mosque to his home with the aid of a stick. Pavlo Lapshyn, 25-year-old Ukrainian student, pleaded guilty to the murder of Mohammed Saleem, as well as plotting to cause explosions near mosques in Walsall, Tipton, and Wolverhampton in June and July 2013. Lapshyn is now serving 40 years in prison for acts of terrorism. He was charged under terrorism laws.

In addition to potentially suffering physical injury, victims of Islamophobic hate crime can be affected emotionally. There are distinct emotional impacts associated with this victimisation including feelings of fear, insecurity, anxiety, vulnerability, isolation, and depression. Given that they are targeted because of their Muslim identity – which is often identifiable because of their Muslim appearance and/or Muslim name (or other forms of identification such as stating that the individual is Muslim) either in the virtual world or in the physical sphere – victims are unable to take comfort in the belief that what happened to them was simply random and 'could have happened to anyone'. Rather, they are forced to view this abuse as an attack on their Muslim identity and this has implications for their levels of confidence and self-esteem as well as their feelings of belonging and safety.

Using a variety of different research methods, including questionnaire surveys, individual interviews, and social psychological experiments, Paterson et al. (2018) examined the (in)direct impacts of hate crimes – how hate attacks on members of a community affect the thoughts, emotions, and behaviours of other members of that community. The project focused on hate crimes targeted against LGBT and Muslim communities. With respect to the impacts of direct hate crime victimisation on individuals, Paterson et al. (2018) found that it can:

- Alter their sense of safety making them feel more vulnerable and anxious
- Increase feelings of anger and injustice
- Lead to increased suspicion and social withdrawal
- Motivate increased community engagement through specialist groups and charities.

Furthermore, a key finding in research conducted by Awan and Zempi (2015) was that participants were multiple and repeat victims of both online and offline Islamophobic hate crimes. Rarely did participants describe Islamophobic hate crime as 'one-off'; rather there was always the sense, the fear, the expectation of another attack. Repeat incidents of cyber and/or physical world Islamophobic hate increased feelings of insecurity, vulnerability, and anxiety amongst victims (Awan and Zempi 2015). Bowling (2009) states that repeated or persistent victimisation can undermine the security of actual and potential victims, and induce fear and anxiety. The distressing nature of Islamophobic hate crime coupled with the frequency with which these acts are committed create high levels of fear amongst actual and potential victims. Participants in this study also highlighted the relationship between online and offline Islamophobic hate crime, and described living in fear because of the possibility of online threats materialising in the 'real world' (Awan and Zempi 2015). Clearly, the Internet allows people to take on a new and anonymous identity, and to bypass traditional editorial controls, to share their views with millions. Online Islamophobic hate messages can be sent anonymously or by using a false identity, making it difficult to identify the offender. The anonymity aspect in cases of online Islamophobic hate messages is extremely frightening as the perpetrator could be anyone and the online threats can escalate into the physical space.

In light of the profound negative impacts of Islamophobic hate crime, it is clear that the emotional scars can last for a long time. When another incident takes place, victims relive previous incidents of Islamophobic hate crime. As a result, some individuals might suffer from depression, eating disorders, sleep pattern disturbances including insomnia and nightmares, flashbacks, and memory lapses. The continual threat of abuse can be emotionally draining for victims who not only relive past incidents but also feel the need to be constantly on the alert. This shows that Islamophobic hate crime can result in a cumulative experience of psychological trauma and emotional burnout over time. Seen in this context, Islamophobic hate crime disrupts notions of belonging whilst maintaining the boundaries between 'us' and 'them'. This highlights the immediate effect of Islamophobic hate crime which is to undermine victims' sense of security and belonging whilst the eventual impact is to create fear about living in a particular locality and to inspire a wish to move away (Bowling 2009). In this way spaces and places are created in which 'others' are made to feel unwelcome and vulnerable to attack, and from which they may eventually be excluded (Bowling 2009). Correspondingly, an additional cost that victims of Islamophobic hate crime often experience is a change in their routines and lifestyles. In this case, the threat of both online and offline hate crimes is so 'real' that it can cause individuals to change the way that they live their lives and even take steps to become less 'visibly' Muslim.

Identity management

Victims' responses to Islamophobic hate crime may include downplaying or perhaps denying parts of their self so as to reduce the potential risk for victimisation, which may lead to the 'invisibility' of certain identities (Spalek 2008). As Perry and Alvi (2012, p. 68) observe, hate crime often results in a careful crafting of victims' self-identities so that "they are less visible, and thus less vulnerable". According to this line of argument, actual and potential victims may attempt to make themselves as 'invisible' as possible to try and reduce the potential for abuse. A decision not to veil, a decision to reduce travel by foot and public transport, and a decision to avoid visiting specific public places are all ways of trying to reduce the risk and manage the fear of Islamophobic victimisation.

Indeed, experiences of Islamophobic victimisation impact upon the way in which Muslim women and men express their 'Muslimness' particularly in relation

118 Impacts of Islamophobic hate crime

to their outward displays of faith, body presentation, and dress (Mythen, Walklate, and Khan 2009). Mythen, Walklate, and Khan (2009) found that visible and audible differences such as dress, language, and skin colour increase the risk of becoming a victim of Islamophobic hate crime. Participants in this study revealed downplaying their 'Muslimness' by modifying or removing traditional clothing (the niqab for women and the jubba for men), wearing Western clothing, speaking in English, and reducing the use of Urdu in certain public places (Mythen, Walklate, and Khan 2009). Along similar lines, Afshar (2008) argues that some Muslims have been driven to adopt Western names and pretend not to be Muslims at all. Some Muslim organisations advised their members to keep a low profile and for Muslim women to refrain from veiling in public places post-9/11 (Allen and Nielsen 2002). Similarly, after the 7/7 bombings Muslim leaders advised women to remove their veils, fearing possible reprisals against them (Braybrooke 2011). This line of evidence demonstrates that a common way of avoiding Islamophobic hate crime may be to appear less 'Muslim' and more 'Westernised'.

In this context, individuals appear to manage impressions of their Muslim identity in public spaces (and online) mainly through concealment with the aim to reduce the risk of future abuse. Zempi (2014) found that Muslim women who wear the niqab often try to become less 'visible' by taking the niqab off. The constant threat of Islamophobic hate crime had forced participants to adopt a siege mentality and keep a low profile when in public in order to reduce the potential for future attacks. Taking the niqab off seemed to be a promising strategy for helping participants to erase the perceived source of their vulnerability and as a result reduce the risk of future attacks (Zempi 2014). Similarly, Allen (2010) observes that veiled Muslim women often try to become less 'visible' and as such less vulnerable by taking the veil off. In this context, veiled Muslim women appear to manage impressions of their Muslim identity in public mainly through concealment with the aim to reduce the risk of future abuse (Ghumman and Ryan 2013).

It is important to point out that participants in Zempi's (2014) research made reference to changing patterns of social interaction, which often culminated in isolation and withdrawal. As Hindelang (2009) points out, for an experience of victimisation to occur, the prime actors – the offender and the victim – must have the occasion to intersect in time and space. By removing themselves from the public space or by reducing the time spent in public places, participants reduced the probability of Islamophobic victimisation (Zempi 2014). Accordingly, participants spoke of feeling safe by confining themselves to their home as much as possible, as this provided them with immutability from being attacked in public. Many participants explained that they would only go out if it was deemed absolutely necessary. In this case the home was understood as a retreat from the hostility of the outside world and a key source of personal sense of security (Magne 2003). However, some participants suffered from damage to their property such as windows smashing, persistent door-knocking, egg-throwing, and graffiti, and this had a cumulative effect upon themselves and their families. Attacks on property violate the security of the place where an individual is considered safest (Bowling 2009). In this regard, the physical fabric of a house provides only an illusion of defence against attacks (Bowling 2009). From this perspective, the tangible fear of being assaulted limits pivotal aspects of identity building such as visiting friends, going to university, and attending the mosque (Mythen, Walklate, and Khan 2009). The threat of violence deprives actual and potential victims of freedom of movement and engagement out of their safe spaces and places (Perry 2005).

The threat of Islamophobic hate crime had long-lasting effects for individual victims including making them afraid to leave their homes and feeling like 'social lepers' and 'social outcasts' (Zempi 2014). As a result, a common sensation cited by veiled Muslim women was that of panic attacks, worry, extreme anxiety, and depression, which was said to derive from the fear of having to endure future victimisation when in public. They were often reluctant to leave the house through fear of being attacked, particularly on the street, in parks, in shops, and on public transport. Some veiled Muslim women described feeling like 'prisoners in their own home' (Zempi 2014). Although the experience and fear of victimisation had led those participants to withdraw from wider social participation, this was seen as the 'only way' to decrease their sense of vulnerability as they felt that there was nowhere else that they could be safe from the threat of abuse. Seen in this context, negotiations of personal safety can create a sense of 'imprisonment' on the basis that they restrict veiled Muslim women's participation in society, despite decreasing exposure to Islamophobic hate crime in public. For those veiled Muslim women who are victims of domestic abuse they are likely to feel that nowhere is safe for them.

Community impacts

As discussed earlier, Islamophobic hate crime may damage victims' self-esteem, confidence, and feelings of security far more than 'normal' crimes. In this regard, it is victims' intrinsic identity that is targeted; something which is central to their sense of being and which they cannot or do not wish to change. However, the emotional, psychological, and behavioural harms associated with Islamophobic hate crime are not restricted to victims; rather, the harm extends to the wider Muslim community, locally, nationally, and globally. Correspondingly, the individual fear and vulnerability discussed earlier is accompanied by the collective fear and vulnerability of all Muslims, particularly those individuals who have a 'visible' Muslim identity.

According to Paterson et al. (2018), a key reason why Islamophobic hate crimes are likely to impact Muslim individuals more than non-hate crimes is because group members feel more emotionally connected to the victim. In all their experiments, participants reported more empathy for the hate crime victim from their community than the victim of a non-hate crime. Paterson et al. (2018) noted that hate crimes can harm entire communities because an attack reverberates through the deep emotional ties that community members are likely to feel towards one another. These emotional ties extend well beyond local and national communities, reaching out to entire global identity groups (Paterson et al. 2018).

120 Impacts of Islamophobic hate crime

Awareness of the potential for Islamophobic hate crime enhances the sense of fearfulness and insecurity of all Muslims due to their group membership. Interviews with members of targeted communities show that hate crimes against others in their communities leave them feeling angry that their group is under attack and vulnerable as they fear that they too will be targeted (Perry and Alvi 2012). Consequently, the threat of Islamophobic hate crime impacts upon notions of belonging and cohesion amongst Muslims, who are reminded of the appropriate alignment of 'us' and 'them'. This shows that Islamophobic hostility affects not only the individual victim but also the community to which victims belong. Indeed, as Perry (2001) points out, hate crimes are 'message crimes' whereby a message of hate, terror, and vulnerability is communicated to the victim's broader community. Within this framework, incidents of Islamophobic hate crime send out a terroristic message to the wider Muslim community. Specifically, the intent of hate crime offenders is to send a message to multiple audiences: the victim, who needs to be punished for his/her inappropriate performance of identity; the victim's community, who need to learn that they too are vulnerable to the same fate; and the broader community, who are reminded of the appropriate alignment of 'us' and 'them'. This emphasises the *in terrorem* effect of hate crime: intimidation of the group by the victimisation of one or a few members of that group (Weinstein 1992).

In Zempi's (2014) study, several participants explicitly acknowledged the nature of their experiences of Islamophobic victimisation as 'message crimes'. As such, the 'message' was received loud and clear. Participants were conscious of the fact that they were liable to abuse and harassment on account of their group identity as followers of Islam. Throughout interviews and focus group discussions the consensus view amongst participants was that the wider Muslim community is under attack by virtue of the fact that 'an attack on one Muslim is an attack on all' (Zempi 2014). For Muslims, this is a crucial aspect of their faith; they are one body in Islam and 'when any part of the body suffers, the whole body feels the pain'. Respectively, Islamophobic victimisation is unique in the consciousness of the wider Muslim community through notions of a worldwide, transnational Muslim community, the *ummah*, which connects Muslims in the UK with other Muslims throughout the world. In this sense Islamophobic hate crime is seen as an attack upon the fabric of the wider Muslim community.

Paterson et al. (2018, p. 2) noted that the indirect effects of hate crimes (that is, how hate attacks on members of a community affect the thoughts, emotions, and behaviours of other members of that community) can be described as a process:

- Hate crimes increase feelings of vulnerability and empathy
- Feelings of vulnerability and empathy then increase emotional reactions (anger and injustice about hate crimes, anxiety, shame)
- These emotional reactions motivate specific behavioural responses:

  ○ Anger leads to proactive behaviours and less avoidance (e.g. wanting to be more proactive within the community, for example, by joining community organisations and charities, and/or trying to raise awareness of the hate crime throughout the community, for example, by using social media)

○ Anxiety leads to avoidance and security concerns (they were more likely to avoid certain places and locations and also, they were more security conscious)

○ Shame, although not always felt strongly, is linked to avoidance, proactive behaviours, security concerns, and uniquely to retaliation-based conduct.

With respect to the impacts of hate online, Paterson et al. (2018) found that similarly to hate offline, instances of hate online were linked to emotional and behavioural responses. Specifically, viewing hate online generated feelings of anger and anxiety amongst participants, and was more likely to provoke help-seeking responses (e.g. discussing and reporting online abuse) and avoidant behaviours (e.g. ignoring the abuse, changing their profile) rather than retaliatory actions (e.g. insult them back, be more aggressive). Viewing hate materials made people angrier and more likely to engage in proactive behaviours than viewing similarly unpleasant material, which was unrelated to their community (Paterson et al. 2018).

Perry (2001) notes that hate crime can simultaneously be used for punitive purposes and to ensure subordination. Following this line of argument, the use of violence by perpetrators enhances their authority in the eyes of the communities of both the victim and the offender. As such, violence is 'empowering' for its users as physical domination, especially in the public sphere, demonstrates a corresponding 'cultural mastery' (Perry 2005). Ultimately, the perpetrator (male or female) becomes empowered and gains control through the use of violence. Accordingly, targeted violence provides a context in which the perpetrator can reassert his or her hegemonic identity, whilst at the same time, punishing the victim for the individual or collective performance of their identity (Perry and Alvi 2012). This mechanism reaffirms the boundaries between dominant and subordinate groups by reminding the victim of their 'proper' place. This discussion emphasises the significance of the victim's group identity, whereby manifestations of Islamophobia are designed to spread fear and reinforce the hegemonic identity of the perpetrator and the boundaries between 'us' and 'them'.

Hindelang (2009) observes that the ability of individuals to isolate themselves from people with offender characteristics affects the probability of victimisation. Mythen, Walklate, and Khan (2009) found that the fear of abuse restricted Muslims' freedom of movement in public, use of community facilities, and visits to 'hostile' areas. Similarly, Tarlo (2007) highlights the reluctance of both hijab and niqab wearers to visit areas in London where they will be in a sartorial minority. Whilst looking at women who have experienced homophobia or transphobia in London, Paterson et al. (2018) found that victims felt safer in their local area than they did in other public spaces. According to Perry and Alvi (2012), Islamophobic victimisation also limits the desire of actual and potential victims to interact with others, to the extent that they may choose to limit interactions with those 'like'

122 Impacts of Islamophobic hate crime

their perpetrators. This line of argument indicates that the fear of Islamophobic victimisation limits both the movements and social interactions of 'visible' Muslims, potentially resulting in withdrawal, isolation, and ultimately segregation.

This discussion demonstrates how the enactment of physical geographical boundaries impacts upon 'emotional geographies' in relation to the way in which participants perceived the spaces and places inside and outside their 'comfort zones' (Hopkins 2007). Rather than risk the threat of being attacked many actual and potential victims choose to retreat to their 'own' communities and as a result become reclusive. Unarguably, this limits the behavioural options and life choices of individuals as it determines the area of residence, their vocational pursuits and leisure activities, their mode of transport, and even their access to educational opportunities. Ultimately, this reality has resulted in segregation in housing, transportation, education, employment, and leisure activities. However, as Perry and Alvi (2012) point out, this is not a voluntary choice; rather, it is the 'safe' choice. They explain that the potential for future victimisation creates social and geographical, yet 'invisible', boundaries across which members of the Muslim community are not 'welcome' to step (Perry and Alvi 2012). From this perspective, Islamophobic victimisation acts as a form of emotional terrorism on the basis that it segregates and isolates Muslims, particularly in terms of restricting their freedom of movement in the public sphere and changing their patterns of social interaction. Ultimately, the fear of attack reinforces these emotional and geographical boundaries whilst promoting patterns of segregation between 'us' and 'them'.

Societal impacts

As indicated earlier, Islamophobic hate crimes can have a greater emotional impact on the victim than comparable non-hate crimes, and can cause increased levels of fear and anxiety that can also permeate through wider communities. As Paterson et al. (2018) point out, hate crimes are particularly dangerous to society not only because of the significant trauma that they cause to victims but also because they are likely to cause vicarious harms to entire communities. According to Alexander (2017), it is crucial that we recognise that Islamophobia is not simply 'a Muslim problem' but that it implicates and affects everyone. Islamophobia divides the world into two homogeneous groupings, 'us' and 'them', whist failing to recognise that the wider Muslim community comprises a number of fluid, overlapping, and internally diverse national, racial, and ethnic communities, which cut across any simple majority/minority division. The impacts of Islamophobic hate crime extend to society as a whole by promoting a separation between 'us' and 'them' (Zempi and Chakraborti 2015). In other words, the separation of communities based on this dichotomy promotes a situation where both Muslims and non-Muslims live in fear of each other. This separation prevents 'us' and 'them' from interacting with each other and increases fear of engagement on both sides. The individual and societal impacts of Islamophobic hate crime create disruption, fear, hostility, suspicion, and isolation for both 'us' and 'them'.

Impacts of Islamophobic hate crime **123**

As such, Islamophobic hate crime promotes the notion of 'parallel lives' and self-enclosed communities. The separation between 'us' and 'them' means that Muslims and non-Muslims have little or no experience of each other's daily existence (Zempi and Chakraborti 2015). In addition, this separation infers that there is a lack of shared experiences, with little opportunity for the emergence of shared values.

Islamophobic hate crime also affects British society on the basis that it undermines the quintessential 'British' qualities of tolerance and multiculturalism that this country is proud of. The Runnymede Trust (1997) report noted a particularly dramatic aspect of social exclusion, the vulnerability of Muslims to physical violence and harassment. They argued that whatever the motivations of racist attackers may be, the consequence of this kind of violence for Muslims is that they are unable to play a full part in mainstream society. Viewed from this perspective, Islamophobic hate crime can have a broad negative impact upon British society that does not apply with other types of conventional crime on the premise that it undermines the multicultural fabric of society (Iganski 2001).

Key questions

- What are the impacts of Islamophobic hate crimes on individual victims?
- What are the impacts of Islamophobic hate crimes on the Muslim community?
- What are the impacts of Islamophobic hate crimes on society at large?

Further reading

- Awan, I. and Zempi, I. 2015. I will blow your face off. *Virtual and Physical World Anti-Muslim Hate Crime. British Journal of Criminology.* DOI: doi:10.1093/bjc/azv122.
- Herek, G., Cogan, J., and Gillis, R. 2002. Victim experiences in hate crimes based on sexual orientation. *Journal of Social Issues*, 58(2): 319–339.
- Iganski, P. 2001. Hate crimes hurt more. *American Behavioural Scientist*, 45(4): 626–638.
- Mythen, G., Walklate, S., and Khan, F., 2009. "I'm a Muslim, but I'm not a terrorist": Victimisation, risky identities and the performance of safety. *British Journal of Criminology*, 49(6): 736–754.

References

Afshar, H. 2008. Can I see your hair? Choice, agency and attitudes: The dilemma of faith and feminism for Muslim women who cover. *Ethnic and Racial Studies*, 31(2): 411–427.

Allen, C. 2010. *Islamophobia.* Surrey: Ashgate.

Allen, C. and Nielsen, J. 2002. *Summary Report on Islamophobia in the EU after 11 September 2001.* Vienna: European Monitoring Centre on Racism and Xenophobia.

Alexander, C. 2017. Raceing Islamophobia. In: Runnymede Trust (ed.) *Islamophobia: Still a Challenge For Us All.* London: Runnymede Trust, pp. 13–16.

Awan, I. and Zempi, I. 2015. I will blow your face off. *Virtual and Physical World Anti-Muslim Hate Crime. British Journal of Criminology.* DOI: doi:10.1093/bjc/azv122.

Bowling, B. 1999. *Violent Racism: Victimization, Policing and Social Contexts.* Oxford: Oxford University Press.

124 Impacts of Islamophobic hate crime

Bowling, B. 2009. Violent racism: Victimisation, policing and social context. In: B. Williams and H. Goodman-Chong (eds) *Victims and Victimisation: A Reader*. Maidenhead: Open University Press.

Braybrooke, M. 2011. Respect in a plural society. In: T. Gabriel and R. Hannan (eds) *Islam and the Veil*. London: Continuum.

Chakraborti, N. 2010. Crimes against the 'Other': Conceptual, operational and empirical challenges for hate studies. *Journal of Hate Studies*, 8(1): 9–28.

Corcoran, H., Lader, D., and Smith, K. 2015. *Hate Crime, England and Wales, 2014/2015*. London: Home Office.

Craig-Henderson, K. and Sloan, L. R. 2003. After the hate: Helping psychologists help victims of racist hate crime. *Clinical Psychology: Science and Practice*, 10(4): 481–490.

Ehrlich, H. J. 1992. The ecology of anti-gay violence. In: G. M. Herek and K. T. Berrill (eds) *Hate Crimes: Confronting Violence Against Lesbians and Gay Men*. London: Sage.

Garofalo, J. 1997. Hate crime victimisation in the United States. In: R. C. Davis, A. J. Lurigio, and W. G. Skogan (eds) *Victims of Crime*. Thousand Oaks, CA: Sage Publications.

Ghumman, S. and Ryan, A. M. 2013. Not welcome here: Discrimination towards women who wear the Muslim headscarf. *Human Relations*, 66(5): 671–698.

Herek, G., Cogan, J., and Gillis, R. 2002. Victim experiences in hate crimes based on sexual orientation. *Journal of Social Issues*, 58(2): 319–339.

Herek, G., Gillis, J. R., Cogan, J. C., and Glunt, E. K. 1997. Hate crime victimisation among lesbian, gay, and bisexual adults: Prevalence, psychological correlates, and methodological issues. *Journal of Interpersonal Violence*, 12(2): 195–215.

Hindelang, M. 2009. Towards a theory of personal criminal victimisation. In: B. Williams and H. Goodman-Chong (eds) *Victims and Victimisation: A Reader*. Maidenhead: Open University Press.

Hopkins, P. 2007. Young Muslim men's experiences of local landscapes after 11th September 2001. In: C. Atkinson, P. Hopkins, and M. Kwan (eds) *Geographies of Muslim Identities: Diaspora, Gender and Belonging*. Aldershot: Ashgate.

Iganski, P. 2001. Hate crimes hurt more. *American Behavioural Scientist*, 45(4): 626–638.

Kelly, L. 1987. The continuum of sexual violence. In: J. Hanmer and M. Maynard (eds) *Women, Violence and Social Control*. London: Macmillan.

Magne, S. 2003. *Multi-Ethnic Devon: A Rural Handbook – The Report of the Devon and Exeter Racial Equality Council's Rural Outreach Project*. Devon: Devon and Exeter Racial Equality Council.

McDevitt, J., Balboni, J., Garcia, L., and Gu, J. 2001. Consequences for victims: A comparison of bias-and non-bias-motivated assaults. In P. Gerstenfeld and D. R. Grant (eds) *Crimes of Hate: Selected Readings*. London: Sage.

Mythen, G., Walklate, S., and Khan, F., 2009. "I'm a Muslim, but I'm not a terrorist": Victimisation, risky identities and the performance of safety. *British Journal of Criminology*, 49(6): 736–754.

Paterson, J., WaltersM. A., Brown, R., and Fearn, H. 2018. *The Sussex Hate Crime Project*. Sussex: University of Sussex.

Perry, B. 2001. *In the Name of Hate: Understanding Hate Crimes*. London: Routledge.

Perry, B. 2005. A crime by any other name: The semantics of hate. *Journal of Hate Studies*, 4 (1): 121–137.

Perry, B. and Alvi, S. 2012. 'We are all vulnerable': The in terrorem effects of hate crimes. *International Review of Victimology*, 18(1): 57–71.

Rowe, M. 2004. *Policing, Race and Racism*. Cullompton: Willan Publishing.

Runnymede Trust. 1997. *Islamophobia: A Challenge for us All*. London: Runnymede Trust.

Spalek, B. 2008. *Communities, Identities and Crime*. Bristol: Polity Press.

Tarlo, E. 2007. Hijab in London: Metamorphosis, resonance and effects. *Journal of Material Culture*, 12(2): 131–156.

Weinstein, J. 1992. First amendment challenges to hate crime legislation: Where's the speech? *Criminal Justice Ethics*, 11(2): 6–20.

Zempi, I. 2014. *Uncovering Islamophobia: The Victimisation of Veiled Muslim Women*. Leicester: University of Leicester.

Zempi, I. and Chakraborti, N. 2015. "They make us feel like we're a virus": The impact of Islamophobic victimisation upon veiled Muslim women. *International Journal for Crime, Justice and Social Democracy*, 4(3): 44–56.

10

ISLAMOPHOBIC HATE CRIME IN EUROPE

Introduction

Evidence indicates that Islamophobic hate crime in Europe is on the rise. Drawing on the European Union Minorities and Discrimination Survey reports (FRA 2009; 2017) and the European Islamophobia Report Project (Bayrakli and Hafez 2017), this chapter examines the nature and extent of Islamophobic hate crime in Europe. The evidence shows that Muslims living in Europe face victimisation and discrimination in a broad range of settings and particularly when looking for work, at work, and when trying to access public or private services (FRA 2017). However, all the available data and statistics about Islamophobic hate crime in Europe show only the tip of the iceberg. The vast majority of States in Europe do not record hate crime or Islamophobic incidents as a separate category of hate crime.

European Union Minorities and Discrimination Survey

Muslims make up roughly five per cent of the population in Europe (Pew Research Centre 2017). Specifically, the largest numbers of Muslims live in France and Germany (with 5.7 million and 5 million, respectively) (Pew Research Centre 2017).

Evidence shows that Muslims living in Europe face victimisation and discrimination in a broad range of settings and particularly when looking for work, at work, and when trying to access public or private services (FRA 2017). The report entitled 'Second European Union Minorities and Discrimination Survey (EU-MIDIS II) Muslims – Selected findings' (FRA 2017) examined how characteristics – such as an individual's first and last name, skin colour, and the wearing of visible religious symbols may trigger discriminatory treatment and harassment. In addition to discrimination, the report also explored issues ranging from citizenship, trust, and tolerance, through harassment, violence, hate crime, police stops based on an individual's ethnic background to rights awareness. The report drew on the experiences of more than 10,500 first- and second-generation Muslim immigrants living in 15 EU Member States, namely Austria, Belgium, Cyprus, Denmark, Finland, France, Germany, Greece, Italy, Malta, the Netherlands, Slovenia, Spain, Sweden, and the UK (FRA 2017). The survey asked respondents if they felt discriminated against in the following domains and activities:

- when looking for work;
- at work;
- in education or when in contact with school personnel of children;
- in access to healthcare;
- housing;
- when using public or private services (such as public transport, administrative offices, when entering a night club, restaurant or hotel, and when being in or entering a shop).

Before examining the findings in more detail, it is important to point out that this report (FRA 2017) is part of FRA's second European Union Minorities and Discrimination Survey of around 26,000 migrants and ethnic minorities in 28 EU Member States. As such, FRA (2017) builds on the first European Union Minorities and Discrimination Survey (FRA 2009), which was conducted in 2008 and asked about experiences of discrimination, harassment, police stops, and rights awareness as well as markers of integration such as a sense of belonging and trust in public institutions. The first European Union Minorities and Discrimination Survey was a timely report, which provided a unique insight into the experiences and perceptions of the EU's Muslim population in 2008. The results from FRA's first European Union Minorities and Discrimination Survey (EU-MIDIS I) revealed barriers to integration, such as high levels of discrimination and racist victimisation, particularly affecting young people, as well as low levels of rights awareness and knowledge of, or trust in, complaints mechanisms and law enforcement (FRA 2009). The results from FRA's (2017) second European Union Minorities and Discrimination Survey showed little progress in terms of discrimination and hate crime. As outlined below, the findings showed that Islamophobic hate crime manifested in physical violence and harassment persists whilst discrimination against Muslims remains high, especially when looking for work. Specifically, key findings from FRA's (2017) second European Union Minorities and Discrimination Survey (EU-MIDIS II) include:

- Four out of ten respondents (39 per cent) reported being discriminated against in the five years before the survey because of their ethnic or immigrant background – including skin colour, ethnic origin or immigrant background, and religion or religious belief – in one or more areas of their daily lives, and one in four (25 per cent) experienced this in the 12 months preceding the survey.

Discrimination was a recurring experience, with those who felt discriminated against reporting that this happened, on average, at least five times a year.

- Nearly one in five respondents (17 per cent) reported experiencing religious discrimination in the five years before the survey – whether when looking for work or at work, in access to housing, and when in contact with school authorities as parents or guardians. Specifically, 19 per cent of Muslim women and 16 per cent of Muslim men felt discriminated against on this ground.
- Respondents' first or last names, their skin colour, and/or physical appearance triggered discrimination in all areas of life but especially when looking for work or housing. More than half of Muslim respondents (53 per cent) who looked for housing reported being discriminated against because of their first or last names, and slightly less than half (44 per cent) of those who looked for work.
- Clothing was a key factor for Muslim women with respect to experiencing discrimination in employment and healthcare. For example, 35 per cent of Muslim women – compared with 4 per cent of men – cited the way they dress as the main reason for discrimination when looking for work and 22 per cent of Muslim women cited their clothing as triggering discrimination when at work, compared with 7 per cent of Muslim men.
- Around 12 per cent of respondents who were at work in the five years preceding the survey were not allowed to take time off for an important religious holiday, service, or ceremony, and 9 per cent were prevented from expressing or carrying out religious practices and customs, such as praying or wearing a headscarf or turban.
- Only 12 per cent of respondents reported their experiences of discrimination to any relevant authority. Respondents who did report discrimination incidents mostly addressed their employer (39 per cent), followed by the police (17 per cent), and trade unions (16 per cent). Only 4 per cent of all respondents who reported an incident filed a complaint or reported the incident to an equality body, which could be explained by the very low awareness level amongst respondents about the existence of equality bodies.
- Over one quarter (27 per cent) of respondents reported experiencing harassment because of their ethnic or immigrant background in the 12 months before the survey, and 45 per cent of those individuals experienced six or more incidents during the same period. Two per cent of respondents reported having been physically assaulted in that period.
- Just under one tenth of respondents (9 per cent) reported harassment to any relevant authority. Less than a quarter of respondents (23 per cent) reported physical attacks to the police or other organisation. The main reason respondents gave for not reporting incidents was that nothing would change or happen as a result of reporting (47 per cent). The majority of respondents (81 per cent) who reported a physical assault to the police were dissatisfied with the police's handling of the matter while only 13 per cent said they were satisfied.

- Respondents who felt discriminated against and/or experienced harassment or violence indicated lower levels of trust in the legal system and the police, as well as a lower level of attachment to their country of residence.

European Islamophobia Report Project

In addition to FRA's European Union Minorities and Discrimination Surveys (FRA 2009; 2017), another important piece of research is the European Islamophobia Report Project, which analyses the trends and developments in Islamophobic hate crime yearly, in almost all States in Europe from Russia to Portugal, and Malta to Norway. Although it is not possible to discuss Islamophobic hate crime in every country cited in the European Islamophobia Report Project (Bayrakli and Hafez 2017), a snapshot of the nature and extent of Islamophobic hate crime is provided in the following with regards to some of the countries mentioned in this report.

Austria (Hafez 2017)

It is argued that 72 cases of Islamophobic incidents were reported to the Antidiscrimination Office Styria whilst 28 cases of Islamophobic discrimination were reported to the Initiative for a Discrimination-Free Education, an NGO based in Vienna. Hafez (2017) documented 143 Islamophobic cases, the majority of them occurring in the institutional field (30 per cent), followed by media (23 per cent), and education (20 per cent). Islamophobic hate crimes in Austria also included acts of vandalism (specifically graffiti) which were spotted on the walls of a mosque, a Turkish cultural association, and the University of Vienna, stating 'Islam out', 'Muslims leave!', and 'F*** Islam', accordingly. Following the introduction of the veil ban in Austria, passersby on the street have felt justified in making veiled Muslim women aware of the ban by verbally and/or physically attacking them.

Belgium (Easat-Daas 2017)

In the month following the terror attacks in Brussels, 36 Islamophobic incidents were recorded by the Collective against Islamophobia in Belgium (CCIB). Manifestations of Islamophobia in Belgium include violent attacks, a growth in Islamophobic hate speech, and numerous State-led policies and legislative measures which sought to regulate the practice of Islam in Belgium (namely the ban on ritual slaughter including halal slaughter) in Wallonia and Flanders, and the proposed State takeover of the Grand Mosque of Brussels. It is also argued that Islamophobia in Belgium has a distinctly gendered nature. An example of this includes the European Court of Justice preliminary judgments on the permissibility of dismissing women who wear the hijab in employment issued in March 2017.

France (Louati 2017)

It is argued that in France, laws are becoming ever more repressive, particularly in terms of targeting public visibility of the Muslim faith on the basis of fighting 'radical Islam'. Censorship and political repression are becoming ever more normalised as manifestations of Islamophobia in France. The 2015 and 2016 terrorist attacks have led to a permanent state of emergency, which has turned France into a country where the rule of law is under serious threat. It is estimated that 19 Muslim places of worship have been closed by the government, 749 individuals were placed under house arrest, over 4,500 police raids were conducted, and 25,000 individuals have been placed under government surveillance. The backlash against Muslims by the French State – including house raids, house arrests, shutting down of Muslim places of worship, surveillance, criminalisation of activists, attacks against civil liberties – has further polarised French society. The passing of the state of emergency into the common law – hence rendering permanent its exceptional powers – has allegedly contributed to rendering France a 'Police State'.

Germany (Younes 2017)

The police recently included Islamophobia as a subcategory of 'hate crimes' in the official police statistics of 'politically motivated criminal acts'. The first statistics, which were published in 2017 showed that there were 71 attacks on mosques and 908 crimes against German Muslims (ranging from verbal to physical attacks and murder attempts). Moreover, official statistics showed that there were 1,413 attacks on refugees in the first 273 days of 2017 (Younes 2017). An NGO in Germany, DITIB, listed 101 attacks on mosques in Germany for 2017.

Norway (Døving 2017)

In 2013, the Oslo Hate Crimes unit was established in Norway; it records crimes according to the categories 'religion', 'ethnicity', and 'gender'. It is argued that the Oslo Hate Crimes unit have prosecuted and successfully led cases involving hate crimes against Muslims to conviction. Norway has a coalition government consisting of the liberal Conservative Party (Høyre) and the right-wing populist Progress Party (Fremskrittspartiet). The Progress Party has been using anti-Muslim and anti-immigration rhetoric and arguing for such policy to be implemented; however, such rhetoric incites Islamophobic sentiments in the population. In 2017, a public survey on Islamophobia in Norway found that between one fifth and one third of respondents scored high on negative attitudes towards Muslims. Specifically, the survey measured attitudes based on three dimensions: a cognitive dimension (prejudices), an affective dimension (feelings such as sympathy and antipathy), and one that measures degree of social distance (friends or neighbours). The findings showed that 34.1 per cent of respondents displayed marked prejudices towards Muslims whilst 48 per cent of respondents agreed with the statement 'Muslims largely have themselves to blame for the increase in anti-Muslim harassment'; 42 per cent agreed with the statement 'Muslims do not want to integrate into Norwegian society'; 39 per cent agreed with the statement 'Muslims pose a threat to Norwegian culture'; and 31 per cent agreed with the statement 'Muslims want to take over Europe'. Also, 27.8 per cent of respondents stated that they disliked Muslims and 19.6 per cent would dislike having Muslims as neighbours or in their circle of friends. Islamophobic attitudes were more prevalent amongst men than amongst women, older individuals, and those with lower levels of education.

Poland (Piela and Łukjanowicz 2017)

According to statistics released by the National Prosecutor's Office, Muslims were the most targeted religious group; they represented 20 per cent of all hate crime cases in Poland in 2017. According to the Ministry of Interior statistics, between January and October 2017, there were 664 hate crime proceedings regarding attacks against Muslims, and 193 (29 per cent) of those resulted in an indictment. Third-sector activists agree that these numbers are steadily escalating. Indeed, in 2015 there were three times as many incidents as in 2014. In the Polish workplace, visible Muslim symbols may trigger Islamophobic discrimination. Muslims working in food outlet workers, for example kebab shop employees, are at high risk of attacks. Although racism and Islamophobia are on the rise across Europe, Poland is an example of a country where racism and Islamophobia are not just ignored but actively fuelled by the government, state institutions, state-controlled media, and the extreme fringes within the Catholic Church. The Church in Poland plays an important role in the Polish socio-political scene. Under the ruling party (Law and Justice Party), the government promotes anti-Muslim and anti-refugee attitudes by refusing to accept refugees from Muslim countries. It is argued that these attitudes translate into a fast-growing number of hate crime incidents, including physical and verbal abuse as well as criminal damage.

Sweden (Gardell and Muftee 2017)

It is argued that there were 6,415 hate crimes reported to the police in Sweden in 2016; the majority of these (4,609) were classified as hate crimes with xenophobic/racist motives (72 per cent) and 439 hate crimes (7 per cent) with Islamophobic motives. Drawing on the Swedish Crime Survey on self-reported victims of crime and an analysis of police reports with identifiable hate crime motives, the Hate Crime Report by the Swedish National Council for Crime Prevention published in 2017 found that 145,000 individuals had been exposed to 225,000 hate crimes with racist or xenophobic motives, and 47,000 individuals had been exposed to 81,000 hate crimes with anti-religious motives, including Islamophobic motives; however, only 17 per cent of hate crimes with racist/xenophobic motives were reported to the police. A report by Equality Ombudsman on the experiences of Islamophobia amongst real and perceived Muslims found that out of 217 cases of

132 Islamophobic hate crime in Europe

discrimination reported to them, 64 cases involved discrimination in the labour market; specifically, about 50 per cent of these cases involved discrimination during the recruitment whilst other cases involved cases around harassment by colleagues. It is also argued that applicants with Muslim-sounding names have fewer chances of being called for a job interview compared to applicants with 'Swedish' names. Also, Muslim women who wear the hijab are more likely to experience discrimination in the labour market. This has led Muslims to take measures such as changing their names or taking the hijab off in order to be viewed as less Muslim and thus avoid discrimination.

Netherlands (Yıldırım 2017)

It is argued that 364 incidents of discrimination against Muslims were reported in the Netherlands in 2016 according to Verwey Jonker Institute and Anne Frank Foundation. In 2015, the number of incidents of Muslim discrimination was 466, a tripling of the number of incidents compared to 2014 (142 incidents). It is also argued that Islamophobia the Netherlands is evident in politics but also in other areas such as the media, the judiciary, education, and the labour market. In 2016, MIND (Internet complaint line) received 918 complaints, which is an increase of 41 per cent compared to the year before. The Monitoring Muslim Discrimination project has also reported an increase in Islamophobia.

Key questions

- What patterns can you identify in terms of Islamophobic hate crimes in European States?
- What are Muslims' experiences of hate crime and/or discrimination when looking for work or at work in European States?
- What are Muslims' experiences of hate crime and/or discrimination when accessing services in European States?

Further reading

- Bayrakli, E. and Hafez, F. (2017) (eds) *European Islamophobia Report*. Istanbul: SETA.
- FRA (European Union Agency for Fundamental Rights). 2009. *European Union Minorities and Discrimination Survey: Muslims, Data in Focus Report*. Luxembourg: Publications Office.
- FRA (European Union Agency for Fundamental Rights). 2018. *Second European Union Minorities and Discrimination Survey (EU-MIDIS II) Muslims – Selected Findings*. Luxembourg: Publications Office.

References

Bayrakli, E. and Hafez, F. (eds) 2017. *European Islamophobia Report*. Istanbul: SETA.
Døving, C. A. 2017. Norway. In: E. Bayrakli and F. Hafez (eds) *European Islamophobia Report*. Istanbul: SETA.

Easat-Daas, A. 2017. Belgium. In: E. Bayrakli and F. Hafez (eds) *European Islamophobia Report*. Istanbul: SETA.

FRA (European Union Agency for Fundamental Rights). 2009. *European Union Minorities and Discrimination Survey: Muslims, Data in Focus Report*. Luxembourg: Publications Office.

FRA (European Union Agency for Fundamental Rights). 2017. *Second European Union Minorities and Discrimination Survey (EU-MIDIS II) Muslims – Selected Findings*. Luxembourg: Publications Office.

Gardell, M. and Muftee, M. 2017. Sweden. In: E. Bayrakli and F. Hafez (eds) *European Report on Islamophobia*. Istanbul: SETA.

Hafez, F. 2017. Austria. In: E. Bayrakli and F. Hafez (eds) *European Islamophobia Report*. Istanbul: SETA.

Louati, Y. 2017. France. In: E. Bayrakli and F. Hafez (eds) *European Islamophobia Report*. Istanbul: SETA.

Pew Research Centre. 2017. 5 facts about the Muslim population in Europe. Available at: www.pewresearch.org/fact-tank/2017/11/29/5-facts-about-the-muslim-population-i n-europe/

Piela, A., and Łukjanowicz, A. 2017. Poland. In: E. Bayrakli and F. Hafez (eds) *European Islamophobia Report*. Istanbul: SETA.

Yıldırım, L. 2017. Netherlands. In: E. Bayrakli and F. Hafez (eds) *European Islamophobia Report*. Istanbul: SETA.

Younes, A-E. 2017. Germany. In: E. Bayrakli and F. Hafez (eds) *European Islamophobia Report*. Istanbul: SETA.

11

CONCLUSION

Introduction

This chapter draws together the themes and concepts that are developed and interwoven in the previous chapters. It then takes a forward look at what may develop in the areas of Islamophobic hate crime studies, future legislation, trends and strategies, and developments on tackling Islamophobic hate crime. It also draws upon revision checklists, guidance, essay writing, and getting the most out of lectures and seminars. As social scientists we are aware that human societies are characterised by diversity yet some minority groups have radically different experiences of offences that are motivated by prejudice and hate. It is also the case that criminal justice responses tackling crimes of prejudice sometimes fail to meet their stated outcomes and, in some cases, worsen the experiences of victims. The nature of prejudice, such as Islamophobia and hate crimes, legislative and policy responses to such behaviours, is important when assessing the impact of the intersectionality that exists between social divisions within the UK (and beyond).

Islamophobia in a global context, particularly in relation to the US election and Donald Trump, as well as the recent Muslim travel ban in the US outlines the international dynamics of Islamophobic hate crime, which becomes highly pertinent in a globalised world. Traditionally, the view that Islamophobic hate crimes only target those people who are Muslim has changed in recent times. Increasingly, Islamophobia through forms of racialisation has led to 'Muslim-looking' individuals also being the victims of this type of hate crime. Therefore, anyone who may have a similar disposition to a Muslim, i.e. either through ethnicity, appearance, or race, is more likely to be a target for Islamophobic hate crimes. This may include people from a Middle Eastern or South Asian heritage. According to Parvaresh (2014, p. 1313): "...not only have Middle Eastern Muslims been targeted, but so also have been non-Arabs, non-South Asian Muslims, and non-Muslim Arabs and South

Asians, leading all three groups to be racialized into one." In such a climate, political statements and rhetoric can also have a detrimental effect on victims of Islamophobia. This is considered in the following section in response to the recent statements made by the President of the US (at the time of writing) Donald Trump.

Donald Trump and the Muslim travel ban

In 2016, Donald Trump was elected the President of the US and one of his early pledges was the reduction of Islamist extremists travelling to the US. Trump went a step further and proposed a total and complete shutdown of Muslims entering the US and during his 2016 presidential campaign he argued that a database of all Muslims in America was required. In practice, Trump planned to issue a worldwide ban, which impacted nationals coming to the US from Iran, Libya, Somalia, Syria, and Yemen. Trump's announcements came with a wide backlash on the basis of discrimination and a breach of international law and freedom of movement. Despite those concerns, the US Supreme Court has allowed Trump's travel ban to come into full effect. Trump's ban also lists Syria, a country where refugees wanting to come to the US had originally also been banned indefinitely. The revised order, however, now means the indefinite ban on Syrian refugees has been lifted. The court ruling stated that:

> In practical terms, this means that [the executive order] may not be enforced against foreign nationals who have a credible claim of a bona fide relationship with a person or entity in the United States…. All other foreign nationals are subject to the provisions of [the executive order].
>
> *(BBC News 2017)*

According to Donald Trump, the countries listed in the travel ban had a significant terrorist presence and therefore were viewed as being problematic. Interestingly, whilst evidence for this may be true, it could equally be argued that countries such as Saudi Arabia and Egypt have a long history of terrorism, but they were not included in the list. This is significant, because it reveals how Islamophobia has become politicised and mainstream. Following the travel ban that targeted a number of Muslim countries, Donald Trump took to social media to endorse and retweet the far-right organisation Britain First.

The retweeting of far-right group Britain First by the US President

Britain First is a far-right national group that promotes anti-Muslim hostility and has incited racial and religious hatred. The group has been led until recently by Jayda Fransen and Paul Golding. In fact, the group's main ethos has been related to British patriarchy and the role of being British. The group's credentials are seriously undermined by the recent convictions of its two leaders and it continues to be the

136 Conclusion

voice for Islamophobia in Britain today. Despite the concerns raised earlier about the group, the US President Donald Trump retweeted three videos from the Britain First social media account related to alleged Islamist violence. The three videos purported to show a Muslim man destroying the Virgin Mary statute, another video showed a Muslim migrant attacking a boy on crutches, and a third video showed Muslim men pushing a boy off a building. The videos clearly were horrific and showed an anti-Muslim stance that quickly descended into anti-Muslim hostility. However, the problem was that all the videos were in fact fake. The videos had all originally been posted by Jayda Fransen, the leader of the far-right group Britain First. In fact, Britain and its social media accounts are littered with short videos depicting violence perpetuated by Muslims.

Jayda took to social media to endorse her approval of Donald Trump and sent the following message to her followers: "GOD BLESS YOU TRUMP!" and "GOD BLESS AMERICA!"

Trump's decision to become a megaphone for Islamophobia also led to world-wide condemnation from political leaders including Sadiq Khan, the Mayor of London (at the time of writing).

Furthermore, in a statement issued from Downing Street the British Prime Minister stated that: "Britain First seeks to divide communities by their use of hateful narratives that peddle lies and stoke tensions. They cause anxiety to law-abiding people ... It is wrong for the president to have done this" (Reuters 2017). Trump, however, responded to the Prime Minister's concerns by stating that Britain should be focused on tackling radical Islam. Social media companies such as Twitter and Facebook have taken action against the leaders of far-right groups such as Tommy Robinson (former leader of the English Defence League) who has had his Twitter account removed and the Britain First Facebook page has also been removed. It is important that hateful rhetoric is challenged; however, Donald Trump has only further exacerbated anti-Muslim hate.

Political rhetoric can lead to Islamophobic hostility

The Council on American-Islamic Relations has stated that Trump's anti-Muslim sentiment is a contributing factor towards Muslims feeling a level of anxiety and apprehension. The Council specifically cites how Muslim women are now deciding not to appear in public wearing the veil due to fear that they will be targeted for Islamophobic attacks (Foren 2016). The Council also noted that President Trump's failure to tackle white supremacy and Neo-Nazi violence in the US was leading to a view that Muslims in America were being failed. In a series of cases the rise of Islamophobia in America has been steadily increasing fear and perpetuating anti-Muslim hostility. For example, in 2015 Deah Barakat, 23, Yusor Abu-Salha, 21, and Razan Abu-Salha, 19, who were Muslim, were shot dead.

The 46-year-old suspect, Craig Stephen Hicks, has been charged with the murder. The father of the female victims, Mohammad Abu-Salha, stated the

Conclusion   137

following: "We have no doubt that the way they looked and the way they believed had something to do with this" (Talbot 2015).

In another case, Jeremy Joseph Christian became enraged when he saw a young Muslim woman wearing a hijab on a commuter train and began verbally abusing her and used a knife to kill two passengers who tried to intervene. Ricky John Best and Taliesin Myrddin Namkai Meche, and a third, Micah David-Cole Fletcher, was seriously wounded. Mr Christian was charged with two counts of aggravated murder but defended the killings in court. He stated that: "Death to the enemies of America. Leave this country if you hate our freedom," he said. "You call it terrorism, I call it patriotism" (Rozsa 2017).

Similarly, attacks across the world of anti-Muslims has left Muslims in fear; for example, in Quebec City, Canada, six people were killed and ten others injured after a lone gunman opened fire in January 2017. Between January and September 2017, the Council for American Muslim Relations recorded 1,656 so-called "bias incidents" and 195 hate crimes. That represented a 9 per cent increase in bias incidents and a 20 per cent rise in hate crimes compared to 2016. They stated that:

> Based on preliminary estimates, it's fair to say that 2017 is gearing to be the worst year on record for incidents of anti-Muslim bias since we began our current system of documentation.... Additionally, this year we've noted a disturbing trend of perpetrators invoking Trump to express racial and religious animosity.
>
> *(Buncombe 2017)*

The rise of Islamophobic incidents following political statements in Europe and in America also shows a revealing pattern of attacks that have been conducted against Muslims. In looking at the future landscape it is crucial that Islamophobia through a globalized lens is dealt with and tackled from the outset.

The Hate Crime Action Plan (2016–2020)

The UK Government's plan for dealing with hate crime in England and Wales is part of the Hate Crime Action Plan. The Government has made it a priority to tackle hate crime including the impact on victims, families, communities, and wider society. The Hate Crime Action Plan was published in 2016 and later updated in 2018, and was part of a four-year programme, which focused on five themes: preventing hate crime by challenging beliefs and attitudes; responding to hate crime within our communities; increasing the reporting of hate crime; improving support for victims of hate crime; and building our understanding of hate crime. Recent statistics have shown that the majority of hate crimes identified in the Crime Survey for England and Wales were race related. The greater proportion of anti-Muslim reports, according to the data, are from female victims and there is a range of perpetrator motivations for hate crime. The Government has recognised that this can manifest itself into physical and online crimes. Specifically, in relation to Islamophobia the Government has stated it will work with

138 Conclusion

the Cross-Government Working Group to Tackle Antisemitism and the Cross-Government Working Group to Tackle Anti-Muslim Hatred, because these relationships help to engage and reassure communities – in times of heightened concern – which is invaluable.

How do you report Islamophobia?

Victims of Islamophobia can often minimise their experiences, because of their everyday experience of suffering hate crimes. The normalisation of targeted harassment and violence can also lead to different types of hostility. For example, where victims suffer an Islamophobic hate crime, they are unlikely to report this to the police, due to fear of being victimised again. In instances of Islamophobic hate crimes, a number of third party reporting centres have now emerged, which provide an alternative system for victims to report incidents. The use of a third party reporting mechanism is meant to make things easier for victims of hate crime. We argue that for victims, therefore, better signage and visible posters displayed across public platforms could have a direct and indirect impact on helping dismantle some of the barriers towards reporting Islamophobic hate crimes. Indeed, in 2015, the British Prime Minister, announced that all police forces in England and Wales must record Islamophobic hate crimes as a separate category within their central recording systems. It was envisaged that this will mean that a more accurate picture could be ascertained in regards to incidents of Islamophobic hate crimes. This does therefore raise further questions about reporting and recording incidents of Islamophobia.

When considering Islamophobic hate crimes, a number of barriers also remain difficult to dismantle. For example, these include fear of being stereotyped, fear of prejudice, fear of mistreatment, and issues around mistrust and cultural barriers (Iganski 2008). One of the ways barriers can be challenged is through a better awareness and knowledge from a cultural and religious perspective of victimisation. In understanding the reporting mechanisms of hate crime, far too often is the emphasis based on victims. However, a multiagency approach requires the police and other stakeholders to empower a multicultural and open dialogue with different communities. We argue that diverse cultural units should be helping build relationships with those seeking assistance and support. Multicultural training programmes can promote a sense of awareness and skills and can be important in giving confidence to different people.

Victims of Islamophobic hate crimes face multiple levels of prejudice. They include secondary victimisation such as discrimination in the workplace, loss of earnings, and being mistreated within the criminal justice system. Primary victimisation focuses on the physical and verbal attacks they have suffered. However, further victimisations by society, friends, and the far-right perpetuate a further bias against them. These are consequences of societal islamophobia which has become more mainstream and part of the secondary victimisation they suffer for being Muslim.

Conclusion **139**

We make the case that for victims of hate crime, public policy must offer tangible solutions and ideas for victims of hate crime. For example, the notion of cultural diversity and awareness training. Efforts to help reduce such barriers have become more prevalent following the Hate Crime Action Plan (2016). Victims of hate crime also require reassurance and political will but when secondary forms of victimisation become a norm than as a result, they are unlikely to report such incidents to the police.

Islamophobic hate crimes in general are under-reported and Muslim communities are less likely to report incidents to the police or third party reporting agencies. The same can be said about other forms of hate crime, which also have similar concerns such as disability hate crime and transgendered forms of hate crime.

Berrill and Herek (1990) cites the case of how secondary victimisation occurs within a court room using the example of homosexual panic defense victims of hate crime who are often targeted because of provoking or inviting an attack. In shifting the responsibility from the perpetrator to the victim, Islamophobia can also be deemed to be part of cultural stereotypes of Muslims being dangerous. We argue that similar views can be used to describe the Islamophobia panic defence, which implies less harsh sentences and a mistrust within the criminal justice system.

We argue that barriers to Islamophobic hate crime can be reduced if victims have confidence. They cite the need for harsher prison sentence, and legislation is required to promote culture and diversity within schools and education. Having such legislation is likely to give confidence and send out a clear message. As home office data continues to show a high level of under-reporting of incidents, we do not have a clear picture of the scale of the problem and this is just the tip of the iceberg. We argue that intersection programmes and aftercare are also pivotal in helping give victims of hate crime confidence. Incidents must be monitored closely and specialist units and teams must be used.

Study skills and top tips

Checklist for essay writing – top ten golden rules

1. **Reading! Reading! Reading!** The best essays are often the ones that can show that students have done extensive reading and provided evidence of integrating appropriate supplementary sources.

   Tip: A number of online websites and resources can directly link you to free open access academic journal articles.

2. A good essay will always start with information and detail on how we understand the problem under consideration, i.e. contextualising Islamophobia and the nature of it.

140 Conclusion

> **Tip:** Read the APPG British Muslims (2018) Islamophobia Defined Report and the Runnymede Trust Report (2017) definition of Islamophobia and problems around understanding Islamophobia.

3. Outline key policy developments, while providing an evaluation of their likely impact on the individuals, group, or community and wider society.

> **Tip:** Islamophobia is a 'message' crime – which impacts more than one person in many cases.

4. A strong essay will always use theory to compliment and help us to understand this phenomenon.

> **Tip:** See the scapegoat theory, strain theory, and Allport's scale of Prejudice.

5. Essays must include key developments and issues around contemporary society.

> **Tip:** See new policies via Government websites and policy developments via National Security Council, the UN, third party charities, police official data, and the Home Office.

6. **YOUR VIEWPOINT:** Students often think they must be critical and argue both sides without coming to their own conclusion. A good essay, however, is one that uses your viewpoint and substantiates this with evidence.

> **Tip:** Think beyond being critical and focus on being reflective in your essay in relation to the arguments you have made.

7. A good essay will always demonstrate an understanding of the subject matter and content.

> **Tip:** Bullet point a list of the key arguments in relation to Islamophobia and victimisation. See if you can spot any trends and patterns in relation to victims and perpetrators.

8. Essays must be able to adopt an analytical approach, rather than a merely descriptive approach. Avoid being too descriptive!

> **Tip:** Make sure after every point you make that you find an appropriate source and evidence for it.

9. Good essays should provide an insightful evaluation and synthesis of issues and material, which includes an original and reflective approach.

> **Tip:** Extensive evidence of relevant and perceptive application of theory, and/or empirical results, where applicable.

10. The best essays are always those that are clear and concise.

> **Tip:** Avoid the use of slang and make sure you proof-read your essay more than once.

Debate: defining Islamophobia

Two groups:

1. 'Pro' Definition of Islamophobia
2. 'Anti' Definition of Islamophobia

If arguing AGAINST the notion that we should define Islamophobia:

Why might legislating against Islamophobia be considered to be a bad idea?
Consider the following:

- What is the definition intended to achieve?
- Issues regarding deterrence (or lack of).
- Who are we protecting? – Drawing the line!
- Hatred and prejudice are a lot less easy to understand now than it was in the past – problem of causality (and definitional problems).
- 'Reasonable' versus 'unreasonable' Islamophobia.
- 'Thought crime'?
- Might it send out the wrong message about Islamophobia?
- Negative unintended consequences.
- Should we call it anti-Muslim hate crime?

If arguing FOR the notion that we should define Islamophobia:

Why might defining Islamophobia be a good idea?
Consider the following:

- The deterrent effect.
- Symbolic effect – what is the message we are putting out as a society.
- Promoting social cohesion.
- Might it mean that the Criminal Justice System changes its practices and therefore deals with crimes motivated by Islamophobia more effectively?
- Disproportionate effect on victims of Islamophobia and society at large.
- Media reporting and coverage will be taken seriously.

Revision hints

The process of doing an examination can be one of the most anxious and difficult experiences any student goes through. The good news, however, is that if you can follow some basic tips the idea and pressure of an examination can be lifted. For example, having a required reading plan and essay plan in advance can be really important when preparing for an examination. Using a pre-planned essay plan related to several themes and topics can also be very useful for revision purposes.

142 Conclusion

Setting yourself spare time at the end of every lecture and seminar to prepare an essay is crucial. For example, try using one side of A4 to plan an essay with the key checklist around essay writing which will allow you to have the necessary tools to complete an essay. In terms of wider academic and educational pedagogy, there are a number of ways students best prepare for an examination. For example, this includes:

- Using recorded material to present and deliver your ideas.
- Completing a pre-planned essay based on one of the themes you are covering.
- Using visual and audio material to present your answers.
- Picking up an original idea and using that new material.

Top tips for revision

- Make sure you know which topics you need to revise for each subject. Use your assessment specifications as a revision list.
- Make your revision active. Don't just read notes. You could make flash cards, mind maps, or use notes.
- Test yourself by completing past papers or asking a friend to test you! This will identify areas of strength and weakness.
- Build in rewards for your revision; for example, your favourite snack or using social media.
- Always take a **BREAK!**

How to structure an essay

1. **Introduction** – Introduce the reader to your ideas and the essay title. Make sure the introduction is a summary of what you are going to argue throughout. Keep it brief.
2. **Main text** – This should be a concise synthesis of the arguments you are making. Ensure that you are reflexive, and analytical by evaluating the evidence and the claims you have made.
3. **Conclusion** – A good conclusion will be more than just a summary of the facts presented. Try and offer some practical recommendations here and also a way forward in terms of what future research/policy should look like.
4. **References** – Don't forget that references are important because they show the amount of wider reading you have done. Use what is available in terms of recommended reading but also produce wider evidence of reading.

The disjointed essay

If you follow the previous steps you are likely to be able to write a concise and well written essay. However, the following are the most common errors when it comes to essay writing. These include:

Conclusion **143**

- Failure to answer the question
- A lack of wider academic reading
- A reliance on media sources
- Failure to be reflexive and analytical
- A poor structure with grammatical errors
- The reference list including multiple mistakes
- Spelling errors

Using academic journal articles

There is a wide range of literature around Islamophobia and hate crime, but there is no student textbook that brings all these concepts and areas into one student textbook. Our student textbook, therefore, is a one-stop text for all aspects of understanding, defining, and understanding Islamophobic hate crime in the world and examines international strategies at tackling this phenomenon. Moreover, most of the literature on Islamophobia consists of responses to the 9/11 attacks and how Muslims have been viewed. Our book, however, goes a step further and tackles a wide range of issues that make this is a must-read student textbook. Did you know there are a range of journals that have a wealth of information in relation to Islamophobia? For example, the following journals are a great starting point for your journey:

The British Journal of Criminology
The European Journal of Criminology
Patterns of Prejudice
Ethnic and Racial Studies
International Review of Victimology
Policy & Internet
Social Media and Society
Policing and Society
Transferable Skills and Employability

Some of the key skills you will gain at University are the ability to develop critical thinking, develop your ability to write critical and convincing arguments, working and discussing ideas as part of a team and presenting these ideas to your peers as part of whole class presentations. This is a really important skill-set to gain and you should use your knowledge about Islamophobia victimisation to be able to transfer those skills as an employability skill. As students you are expected to attend all lectures and seminars, so you can gain as much information as possible because there is so much information you can glean within these sessions. The following is a list of key skills that are both transferable and can be used for your CVs and future employability skills. They are:

- To think critically
- To develop the ability to write critical and convincing arguments

144 Conclusion

- To discuss ideas as part of a team
- To present ideas to your peers as part of whole class presentations
- The opportunity to formulate questions
- To work in groups
- To consider the practical elements of tackling different forms of cybercrime
- Team working skills
- Motivation, enthusiasm, and drive
- Interpersonal and communication skills
- Practical awareness
- To be able to write short and concise assignments.

As you embark upon your careers in working with victims/offenders of hate crime and Islamophobia you too are gaining much needed skills that can help empower people. For example, your ability to develop original, independent, and critical thinking, and the ability to develop theoretical concepts, is a really important skill that employers look for. Furthermore, the ability and knowledge of recent advances in related areas can help you develop an understanding of relevant research and their appropriate application. Most employers such as victim support, courts, police, prisons, and probation service are looking for students to transfer the skills they have gained at University. The following list highlights some of the steps you can use when transferring those skills. For example, they are the ability to:

- Analyse critically and evaluate one's findings and those of others
- Summarise, document, report, and reflect on progress
- Show a broad understanding of the context, at the national and international level
- Demonstrate awareness of issues relating to ethics
- Apply effective management through the setting of goals, milestones, and prioritisation of activities
- Design and collate information through the effective use of appropriate resources and equipment
- Identify and access appropriate bibliographical resources, archives, and other sources of relevant information
- Use information technology appropriately for database management, recording, and presenting information
- Demonstrate a willingness and ability to learn and acquire knowledge
- Be creative, innovative, and original
- Demonstrate flexibility and open-mindedness and self-awareness
- Demonstrate self-discipline, motivation, and thoroughness
- Show initiative, work independently, and be self-reliant
- Construct coherent arguments and articulate ideas clearly to a range of audiences, formally and informally through a variety of techniques
- Develop and maintain cooperative networks

Conclusion 145

- Listen, give, and receive feedback and respond perceptively to others
- Show commitment to continued professional development
- Demonstrate an insight into the transferable nature of skills to other work environments and the range of career opportunities
- Show personal attributes and experiences through effective CVs, applications, and interviews.

Being innovative is really important alongside other key traits around researching and evidence of Islamophobic victimisation. One of the key ways to do this is thinking outside the box and creating innovative and creative ways in tackling Islamophobia. For example, can you think of just one idea that you believe will help reduce Islamophobic victimisation? If you had all the resources at your disposal what would that be? Can you think of a way in which social media can be used to tackle online Islamophobia? Remember as well as researching and investigating Islamophobia part of your wider role as global citizens is to see how you can help shape the world and make it a better place and more tolerant society.

Key questions

- Does political rhetoric lead to Islamophobic hostility?
- Has Donald Trump caused an increase in Islamophobia?
- How should society deal with the far-right?

References

APPG British Muslims. 2018. Islamophobia defined. Available at: www.gov.uk/governm ent/publications/hate-crime-action-plan-2016

BBC News. 2017. Trump travel ban injunction partly lifted by top US court. Available at: www.bbc.co.uk/news/world-us-canada-40409490

Berrill, K. and Herek, G. 1990. Primary and secondary victimization in anti-gay hate crimes. *Journal of Interpersonal Violence*, 5(3): 401–413.

Buncombe, A. 2017. Islamophobia even worse under Trump than after 9/11 attacks, says top Muslim activist. Available at: www.independent.co.uk/news/world/americas/us-poli tics/trump-islam-muslim-islamophobia-worse-911-says-leader-a8113686.html

Foren, C. 2016. Donald Trump and the rise of anti-Muslim violence. Available at: www.thea tlantic.com/politics/archive/2016/09/trump-muslims-islamophobia-hate-crime/500840/

Hate Crime Action Plan. 2016. UK Gov. Available at: www.gov.uk/government/publica tions/hate-crime-action-plan-2016

Iganski, P. 2008. *Hate Crime and the City*. Bristol: The Policy Press.

Parvaresh, R. 2014. Prayer for relief: Anti-Muslim discrimination as racial discrimination. *Southern California Law Review*, 87(5): 1287–1317.

Reuters. 2017. Trump was wrong to retweet UK far-right group: British PM May's spokesman. Available at: www.reuters.com/article/us-usa-trump-twitter-may/trump-wa s-wrong-to-retweet-uk-far-right-group-british-pm-mays-spokesman-idUSKBN1DT2IS

146 Conclusion

Rozsa, M. 2017. Portland stabbing suspect: "You call it terrorism. I call it patriotism!". Available at: www.salon.com/2017/05/31/portland-stabbing-suspect-you-call-it-terrorism-i-call-it-patriotism/

Runnymede Trust Report. 2017. Islamophobia: Still a challenge for us all. Available at: www.gov.uk/government/publications/hate-crime-action-plan-2016

Talbot, M. 2015. The story of a hate crime. *The New Yorker*. Available at: www.newyorker.com/magazine/2015/06/22/the-story-of-a-hate-crime

INDEX

Abu-Ras, W. M. 16
Abu-Salha, Mohammad 136–137
Abu-Salha, Razan 136
Abu-Salha, Yusor 136
academic journals 143–145
accessory offender typology 35
Adebolajo, Michael 34, 102, 103
Adebowale, Michael 34, 103
Ahmad, M. 16
Ahmed, Riz 111
airports 91–92
Akbarzedah, S. 103, 105
Alexander, C. 15, 18, 122
Al Jazeera 102
Allen, C. 21, 105, 118
All Party Parliamentary Group on British Muslims 14
Allport, G. W. 7
Al Noor mosque (Christchurch) 21
al-Qaeda 94, 102
Al-Rahma community centre (London) 34
Alvi, S. 117, 121, 122
'analytic' autoethnography 76
Anne Frank Foundation 132
anomie theory of societies (Merton) 60
'anti-civilisation of Islam' 36
Anti-Defamation League 33
anti-discrimination laws 95
anti-hate webpages 33
'anti-Muslim hate' 14
anti-Muslim narratives 36, 100–101
'anti-Muslim racism' (Elahi and Khan) 14
apprentice offender typology 35

Asians 19
Association of Chief Police Officers (ACPO) 34, 87–88
Austria 129
autoethnography 75–82; case studies 76–80; covert research 82; defining 75–76; 'insider' knowledge 80
Awan, I. 16, 19, 23, 32, 34, 64, 87, 116
Az-Zawarhi, Ayman 102

Baker, P. 100
BAME (Black, Asian, and Minority Ethnic) communities 87
Barakat, Deah 136
Barcelona 52
barriers to integration 127
barriers to reporting crimes 138–139
Bataclan music hall 22
Bayrakli, E. 126
BBC 22
BBC News 135
BBC Panorama 88
BBC Radio 1 Newsbeat surveys 34, 106
Belcacemi and Oussar v. Belgium (ECHR 2017) 52
Belgium 52, 55, 56, 78, 129
Berrill, K. 139
"bias incidents" 137
bin Laden, Osama 102
"Bin Laden's wife" 47
Birmingham 79, 88
Birmingham Medical School 45
Birmingham Metropolitan College 45

148 Index

Black Afro-Caribbean communities 86, 93
Blair, Tony 19, 109
Blakemore, B. 34, 87
Bochner, A. P. 76
The Bodyguard (BBC) 111
Bosnian Muslims 7
Bosnian Serbs 7
Boston (US) 115
Bouteldja, N. 55
Bowling, B. 50–51, 87, 116
'Boycott all Halal products in Australia!'
    (Facebook) 36
Bozarth, M. 101
Brems, E. 56
Brexit 1, 23, 64–65
Britain First 32, 33, 135–136
British National Party (BNP) 33, 53
British Transport Police 20
British values and way of life 15, 45–46
Brixton riots (1981) 86, 87
Brown, R. 12–13
Brussels attacks (2016) 22, 129
Bucqueroux, B. 89–90
Buncombe, A. 137
burka ban poll (YouGov) 53
'burkini' swimsuits 51, 52
Burnap, P. 21–22
Burton Mail 105

Cameron, David 35, 44, 106
Campbell, E. 81
case studies: autoethnography 76–80;
    Mohammed Saleem and Woolwich
    103–104; niqab wearing women 47–51;
    Project Champion 88–91
Catalonia 52
Catholic Church 131
Census 2011 23–24
Chakraborti, N. 11
Chang, H. 75
changing appearances 68
Channel 87–88
ChildLine 39
children: online bullying 39; radicalisation
    87–88
Choudhury, T. 89, 93
Christchurch (New Zealand) 21
Christianity 46
Christian, Jeremy Joseph 137
Clarke, R. 61
'clash of civilisations' thesis 15
clothing 128; *see also* veiled Muslim women
Cogan, J. 115
Cohen, L. E. 60
Cohen model of moral panic 100

Cole, M. 79
Coliandris, G 33
Collective against Islamophobia in Belgium
    (CCIB) 129
collective fear *see* community impacts
College of Policing (England and Wales)
    10–11, 13
colonialism 18, 42–43
'comfort zones' 122
Commission on Racism and Intolerance
    2010 UK country report (ECRI 2016) 18
Communications Act 2003 37
community cohesion agenda 46
community impacts 69–70, 119–122
community-led approaches 89
community policing 89–90
contemporary Islamophobia 18–20
content analysis 103
Cooper, Yvette 91
Co-op supermarket attack (Milton Keynes
    2016) 115–116
Copsey, N. 10
Cornish, B. 62
Cornish, D. 61
Costas, G. 100
Council for American Muslim Relations 137
Council of Europe 18
Council of Europe Parliamentary Assembly 53
Council on American-Islamic Relations 136
counter terrorism 19, 90, 94–95
Counter-Terrorism Act 2018 93
Counter Terrorism and Security Act 2015 93
courts 139
covert research 82
Crime and Disorder Act 1998 (CDA) 17, 37
crime pattern theory 64
crimes against the person 37
Crime Survey for England and Wales
    114, 137
criminal damage 50–51
Criminal Justice Act 2003 (CJA) 17
critical discourse analysis 100
Cross-Government Working Group to
    Tackle Anti-Muslim Hatred 138
Cross-Government Working Group to
    Tackle Antisemitism 138
Crown Prosecution Service (CPS)
    11, 37
Cuerden, G. 22, 23
cultural barriers 138
cyber activism 38
cyber hate 30, 36, 37, 38
cyber Islamophobic hate groups 31
cyberspace 29–39
cybersquatting 33

Daily Mail 100, 101, 109
Dakir v. Belgium (ECHR 2017) 52
death 115–116
'defensive' perpetrators and offences 12
Demos 36
Denmark 78
Denshire, S. 76, 78
Department for Transport 63
depression 69
'difference' and integration 46
direct victimisation 63
discrimination 85, 126–129
disseminator offender typology 35
Dixon, H. 109
Døving, C. A. 130–131
Dowler, Amanda Jane 'Milly' 102
Duncan, P. 20
Dwyer, C. 14

Easat-Daas, A. 129
eating disorders 69
ecological perspective on neighbourhoods
    (Shaw and McKay) 60
education 24, 62
Egypt 135
Ehrlich, H. J. 115
Elahi, F. 14
Ellingson, L. 76
Ellis, C. 76
'emotional geographies' 122
emotional impacts of hate crimes 81,
    114–115, 117, 119
emotional labour 81
England and Wales: Hate Crime Action
    Plan 137–138; racist/religious offences
    23; *see also* United Kingdom (UK)
English Defence League (EDL) 33, 36, 53
Equality Act 2010 94
Equality Ombudsman (Sweden) 131–132
essay writing 142–143
ethnic cleansing 7
ethnic minorities 89, 92
ethnic-sounding names 85
EU referendum (Brexit) 1, 23, 64–65
European Court of Human Rights 52, 92
European Islamophobia Report Project
    (Bayrakli and Hafez) 126–129
European Monitoring Centre for Racism
    and Xenophobia (EUMC) 21
European Union Agency for Fundamental
    Rights (FRA) 127
European Union Minorities and
    Discrimination Surveys (EU-MIDIS I and
    II) 126–129
'evocative' autoethnography 76

'external' factors 64
extremism 88

Facebook 31, 32, 36, 136
Face Coverings Regulations Bill 53
false patriotism 31
Farage, Nigel 53
far-right groups 33, 36, 101–102
fear 7, 121–122
Feldman, M. 29, 30, 33, 38
Felson, M. 60
Fenwick, H. 89, 93
Finsbury Park attacks (2017) 22
Forman, Ian 22
Forum Against Islamophobia and Racism 31
France 51, 55, 78, 130
Fransen, Jayda 135, 136
freedom of movement 68, 121–122
freedom of religious expression 53
freedom of speech 32

Gallacher, David 116
Gardell, M. 131–132
Garland, J. 11, 62
Garofalo, J. 115
gendered Islamophobia 21, 42–56; *see also*
    Muslim women
gender oppression 43–44
geographical boundaries 122
geographical locations 67–68
'The Geography of Anti-Muslim Hatred'
    (Tell MAMA 2016) 20
Germany 52, 130
Ghumman, S. 44
Gillis, R. 115
Githens-Mazer, J. 21, 79
global identity groups 119
globalised contexts 134
Golding, Paul 135
Google bombing 33
Greater Manchester police 11
Greenberg, J. 91
Greenwald, Glenn 91–92
Greer, S. 94
Grillo, R. 52
grounded theory 103
The Guardian 107, 108

Hafez, F. 126, 129
Hale, C. 63
Hall, M. 109
Hall, N. 32
harassment: after veil ban 55–56; Internet
    32–33; reporting 128
Hartnett, S. 90

150 Index

Hate Crime Action Plan 137–138
Hate Crime Awareness Week 1
Hate Crime Report (Swedish National Council for Crime Prevention) 131
hate crimes: defining 10–13; direct impacts 116; emotional impacts 81, 114–115, 117, 119; ensuring subordination 121; EU referendum 64–65; indirect impacts 116, 120–121; on the Internet 32–33; locations for 62–63; 'message crimes' 33, 120; non/under-reporting 70–71; reactions to Woolwich attack 35; typology of perpetrators 12; UK policies 37; US Presidential Election 65; victimisation 11, 115; and wider communities 69–70; see also Islamophobic hate crimes
hate groups 31, 32
hate motivation 37
hate speech 33
hate violence 16
Hayano, D. M. 76
Heider, Karl 76
Herek, G. 115, 139
Hickman, Mary J. 94
Hicks, Craig Stephen 136
Hier, S. 91
Higher Education 24
hijab (headscarves) 77, 129, 137
Hill Collins, P. 80
Hindelang, M. 118, 121
Hindus 16
Hochschild, A. 81
Hodkinson, P. 62
Hollobone, Philip 53
Home Office official data 1, 114
homes 118, 119
homophobia 121
Hooks, B. 80
hostility 17

identity management 117–119
Iganski, P. 69
immigration 23
Imperial College 45
impersonator offender typology 35
Imran (researcher autoethnography study) 78–80
in- and out-groups 12
The Independent 107, 108, 109
indirect impacts of hate crimes 116, 120–121
indirect victimisation 63
individual impacts 114–117

'Industrial Society and Its Future' (Kaczynski) 102
Initiative for a Discrimination-Free Education 129
Innes, M. 90, 94–95
'insider ethnography' 76
insider research 80
institutional Islamophobia 85–95, 131
integration 46–47
'internal' factors 64
Internet 11, 32–33, 117; see also online Islamophobia; social media
intrusion of privacy 92
Irene (researcher autoethnography study) 76–78
Irish communities 93
ISIS 22, 65–66
Islam: as 'culturally dangerous' 15; gender oppression 43–44; identification with terrorism 103, 109; patriarchal religion 44; visual representations 30–31
Islamic swimsuits ('burkinis') 51, 52
'Islamification' 48
'Islamisation' of Europe 52–53
'Islam is Evil' (Facebook) 36
Islamist fundamentalism 44–45
Islamophobia: checklist 6; as 'dangerous' 31; defining 13–14, 141; fear and threats 7; gendered 21, 42–56; key theories 7–8; origins 33–34; as racism 15–16; visibility 21
'Islamophobia' (Runnymede Trust 1997) 13–14, 44, 123
'Islamophobia' (Runnymede Trust 2017) 14
Islamophobic hate crimes 114–123; community impacts 119–122; 'external' and 'internal' factors 64; individual impacts 114–117; ISIS-inspired terrorism 65–66; locations for 20; multiple levels of prejudice 138; operational definition 13; responses to 117–119; societal impacts 122–123; see also hate crimes
Islamophobic victimisation 47, 120
isolation 68
Italy 52
ITV News 102

jilbab (long dress) 76–77
Johnson, Boris 5–6
journalism 100–101

Kaczynski, Ted (Unabomber) 102
Kaplan, J. 13
Keats, C. 32
Khan, F. 118, 121
Khan, Jemima Marcelle 29–30

Index

Khan, O. 14
Khan, Sadiq Aman 136
Khiabany, G. 47
#KillAllMuslims (Twitter) 32

Lagou, S. 69
Lambert, R. 19, 21, 79
Lapshyn, Pavlo 22, 103, 106, 107–108, 116
Law, I. 14–15
Lawrence, Stephen 86
Lee, A. 76, 78
Leicester Hate Crime Project 12
Leichtman, E. 90
Leveson inquiry 18, 37, 100, 102–103
Levin, J. 12
Lewis, J. 99, 110, 111
LGBT communities 116
Linwood Islamic (Christchurch) 21
Littlejohn, Richard 100
Lleida (Spain) 52
Lofland, J. & L. 82
Lombardy (Italy) 52
London 22
London Bridge attacks (2017) 22
London Evening Standard 105
lone actors 31, 33
loneliness 68
Louati, Y. 130
'low-level' hostility 77
Łukjanowicz, A. 131

Macpherson report 86–87
Maisuria, A. 79
Maiziere, Thomas de 52
males: online hate crimes 33; sexual
    harassment 49
Malicious Communications Act 1988 37
Malik, Sabure 92
Manchester Arena attacks (2017) 22
Mancini, L. 46
Mason, P. 99, 110, 111
matriarchal submissiveness 44
May, Theresa 71, 138
McConville, M. 86
McCulloch, J. 89, 90, 94
McDevitt, J. 12, 115
McEnery, T. 100
McKay, H. D. 60
media *see* newspapers; social media
Meer, N. 14
de Menezes, Jean Charles 19
Merkel, Angela 52
Merton, R. K. 7–8, 60
'message crimes' 120
Mexico City Metropolitan 63

micro aggressions 20
Milburn, Alan 85
military model for policing (MPM) 90
Milton Keynes 115–116
MIND (Internet complaint line) 132
Miranda, David 91, 92
misogyny 11, 43
'mission' perpetrators 12
Modood, T. 14, 15
Mohanty, C. T. 80
Moore, K. 99, 110, 111
moral panic syndrome 100–101
mosques 21, 34
mover offender typology 35
Muftee, M. 131–132
multiagency approaches 138
multiculturalism 45, 123
Muslim communities: counter-terrorism-led
    policing 90; impacts of hate crimes 116;
    marginalisation 34; and other religious
    groups 70; policing 87; Woolwich
    attacks 105
Muslim Council of Britain 24
Muslim identity: attacks against 115, 116;
    managing in public spaces 118;
    racialisation 15–16; visibly 21
Muslim immigrants 127
Muslim-looking people 16, 134
'Muslimness' 16, 59–60, 117–118
'Muslim problem' 44
Muslims: as 'culturally dangerous' 15;
    defining 94; 'demonisation' of 19;
    population of Europe 126; post-war
    labels 18; representations in newspapers
    100–101, 103–104; stereotypes 44;
    'suspect communities' 19
Muslim travel bans 6, 135
Muslim women: colonial exploration 42;
    Islamophobic victimisation study 47–51;
    lack of agency 44; name-calling 49–50,
    77, 79; stereotypes 44; visibly identifiable
    21; *see also* veiled Muslim women
Myanmar 7
Mythen, G. 118, 121

Nacos, B. 102
Nadia (*The Bodyguard*) 111
name-calling 49–50, 77, 79
national cohesion 45–47
National Offender Management Service 37
National Police Chiefs Council (NPCC) 23
Neo-Nazi violence 136
Netherlands 52, 78, 132
"New Folk Devils" 23, 100
Newman, Kenneth 86

152 Index

News of the World 102
newspapers 99–112; common adjectives and words 103, 105; critical discourse analysis 100; Leveson inquiry 102–103; moral panic 100–101; negative stories 99–101, 106; oxygen for far-right 101–102; post-9/11 attacks 99; and the 'threat' of Islam 18; use of 'Islam' and 'Islamic' 108–109; use of 'terror' and 'terrorists' 106–109; Woolwich attack 104–108
'new terrorism' 19
Newton, A. D. 62, 63
The New York Times 102
New Zealand 21
Nexis 103–104
Nickels, H. 94
Nielsen, J. 21
night-time economy 20
9/11 attacks 2001 13; *see also* post-9/11 attacks
niqab (face veil) 44–45; autoethnography study 76–78; banning 45; criminalisation 51–54; inter-personal communication 46; religious fundamentalism 45; research after ban 55–56; as a security threat 100; taking off 118; victimisation studies 47–51
nodes (crime pattern theory) 64
Nomis 23–24
non-hate crimes 70, 114–115
non-Muslim men 16, 59–60, 69
non-reporting of hate crimes 70–71
non-visible Muslims 78
Northern League 52
Norton, H. 32
Norway 130–131
Nottinghamshire police 11
Novara (Italy) 52
nurseries 87–88
NUS Black Students' Campaign 45
NVivo (electronic software system) 103–104

offences 33
Office for National Statistics 23–24
online bullying 39
online content behavioural offender typologies 35
online hate crimes 33, 121
Online Hate Prevention Institute 36
online Islamophobia 29–39; approaches to 30; challenging and reporting 36–38; defining 30–31; impacts 32–34; normalised behaviour 38; policing 37–38; repeated victimisation 116–117; under researched 29; Woolwich attack 34–36; *see also* Internet; social media

opportunistic crimes 32
'Orientalism' (Said) 42–43
Oslo Hate Crimes unit 130
the 'other': and colonialism 43; hate crimes 11; perceptions of 7; and racism 15; veil as visible sign of 54
'Othering' 43, 100
'outsider status' 12
'outsider within' status 80–81

'parallel lives' 45, 123
Paris attacks (2016) 8, 22, 32
Parnham, David 6
Parsons Green tube station attacks (2017) 22
Parvaresh, R. 134–135
Paterson, J. 116, 119, 120–121, 122
patriarchal domination 44
perceived Muslim identity 16, 61–62
perceptions of 'threat' 12
Perry, B. 117, 120, 121, 122
personal activity nodes 64
personal safety 67–68
physical attacks 50–51, 61
physical distress 81
Pickering, S. 89, 90, 94
Piela, A. 131
Poland 131
police: approaches to extremism 88; confidence in 72; cyber activism 38; and ethnic minorities 89; institutionally Islamophobic 87; as 'institutionally racist' 86–87; and minority relations 86; recording hate crimes 71–72, 79, 138; reforms 86; social networking sites 31; trust in 87, 90, 129
Police and Criminal Evidence Act 1984 (PACE) 86
Police Service 37
'Police States' 130
policing: in the community 89–90; contemporary typologies 90; cyberspace 37–38
political communication triangle 102
Poole, E. 100
positivism 75
post 7/7 bombings: counter-terrorism policies 89; Islamophobic perceptions 18; removing veils 118
post-9/11 attacks: community policing 90; Islamophobic perceptions 18; media coverage 99–100, 106; 'over policing' 87; veiled female Muslims 43
pre-reform policing model 90
Prevention of Terrorism Act 2005 93
Prevent programmes 94–95

Prison Service 37
'problem-groups' 8
professional offender typology 35
Project Champion case studies 88–91
property damage 118–119
'Prophet Muhammad Still Burns in Hell' (Facebook) 36
psychological trauma 117
Public Order Act 1986 17–18, 37
public parks 62
public policy 139
public transport 20, 62–64, 77
'Punish a Muslim' Day letter 6

qualitative research studies 76–80
quantitative research 75
Quebec City 137

race-based traumatic stress injury model 16
Racial and Religious Hatred Act 2006 94
racialisation of crime 16
'racially motivated' crimes 37, 106
racial profiling 87
racism 14–16
racist abuse 48
racist offences 23
radicalisation of children 87–88
Rashid, N. 44, 45
rational choice perspective 61
reactive offender typology 35
'realistic' threats 12–13
recordable crimes 11
regional newspapers 104, 105–106, 107–108
religious discrimination 128
religious fundamentalism 45
'religiously motivated' crimes 37
religious offences 23
religious symbols 51
reporting discrimination 128
reporting harassment 128
reporting hate crimes 70–72, 138–139
retaliation 12
revision 141–142
Rigakos, G. 90
Rigby, Lee 22, 34, 102, 103
Riz Test 111
Robert, N. 46
Robinson, Tommy 32, 109, 136
Rogers, C. 22, 23
Rohingya Muslims 7
Rotherham scandal 23
Rowe, M. 115
Runnymede Trust 13–14, 44, 123
Ryan, A. M. 44

Sabir, Rizwaan 87
Said, E. 42–43, 109
Saint-Denis attacks (2016) 22
Saleem, Mohammed 22, 103, 106, 107–108, 116
Sallah, M. 48
S.A.S v. France (ECHR 2014) 52
Saudi Arabia 135
scale of prejudice (Allport) 7
scapegoat theory 8
Scarman Report 86
Schedule 7 (Terrorism Act 2000) 91–92
Scotland on Sunday 105, 109
secondary victimisation 139
Second European Union Minorities and Discrimination Survey (EU-MIDIS II) 126–129
'The Secret Policeman' (BBC Panorama) 88
securitisation and fear 30–31
security risks 20
self-enclosed communities 45, 123
self-protectionism 31
self-reflexivity 76
self-segregation 46
sentencing 17
sentry-dataveillant policing 90–91
serious injuries 115–116
7/7 attacks 2005 18, 89, 118
sexual harassment 49
Shah, P. 52
Shaw, C. R. 60
Shepherd, D. 86
Sherman, L. 60–61
Sikes, P. 81
Sikh men 16
Silvestri, S. 94
Simpson, K. 87
Skogan, W. 90
Sky News 102
sleep pattern disturbances 69
Smith, B. 103, 105
Smith, M. 62
social inclusion 70
social interaction and isolation 20, 46, 119, 121–122
social learning theory 8
social media 29; criminal offences 37; global reach 32; hate crimes 11; online hate 35; police use of 31; visibility of location 68; *see also* Internet; online Islamophobia
social mobility 23–25
Social Mobility Commission 23, 24–25, 85
social vulnerability 63
societal impacts 122–123
Spain 52

154 Index

Spalek, B. 19, 89, 90
stereotyping 20
Stockwell station (London) 19
stop and searches 19, 93
Strain theory (Merton) 7–8
'stranger danger' offences 12
Straw, Jack 46
study skills 139–140
Suarez, Z. E. 16
subjugation of women 44
subordination 121
The Sun 100
surveillance 15, 91
'suspect communities' 19, 93, 94–95
'Suspect communities' report (Hickman, Thomas, Silvestri & Nickels) 94
Sweden 131–132
Swedish Crime Survey 131
Swedish National Council for Crime Prevention 131
symbolic threats 13

Taber, N. 82
Tajfel, H. 8
Taras, R. 30, 31, 34
targeted harassment and violence 70, 138
Tarlo, E. 121
Tarrant, Brenton Harrison 21
The Telegraph 105, 106–107, 109
Tell MAMA (Measuring Anti-Muslim Attacks) 6, 20–23, 29–30, 33, 38
'terror attacks' 108
Terrorism Act 2000: Schedule 7 91–92; Section 44 93
Terrorism Act 2006 93, 108
terrorism and terrorists 19, 99–112; conflating arguments 105; media publicity 101–102; news headlines 109; and Pavlo Lapshyn 108; regional newspapers 107–108; Woolwich attack 103–105
Thatcher, Margaret 101
third party reporting centres 138
Thomas, L. 94
'threats' 12
'thrill seekers' 12
Tissot, S. 45
tolerance 70, 123
Tourkochoriti, I. 46, 53
transphobia 121
trawler offender typology 35
'trigger' events 21–23, 30, 33, 64–67
Trojanowicz, R. 89–90
'trolling' 30
'True Vision website' (ACPO) 34

Trump, Donald John 1, 6, 65, 135–136
'The truth about Islam' (Facebook) 36
Turner, J. C. 8
Twitter 31, 35, 136; #KillAllMuslims 32

"UK attitudes toward the Arab world" (YouGov) 16
UK Independence Party 53
ummah 120
Unabomber (Ted Kaczynski) 102
under-reporting hate crimes 70–71
Unitas Report 106
United Kingdom (UK): anti-terrorism strategy 19–20; niqab bans 53; policies on hate crimes 37; policing the Internet 33; qualitative research 78; *see also* England and Wales
United States (US) 16, 65, 135
unwarranted detention 91
urban Islamophobic hate crime 60–64
urban policing model 90
'us' and 'them' dichotomy 42–43, 44, 120, 122–123

Valls, Manuel 51
veil bans 53, 54–56
veiled Muslim women: British and Western values 45–46; colonialism 43–44; lack of agency 44; name-calling 77; as 'other' 77; physical abuse 50–51; post 7/7 bombings 118; post-9/11 attacks 43; qualitative research 77–78; symbol for Islam 43; as terrorists 47–48, 77; *see also* Muslim women
verbal abuse 48, 55–56, 77
Verwey Jonker Institute 132
victimisation: direct and indirect forms 63; emotional impacts 116; and hate crimes 11, 115; repeated 20, 116; secondary forms 139; women in niqab 47–51
Victimisation Survey 2007 63
victims of hate crimes: avoiding 'white' places 67–68; identity management 117–119; impacts 67–69, 114–117; loneliness and isolation 68; minimising experiences 70
victims of non-hate offences 115
victims of parallel crimes 69
Victoria police (Australia) 89
Vilalta, C. 63
'visible' Muslim identity: gendered Islamophobia 21; risk of Islamophobia 118; as terrorists 47–48, 77; triggering discrimination 131; vulnerability 3
'visible' Muslim men 78–80

'visual identifiers' 21
vulnerability 67

Walklate, S. 118, 121
Walters, M. 12–13
'war on terror' 89, 93–94
Warsi, Sayeeda Hussain, Baroness Warsi 6, 29
The Washington Post 102
Western identity 43
Western values 45–46
West Midlands police 87–88
Westminster Bridge attacks (2017) 22, 101
'white' places 67–68
white supremacists 36, 106, 136
Wilders, Geert 52
Williams, M. L. 21–22
Williamson, M. 47

women: homophobia and transphobia 121; sexual attraction 49; *see also* Muslim women; veiled Muslim women
Woolwich attacks (2013) 33, 34–36, 102, 104–108
workplace discrimination 61–62, 85
Wright-Neville, D. 89, 90, 94

xenophobia 48

Yeung, P. 20
YouGov polls: burka ban 53; Muslims as a threat to democracy 105–106; "UK attitudes toward the Arab world" 16
Younes, A-E. 130

Zempi, I. 16, 23, 32, 47, 50–51, 54, 64, 116, 118, 120

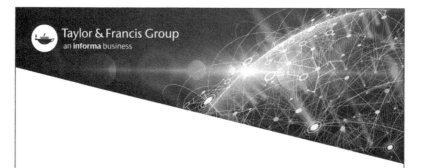